BASIC TEXTS IN COUNSELLING AND PSYCHOTHERAPY

Series editors: Arlene Vetere and Rudi Dallos

This series introduces readers to the theory and practice of across a wide range of topic areas. The books appeal to any psychotherapeutic skills and are particularly relevant to work and related settings. The books are unusual in being rooted in ideas, yet being written at an accessible, readable and introduc theoretical background and guidance for practice, with creative

..ıples.

Published

Jenny Altschuler
COUNSELLING AND PSYCHOTHERAPY FOR FAMILIES IN TIMES OF ILLNESS AND DEATH 2nd Edition

Bill Barnes, Sheila Ernst and Keith Hyde
AN INTRODUCTION TO GROUPWORK

Stephen Briggs
WORKING WITH ADOLESCENTS AND YOUNG ADULTS 2nd Edition

Alex Coren
SHORT-TERM PSYCHOTHERAPY 2nd Edition

Jim Crawley and Jan Grant
COUPLE THERAPY

Emilia Dowling and Gill Gorell Barnes
WORKING WITH CHILDREN AND PARENTS THROUGH SEPARATION AND DIVORCE

Loretta Franklin
AN INTRODUCTION TO WORKPLACE COUNSELLING

Gill Gorell Barnes
FAMILY THERAPY IN CHANGING TIMES 2nd Edition

Fran Hedges
AN INTRODUCTION TO SYSTEMATIC THERAPY WITH INDIVIDUALS

Fran Hedges
REFLEXIVITY IN THERAPEUTIC PRACTICE

John Hills
INTRODUCTION TO SYSTEMIC AND FAMILY THERAPY

Sally Hodges
COUNSELLING ADULTS WITH LEARNING DISABILITIES

Linda Hopper
COUNSELLING AND PSYCHOTHERAPY WITH CHILDREN AND ADOLESCENTS

Sue Kegerreis
PSYCHODYNAMIC COUNSELLING WITH CHILDREN AND YOUNG PEOPLE

Martin Milton
THE PERSONAL IS POLITICAL

Peter Rober
IN THERAPY TOGETHER: FAMILY THERAPY AS A DIALOGUE

continued overleaf...
●

Geraldine Shipton
WORKING WITH EATING DISORDERS

Gerrilyn Smith
WORKING WITH TRAUMA

Laurence Spurling
AN INTRODUCTION TO PSYCHODYNAMIC COUNSELLING 2nd Edition

Paul Terry
COUNSELLING AND PSYCHOTHERAPY WITH OLDER PEOPLE 2nd Edition

Steven Walker
CULTURALLY COMPETENT THERAPY

Jenny Walters
WORKING WITH FATHERS

Jan Wiener and Mannie Sher
COUNSELLING AND PSYCHOTHERAPY IN PRIMARY HEALTH CARE

Shula Wilson
DISABILITY, COUNSELLING AND PSYCHOTHERAPY

Jessica Yakeley
WORKING WITH VIOLENCE

Laurence Spurling
THE PSYCHOANALYTIC CRAFT

Invitation to authors
The series editors welcome proposals for new books within the Basic Texts in Counselling and Psychotherapy series. These should be sent to Arlene Vetere at the University of Surrey (email a.vetere@surrey.ac.uk) or Rudi Dallos at Plymouth University (email r.dallos@plymouth.ac.uk)

THE PERSONAL IS POLITICAL

Stories of Difference and Psychotherapy

MARTIN MILTON

Professor of Counselling Psychology
Psychologist and Psychotherapist

First published 2018 by
PALGRAVE

Palgrave in the UK is an imprint of Macmillan Publishers Limited, registered in England, company number 785998, of 4 Crinan Street, London, N1 9XW.

Palgrave® and Macmillan® are registered trademarks in the United States, the United Kingdom, Europe and other countries.

ISBN 978–1–352–00170–9 paperback

This book is printed on paper suitable for recycling and made from fully managed and sustained forest sources. Logging, pulping and manufacturing processes are expected to conform to the environmental regulations of the country of origin.

A catalogue record for this book is available from the British Library.

A catalog record for this book is available from the Library of Congress.

For Stuart and Jordan, Harry and Jessie – my family.

CONTENTS

CONTENTS

ABOUT THE AUTHOR

Martin Milton Cpsychol, AFBPsS, UKCP Reg, is Professor of Counselling Psychology at Regents University London. He also runs an independent practice in psychotherapy and supervision. Martin received the British Psychological Society (BPS) prize for the promoting of equality of opportunity in 2012.

ACKNOWLEDGEMENTS

No book is the product of one person alone, and this one is no different. It is a long time in the making and comes out of years of discussion – with clients, colleagues, supervisors and friends, all of whom have helped me consider and amend my ideas and conclusions about the role of difference in our lives.

While my appreciation is extended to all those I have learned from, some specific acknowledgement should be made to the following:

To my family, Stuart, Jordan, Harry and Jessie – for inspiration and respite during this process; to all my friends and colleagues who acted as 'Beta readers', questioned me or offered insights and examples – including Marjan Bergstein, Julia Brewer, Stelios Gkouskos, Claire Hinett, Charlotte Ord, Rose Perkins, Caroline Renzulli, Anne Sonnet, Edith Steffen and Margareta Theron. Sarah Young has long acted as supervisor, support and challenger; Adrian Coyle, eagle-eyed critic and perennial provocateur; and Mary-Lynne Ellis for insight into how therapy is meant to be done. And, of course, Arlene Vetere, whose enthusiasm and flexibility helped make this book a reality.

PREFACE

This book has been a long time in the making. Although there was less than eighteen months between contract and delivery, I have been preoccupied with it for the best part of two decades. Over that time I have pondered the place of difference and the political in psychological and psychotherapeutic practice. While I have always loved reading Freud, Jung, Sartre, Beck and others, something was always nagging me; it was the way that our profession could spin these ideas so as to only focus on the internal world, whether it was couched in terms of unconscious processes, thoughts and schema or the notion of the self-contained individual. It wasn't until I found what was to become one of my favourite papers ever – *Cohn's (1989)* 'The place of the actual in psychotherapy' – that the penny began to drop. That paper sparked an enduring interest, and offered relief that there may be a way to think about the inner and outer, personal and public, subjectivity and objectivity in relation to one another.

Much of my professional writing, and my work as a trainer, has been driven by questions and quandaries about the ways in which we understand people in their environment, how we might take seriously the notion of *Being-in-the-world*, and that the world is as important to consider as the personal. I have also wrestled with difference beyond the consulting room, with its place in my personal and public life too. I grew up affected by politics (as we all do): one migration was to escape the demoralised, broken Britain of the 1970s, another was to flee complicity in the horror of apartheid. Growing up in South Africa in the 1970s and 1980s meant experiencing significant pressure to limit oneself – racial hierarchies were, of course, most strongly policed, but all forms of difference were under scrutiny: gendered and sexual identities, the pressure to be a certain type of man, to expect a certain type of femininity and to embody a rather bland, rigid and predictable heterosexuality too. Moving to the USA and back to the UK were also rude awakenings as, while *less* rigid and overt in some ways, both cultures seemed to be equally wrapped up in what or who to be.

So, whether personally or professionally, the dilemmas of sameness and difference, opportunity and oppression, privilege and privation have long called my attention, both for myself and for others and have led to this book.

I should probably also comment on the structure of this text, as I can imagine readers wondering why – if the dilemmas of incorporating attention to both the personal and the political are so long-standing and still so problematic – would I not address them in a traditional, academic framework and utilise some professional or research authority to assert my findings? Well, I could have, but as a practitioner I fear that, very often, the voice of the client, the curiosity of the therapist and the efforts of their work together often get overlooked, subsumed into bodies of knowledge and statements of evidence. Yet that's often not helpful back in the consulting room where it matters. Research and practice are different languages, separate frameworks that require translation for those negotiating these issues in the consulting room. Therapy is where a client needs help and where an ill-attuned therapist can do significant damage. So the book needs to highlight the consulting room and everyday practice beyond that.

In addition, I have to note that I am as worried about the academy as I am about the health and political domains. I have after all, been a trainer for over twenty years and seen the training context change alongside that of health and social care. The training context increasingly faces a demand to 'do' more, whether that is actually feasible or not. We face demands to limit length of trainings yet to 'produce' 'expert' therapists, supervisors and leaders. Ironically, that means that trainees – and training courses – now struggle to find time to devote to pondering, thinking and reflecting. There are formal requests from colleagues and from students to *not* have to read, to find short chapters that 'sum up' complex matters of being human. As academics we write the importance of reading and thinking into course standards and trainees incorporate comments about this in reflective pieces of work, but the demands mean that there is very little time for this and there are innumerable pieces to write, and learning outcomes that have to be 'ticked off' at certain points in a training journey. I am fearful that standardisation is increasingly infecting syllabi, and creating a reliance on form-filling and box-ticking, and prioritising instruction over imagination. It is getting to the stage where trainees look forward to qualification to really read the books they have had a taste of or to make sense of what they have been tasked with learning. So, a traditionally structured book that said 'this is what has been found' runs the risk of being read as 'this is what must be done'. Instead, I wanted to turn back time, revert to basics and take advantage of the age-old facility that humanity has thrived on. Storytelling. The Oscar-winning scriptwriter Dustin Lance Black has reminded us that 'stories are the most powerful thing we have to communicate, to change minds, to change hearts. If you can do that, you can start to change communities, states, countries, the world. I just think that they are the most potent thing we have' (Whatascript, 2016).

I have set these stories in actual professional contexts, with clients that are an amalgamation of people that my colleagues and I meet regularly. But they are stories; they are not a template for the clients that readers are currently working with or those they may meet in the future. The function of stories is – and always has been – to offer insight, provoke imagination and whet the appetite to get out and encounter the world. I can't think of a better ambition to have for readers.

1

INTRODUCTION

Politics and the consulting room

I

It's London, late afternoon, Friday, 24 June 2016. I close my consulting room door, lean against the wall, close my eyes and breathe. Fridays often weigh heavy but today I ache, feel beaten, depleted and ready to drop. I have felt a gamut of emotions today – anger, fear, hopelessness, disgust, and anxiety.

As I lean, I realise that every single client has commented on Brexit,[1] some fleetingly, others as an issue that needed our full attention. With some it proved to be a way to understand their psychological splits and divisions, for others it was an urgent need to explore the world we live in. I heard, 'Could I have really gotten it this wrong?', 'I didn't know how many people I am different to', and most desperately, 'How can I survive with all this hate out there?'

But let's go back to the morning ...

It is 7.45 am and I am driving to work. I am reeling from the shock of the result of the referendum. Like so many people, I have been disturbed by the enormity of the question and the tenor of the 'debates'. It has been nasty and full of lies; obfuscation and deceit have been utilised and accepted as seldom before.

I have to manage myself as best I can; I need to be able to listen, to tune into client concerns rather than be too affected by this and what it will, might, could or won't mean.

At 8.30 am I let Will into the clinic. He is a young American client, over here on a year's exchange programme. His opening line today ... Brexit.

'Bet you weren't expecting that, were you?' he laughs. 'What did you vote? If I'd had to vote I am not sure what I would have done; my head would have said one thing, my heart another.'

I don't respond, or at least I say nothing, but that is a response all in itself. Will often tries to get me to talk about events of the day. I have been invited to comment on the weather, on the train service and on *The Revenant* – we

---

[1] The term 'Brexit' came into being in the run-up to Britain's referendum on whether to stay in or exit Europe, that is, 'Britain's exit = Brexit'.

1

have recognised that this is a way of him distancing himself from his worries. His question – and my silence – helps me realise that I don't yet know what I am comfortable saying, to him or to anyone else. On one level it is a matter of what is professional of course. He isn't here to examine my political opinions. On another, more visceral level though, it is that I don't know whom I can trust anymore.

Will moves us on: 'Well, my week hasn't been too bad and I haven't felt too anxious ... which is a good thing.'

From that point we are back on familiar ground but I haven't forgotten his telling comment about how his head and heart are sometimes quite divided. That's useful for understanding the root of his anxiety across a range of issues.

My second client is Jacinta. I am still closing the door as she tells me, 'I am gutted'.

I don't want to assume too much, so I ask 'about?'

With raised eyebrows she says, 'the vote of course, the fucking Brexit vote'.

I am not surprised that she has raised this so strongly and so quickly. Jacinta is from Spain; she lives here and works in Europe part of the time. Her life is wrapped up in Europe in a very real way.

During the session her anxiety is almost uncontainable. There are tears, she hyperventilates and there is a stark terror in the face of the enormity of the unknown. 'What is going to happen?', she asks.

There is no point in me trying to answer that question with any political facts (even if I did think I knew) as she immediately asks, 'How am I going to survive?' And then most painfully she questions, 'Why have we done this? What have we ... me and people like me, ever done ...?' The rest of that sentence, 'to people like you', hangs unspoken in the air.

During the session I feel so limited. Sure I can listen to the questions and to the underlying themes that she brings. I try hard to think about what this tells me about her now but also what this adds to what I already know about Jacinta and her distress. But I feel slow, stagnant, impotent even. I manage to nod, to agree a few times and make a couple of comments to acknowledge that I am here and that I understand the fear, and that there are grounds for such fears – 'normalisation' as therapists sometimes call it. But that's about all I can manage. I find myself momentarily regretting that I am a mere muggle; I want the talents of Madam Pomfrey, reaching into a magical bag of psychological spells to make her feel calm again. I know better. I know so much better, but it's hard to be with someone so distressed and not be able to offer some relief. As Jacinta leaves we acknowledge how much we do not know, and the importance of thinking of how to support herself, to accept that she is scared and that maybe that's OK for now.

Andrew and Sandy are next, and slightly late for their appointment. They often are. But this time Andrew comments on it. 'This morning we lost track of time, listening to the radio and trying to make sense of what is happening. I can't believe that wanker has got away with it.'

'Andrew', Sandy says sharply, she never likes his swearing, at least not in my consulting room.

Andrew doesn't seem to hear her and he carries on, and as he does Sandy seems uncomfortable and purses her lips a great deal. 'Sorry about his swearing, Martin.'

Before I have time to raise an eyebrow or ask why she feels that she has to apologise for him, Andrew says coldly, 'Don't start' and there is an uncomfortable silence.

It's clear that this is a couple who have opposing views on this issue as they do on so much in life: sex, raising their son, finances and even what therapy is for. I often suspect that they are just trying to keep the peace rather than trying to understand how the other one sees the world, and this may not be any different. Getting to understand what Brexit means to Sandy and what staying meant to Andrew may be helpful for them politically but also in terms of their relationship.

I am pleased when lunchtime arrives. I need the break, a walk and to just watch our kittens at play before returning to work.

Mark is my first client this afternoon and he seems perky. His only mention of the vote is that 'people shouldn't be upset. "The people have spoken"', he says with dramatic, grandiose air quotes. 'Let's just get on and do it. It will all be OK.' I am a little surprised by this but a part of me also likes it. It's seductive and I experience relief. Business as usual is good.

Mark talks about how annoyed he is with his boss. 'I had my appraisal last week ... my *development review*', his tone drips sarcasm. 'Like that means anything. I talk, my boss talks and then there's a form and that's what takes precedence. We both think I am doing well, the form says differently. But fuck it ... Tick the box and move on.'

My heart sinks, even if I want not to connect this with the referendum, I know it is connected. This is not to suggest that one necessarily 'causes' the other, but Brexit and the appraisal relate to similar experiences. Once a box is ticked your fate is sealed. There is no going back even if you have no faith in the process.

Mark and I have been here before. It's what he does with so many dilemmas; its typical of his approach to life's problems and while it gets him through the tough spot, in a few days he will experience the kick, the unfairness of it, the powerlessness that he struggles so intensely with. And we know that he will then experience trouble, start taking risks and his passive aggressive retaliations will be evident.

Casey is my last client that day and seems ... 'fine', very involved in therapy, preoccupied almost with the complexity of navigating the rigid expectations of the world. Brexit is mentioned but it seems simply to be another example of the costs of thinking in what they consider a simplistic 'either-or' manner – 'in vs. out', 'British or immigrant', 'Good or bad' ... The same old problem.

It's after Casey leaves that I get to lean against my wall, switch the light off and acknowledge just how much the day has taken out of me.

II

This book focuses on the ways in which people are affected by and navigate difference and the political aspects of life. It explores how we, in the psy-professions, might be of assistance. Psychologists and psychotherapists have a history of struggling with this domain, both politics with a 'big P' (the impact of issues such as elections and referenda, economic policy and the governance of the country) and politics with a 'small p' (everyday issues such as difference and diversity and the way we act towards one another). Among other things, this book explores the experience of disability, race and gender as they are policed and managed in our everyday lives, in that space where the big and small Ps intersect, where the personal is political and the political personal.

In the area of psychotherapeutic theory and practice, some of our models have rejected any focus on real-life politics and diversity, seeing them as a deviation from the practice of *psychological* analysis. The focus in this vision is the 'internal' world, the brain, unconscious drives, cognitive schema and the like. For these world views, thinking about politics can be seen as a collapse into the sociological – it is assumed that it may be a valid focus but one more for social workers and policy makers than for psychotherapists.

Other schools have simply not seen the necessity of attending to the political, assuming that a robust adherence to a manual or application of technique will suffice. This approach, of a universal methodology, is not just thought to be politically neutral, some have argued that it protects against discrimination and oppressive practice (see Milton et al., 2010). This is discussed further in Chapter 2.

However, psychologists, psychotherapists, clients, philosophers, economists, historians and policy makers alike, have all noted how important it is to understand the contexts within which we exist because, without that, it is simply not possible to understand experience, formulate client difficulties, or tailor practice appropriately. Without understanding our embedded-ness in the world, we are working with mere ghosts and projections of experience.

As scientist-practitioners, we also have an enormous amount of research and theory that helps us understand our relational and intentional existence; this body of knowledge and experience reminds us that the notion of the 'self-contained' individual is as problematic as it is inaccurate (see Strawbridge, 1996). Like our mammal relatives, our elephant, dolphin, monkey and ape cousins, we are social animals. We exist in relationships, in personal, community and socio-political interdependencies. When these relationships offer support and validation we do well. When the world is against us, when it excludes or oppresses us, we suffer and that suffering takes the form of community, family and individual distress. While it may be individuals who experience the various manifestations of distress, anxiety, depression, eating disorders and experiences of madness, the roots of this distress can be traced to toxic and oppressive relational and social experiences. Jaspers (1963), Szasz (1960) and Laing (1961) all helped outline this in the 1960s and more recent contributions have been made by Dallos and Draper (2015), Douglas (2010), Johnstone (2014), Langdridge (2014) and Wilkinson and Pickett (2010) among others. This book illustrates some of the areas where the policing of policy and interpersonal freedoms impinges on our psychological well-being.

Politics with a 'big P'

Politics with a big P, has recently been brought into the consulting room like seldom before. We have heard about the impact of austerity, despair in the face of the Syrian genocide, shock and confusion about the referendum result and the election of Donald Trump. Radlett also notes 'soaring unemployment; zero hour contracts/low pay/job insecurity; savage cuts to housing, sickness and disability benefits; profit-gauging landlords demanding extortionate rents; evictions; homelessness; foodbanks' (2017, p. 34).

These issues directly affected therapy, becoming topics in client sessions, supervision groups, in conference discussions, on social media, in the press and on TV. Optimistic visions and their more negative alternatives vied for airtime, and the expression of xenophobia, homophobia and misogyny flourished, as did anxiety and fear about such expression. People suffered from actual, and threatened, xenophobic and racist violence, the overall rate of which was significantly higher than in corresponding periods in previous years (see Stone, 2016). A report by Galop, the Lesbian, Gay and Bisexual Anti-Violence and Policing Group, indicated that a similar process was directed towards gender and sexually diverse communities with a 147 per cent increase in anti-LGBT crime in the three months after the referendum (Antjoule, 2016).

The responses to big and small P politics were raw and full frontal. No one seemed unaffected: individuals were shaken up, families were brought into conflict, Facebook friends were deleted and communities subject to hostility. Clients brought painful material related to Brexit immediately, and of course, that's not the only way it affected therapy. Whatever our own concerns and decisions about Europe, we psychologists, psychotherapists and counsellors, those whose work it is to assist with the psychological well-being of our clients, were already reeling. These events reminded us that it is impossible not to be affected by politics and we can't expect it to mean nothing to our clients either.

Politics with a 'small p'

Psychotherapy is a profoundly personal process, where clients embark on a process of discovery, finding out about themselves, who they are, what lurks in the shadows and who they might become. While it can be an extremely rewarding process, one cannot deny that it can also be an excruciatingly personal process. Yet while it is so personal, it is undertaken in relationship with another, the therapist. This process is one where dilemma is ever present – trust and mistrust, dependence and the urge to be independent, the personal insight and its political ramifications; these are at the very heart of the process because, best will in the world, and one of the reasons psychotherapy works, is that difference is there. It stares you in the face. The client *is not* the same as the therapist and the therapist can *never be* the same as the client. Where difference is relevant, the client and therapist embody it in each other's presence – whether that be through actual or perceived markers of wealth, gender, race, nationality or any other difference that may carry meaning.

One response to this has been to try and limit difference. We sometimes try to match clients on relevant demographics, a black client may prefer to see a therapist of colour, women sometimes request to see a female therapist and LGBT clients often fear the possible homophobia or insensitivity of the heterosexual therapist and so seek out an LGBT therapist. But even these attempts at 'matching' do not avoid the fact that the two people are different and that this will inevitably become apparent. The fact that two people, with profound differences attempt to relate deeply and to understand the client's experiences, choices and ways of being, means that what might seem something personal hidden away in the safety of the consulting room, is actually a profoundly political engagement.

Some in the therapeutic professions recognise that the political dimension is relevant to human well-being and to the therapeutic endeavours of many who are struggling. Indeed, Pearce contends 'that the essence of our work as psychotherapists is political and that it is authentic and therefore ethical [...] that we recognize the work as such' (2017, pp. 29–30).

But, this view cannot be said to be universal. In fact, this view is under attack. Our paymasters, political leaders, health policy makers, interpretations of the medical model of human distress and Pharma companies all come together to encourage, instruct and force therapy to be reductionistic, to see the problem in the individual sufferer and overlook the impact of culture and capitalism, oppression and disavowal.

The contested nature of this field has a number of possible explanations – some are economic, some are related to who is in power (and who wants to keep power), but some are also to do with the fact that while the reductionists have been writing manuals and illustrative cases for years and years, other perspectives have had much less 'airplay'; there are fewer stories and images of what good relational and politically informed therapy looks like.

It seems that many approaches to therapeutic practice have been reactive to the pressures upon us and have been corralled into an apologetic, reactive discussion rather than following the line of our own research and insight. In doing so, we have failed to show – clients, trainees and colleagues – how it makes sense to consider the socio-political in therapy. One real shame is that we have allowed the humble case study to be sidelined and those that recognise the interplay between reality, actual life, political and social factors haven't developed stories that help therapists to think about, and become confident in, including the political in psychotherapy.

The book

This introductory chapter is followed by one that outlines some of the theoretical and professional issues that bedevil the professions; and this in turn is followed by eight chapters that explore psychotherapy alongside issues of power, diversity, politics and oppression and the impact they have on therapeutic work. They are stories of diverse clients and different therapeutic journeys. The socio-political contexts vary between them, both in terms of the subject positions inhabited by the clients and in terms of the context in which therapy was undertaken. However, they are all intended to allow reflection on such aspects of life as race, gender, sexual identity, those that live by expected rules and those that challenge the norm, deliberately or simply by way of their being. Such issues may – or may not – be the core referral or presenting concerns, but they are always a part of the context that it is crucial to be mindful of. I hope that this helps the reader look at the way in which difference, diversity and the socio-political dimensions are seldom far from the work of therapists – whether we choose to see it or not.

The stories in this book are intended to be *contributions* to the ways we think about difference and diversity, the way difference plays out between people – whether that is by way of social inequality on our streets, in our schools, at universities and workplaces or in the consulting room between client and therapist. The book is also about politics, power and oppression and how these might be considered and worked with in practice. These issues may help to illustrate forms of distress and to highlight the way in which theory can helpfully guide our interactions. Of course, none of these will be *exact* blueprints for the work a therapist will do with a particular client who walks through their consulting room door, but it is hoped that readers will use them as imaginative aids to engaging with these issues in their own practice.

The stories in this book explore the paradox that we have been curious about since Carol Hanisch's 1970 essay brought to our attention the fact that 'the personal is political'.[2] It is important that stories of the therapeutic process are available so as to foster a space for therapists to consider and rehearse how they might think about difference, social impact and political matters. Unless we do this clearly and with conviction now, we risk being complicit with movements that reduce everything down to genes, chemicals and individual thought patterns. We need to be *more* curious and *more* imaginative about the ways in which a political contribution can enhance the core tasks of assessment, formulation and practice. Without this we risk psychotherapy receding into the murky shadows as Radlett recently envisioned.

I'm in a room in an NHS surgery, supposedly providing CBT. I check for hidden microphones and cover up the CCTV camera. A new client comes in. First I clarify that s/he is not to blame, and explain what is. Next I tell him/her that as an individual, h/she had no power to prevent or change what's happened. However, despite serious limitations s/he can make choices about how to live on their greatly altered Personal World. I ask the client questions and explore/challenge their responses: are they numbing the pain with alcohol or drugs?; self-harming?; considering suicide?; taking out the fear and frustration on partner or children?; blaming other vulnerable groups – migrants; racial/ethnic populations?

---

[2] While Carol Hanisch is credited with creating the phrase, she has denied that it was her original wording and suggested that it was selected by the editors of the anthology in which her 1970 essay was published.

This investigation may seem much too little, but it is what I believe is ethical for therapy to offer. At the end of six or 12 sessions I have to say goodbye. I wish them courage, fortitude and compassion towards themselves and others. And because I'm a very political person, I'd be tempted to give my client a copy of Lenin's pamphlet, *Imperialism: The highest stage of capitalism.* (Radlett, 2017, p. 46)

Stories ... NOT case studies

The content of the upcoming chapters is conceived of as 'stories' rather than case studies or clinical vignettes and this terminology is deliberate. The terms 'case studies' or 'clinical vignettes' are problematic. Both feel distancing, and are located within a discourse of the 'expert', where the heroic therapist guides the unknowing client back to health. Despite what TV documentaries and tabloids might suggest, this is not the process of therapy as it actually occurs in the consulting room.

As the reader will be able to tell, my view is that the therapeutic process is an intensely personal one and, like other colleagues, I am uncomfortable simply divulging my clients' experiences. That would be the case even if it were not unethical or if clients were so kind to grant me permission. Attempts to reproduce the reality of another are always flawed because we are always 'Other'. Therefore, like others in the field I have settled on the use of fictional stories drawn from my experience, stories that are reflective of the kind of work I have done over my career as therapist and a supervisor, informed by my work as an academic and researcher.

The book attempts to go 'beyond schoolism' (Clarkson, 1998) and to question the assumption that theory leads to definitive practice. In my view, that conclusion is flawed. Theory shapes practice of course, but regardless of intent or desire, we are not automatons, so the claim to work in any single model can only say a *little* about a therapist's practice, regardless of the pressure to adhere to a manual. My analyst's version of psychoanalytic therapy was inevitably different to other analysts; we talk as if CBT is a standard experience rolled out to all suffering from a specific difficulty when of course it cannot be; and humanistic therapists have long called for us to recognise the fact that a large part of psychotherapy is the importance of being congruent to ourselves, our talents and our struggles, thereby individualising the therapeutic process.

I could have chosen to spotlight a particular form of therapy, to compare and contrast approaches, or to take a number of any other foci. This book though has a more modest aim of offering insight into the ways in which therapists might incorporate wider contextual thinking into good practice, as such it is pan-theoretical, or pluralistic in ambition. Having said that, my immersion in the fields of counselling psychology, existential psychotherapy and psychoanalytic therapy mean that these ideas are evident to at least some degree alongside comment on difference and the political. I hope that readers will accept the fact that the limits of my own voice should not be read as a call to limit the scope of these ideas to my specific professions. These are issues for all of us, psychologists and psychiatrists, psychotherapists, psychoanalysts and counsellors alike. So I hope that readers will consider these ideas, digest them and adapt them to their own circumstance, whether that be profession, model of therapy or place of work.

The final consideration to note is that while the book focuses on the ways in which political issues affect clients and therapists alike, and influence therapeutic relationships and service design, this book does not argue that all of the potentially relevant political dimensions can be prioritised at the same time. As in actual therapy, the writing of these stories, meant that some issues were more clearly evident and possible to address. Others lingered in the shadows somewhat, but were not central to a process that prioritised a client's subjective experience. Thus because of the era and the context I could have explored HIV/AIDS stigma more directly with Kenny, but that wasn't the most meaningful issue. Likewise with Taye, I am not oblivious to the fact that class and economic constraints might also have been a beneficial focus or with Ravi that stigmatising assumptions about mental health were relevant.

2

DIFFERENCE AND DIVERSITY IN THE CONSULTING ROOM: THEORETICAL AND PROFESSIONAL PERSPECTIVES

Article 1 of the Universal Declaration of Human Rights states:

All human beings are born free and equal in dignity and rights. They are endowed with reason and conscience and should act towards one another in a spirit of brotherhood.

(United Nations, 1948)

While the following chapters illustrate the moment-to-moment processes of therapy, this one focuses on the ways in which the psychotherapeutic professions have or have not, do or do not, engage with difference and the political domain. It will focus on the meaning of 'political', on the ways that politics impacts on the everyday experiences of people and the practices the psy-professions have adopted in relation to difference and the political.

Being mindful of the binary

It is unfortunate that our understandings of the place of the personal and the political are often seen as mutually exclusive, as an exploration of either one or the other and as such can feel tribal, oppositional and can fail to consider the interaction between the two. This binary, either-or stance, has led to a rather long-held stand-off in the professions and is fostered by government, industry and the markets. Such a stance does no one any favours at all (see Cohn, 1989; Douglas, 2010; du Plock, 2014; Langdridge, 2014; Milton, 2005, Milton, et al., 2010; Pearce, 2017; Samuels, 1993). However, every now and again something happens and we are reminded, sometimes quite powerfully, that we are political beasts too, that the distinction between the personal and political is specious.

Politics and society

The term 'politics' often refers to societal practices such as elections and referenda, economic policy and the governance of the country. Sometimes these get a great deal of attention in therapy and sometimes not. For instance, clients have sometimes brought issues such as austerity (House et al., 2015), which in Europe has led to a surge in psychological distress and suicide (see Antonakakis and Collins, 2014). Others bring their distress in relation to the Syrian refugee crisis or going back in time, the Iraq War, the Cold War or an array of similar issues that affect us. 2016 saw high-impact political events such as a referendum to decide whether the UK would maintain its membership of the European Union or whether it would leave; and in the USA a presidential election was held. The results of both were counter to many polls with the referendum result being in favour of Brexit and the USA voting a non-politician to the position of president. Both of these led to discussions in the consulting room coloured by surprise and confusion, focusing on the prevalence of hate and division.

As well as the reality of significant political change, we also saw an increase in intergroup stress and violence associated with these events. Both of these brought politics, with a big P, powerfully into the consulting room. That these events have a psychological impact was immediately clear, proving to be a delight for some and a terror for others. The expression of xenophobia, homophobia and misogyny flourished, as did anxiety and fear about such expression. We saw death threats being made and the Labour politician, Jo Cox, was killed just a week before the Brexit vote. As mentioned earlier, the overall rate of xenophobic violence increased enormously (Stone, 2016) with a 147 per cent increase in anti-LGBT crime in the three months after the referendum (Antjoule, 2016). These were seen to be reactions to the discourse from the campaign.

Politics and the everyday

The colloquialism 'politics with a small p' is sometimes used to refer to the ways in which political issues are experienced in people's everyday lives. Small 'p' politics often manifests in response to, and management of, difference and diversity, how we engage with human and civil rights, how we address people, access to such resources as schools, bathrooms and such like. Understandings of difference are always in flux and often contested. People have to navigate this fluidity in their daily lives and psychologists and other therapists are often called upon to help manage the confusion and distress that results from the ways in which our world is changing, materially, politically and professionally; this is because oppression and discrimination are often the negative side of the process and create much psychological distress and disturbance.

Difference, policies related to human diversity and the social inequality that results have long been studied and we know that the greater the social inequality, the higher the rates of mental health difficulties, health problems and violence, for individuals and communities (Hamilton, 2004; Wilkinson and Pickett, 2010). Inequality has led to disparities between rates of mental distress for those of racial majorities and minorities (see Brantley, 1983; Kawachi et al., 2005); LGBT people tend to experience greater psychological distress and social oppression (see Bidell, 2005; Ryan and Rivers, 2003; Riggle, et al., 2008); and there are significant differences in relation to the rates of addiction and psychological distress for people in the deaf community compared to those who are not registered as disabled (see Moore and McAweeney, 2006). So it is clear that the impact of difference matters to our everyday lives and is monitored, policed and managed at all levels. As well as impacting groups, it is also a factor in individual well-being and distress. Individuals are traumatised by violence and internalised racism, sexism and homophobia and these lead to self-hate and thwarted potential and manifests in the full range of emotional difficulties, such as anxiety, depression, eating disorders and psychosis.

The psy-professions: Ambivalence to the political domains

The therapeutic professions are coming to recognise that the political dimension is relevant to human well-being and to the therapeutic endeavours of many who are struggling. Our own experience and location within the matrix of human diversity, over a century of theorising, psychological studies and a lifetime of working with real (rather than hypothesised) people and their difficulties bring this absolute embeddedness of the individual, in the wider social and political world, home to us. In addition, a therapist's own personal therapy or analysis, and the intense scrutiny undertaken during many years of training mean that we learn first-hand that context has a huge effect on a person's well-being – whether that be our own or that of the client.

However, this cannot be stated categorically as this view is also under attack. Our models of practice, our paymasters, political leaders, health policy makers, interpretations of the medical model of human distress and Pharma companies come together to encourage, instruct and force us to be reductionistic, to see the problem in the individual sufferer and overlook the impact of culture and capitalism, oppression and disavowal. Our 'citizens are casualties of economic/political forces and the subsequent decisions made in boardrooms on Wall Street, the City of London and Parliament' (Radlett, 2017, p. 35).

Increasingly we are seeing models of practice come into vogue that rely heavily on a more distant, intellectual and rational approach to mental health 'treatment'; these are often written down as manualised, almost scripted, ways to interact with clients. They may offer the promise of economy and instant gratification – what you want (health), when you want it (now) – but client and therapist reports are often that this impersonal approach is a less powerful and less transformative an experience. This push to manualised uniformity is not just a scientific- or scholarly-driven enterprise as proponents suggest; it is driven by the economics of public sector health care and the 'health for profit' ethos in a free market economy. These, in turn, impose particular visions of humanity, health and identity on the population.

This is the preferred focus of many politicians who seem unable to debate mental health without immediate reference to monies available or the impact on 'the economy' of ill health. The experience of the person seldom features. The influential economist, Richard Layard and colleagues have gone as far to note that 'tackling depression and anxiety would be four times as effective as tackling poverty. It would also pay for itself' (Inman, 2016). This separation of outcome (emotional distress) from context (struggles of poverty) is counter to much psychological, sociological and economic science (see BPS, 2015; Hamilton, 2004; James, 2007; Wilkinson and Pickett, 2010), but very appealing to the government as it puts the 'blame' in the individual rather than calling forth a recognition of the impact of economic policy and other contextual factors.

Contested visions and a multitude of players

The contested politics of what it means to be human is at play in these discourses, with political visions of people as exclusively rational beings amenable to being patched up, MOT-style, and returned to work, being favoured by many in this technological era. With this, the irrational and emotional aspects of being are often overlooked, rejected or pathologised. In this way, big P politics directly affects the consulting room (see also Rizq, 2011).

Another way in which the politics (and economics) of health has become a key priority, is through the transformation of mental health and psychological services over the years. In spite of the recent urge to increase access to psychological therapies, many forms of psychotherapy have been moved from the National Health Service (NHS) into the private sector either by design or as the sole way they can be offered. Of course, it is true that service managers have to wrestle not only with the needs of individual clients, but also with increasingly restricted budgets available to them for staff appointments, training and development, and management of site. Thus decisions about approaches made available to clients become financial issues rather than prioritising need or evidence. This is not stated this way by service providers and the Department of Health; the justifications tend to be hijacked by different versions of an 'evidence-based' debate – Lord Layard's views, mentioned earlier, appear to hold much government attention whereas the large body of evidence about the contextual factors underpinning psychological distress appears to go largely unrecognised. Evidence that backs up pre-existing visions appears to be far more attractive than evidence that challenges it. This means that, in essence, policy oftentimes relies on a selective sub-section of the available evidence.

The pharmaceutical companies are similarly wedded to understanding human distress as mental 'illness' and privileging biological explanations and 'treatments', often in areas that are contested by psychologists. The notion that human distress *originates* in genes and 'brain chemicals' is hugely contentious, with very little evidence for this reading. This is even the case with those complex presentations that have a history of being seen as organic in origin. In fact the British Psychological Society report on schizophrenia and psychosis notes that 'to date we do not have firm evidence for any specific biological mechanism underlying psychotic experience' (Cooke, 2014). Contemporary psychology notes a more complex debate about the fact that biology can also be a *response* to toxic environmental and relational difficulties rather than the cause; it recognises that while medication can have helpful effects it can also have problematic physical and psychological impacts too. The levels of investment available to these various perspectives are of course also significantly different (for more consideration of these issues, see Johnstone, 2014; Kinderman, 2014).

As globalisation moves us towards seeing everything in binary terms and ever-greater specialisms, identifiable skills and branded expertise, the psychological professions are also affected. While some therapists manage to maintain a 'generalist' role, many of us find ourselves increasingly located within 'specialist' services or specific models. We become experts in Older Adult Work, we head Children's Services and we find ourselves on the specialist registers of existential, psychoanalytic, systemic or cognitive behavioural therapies. As well as being ways of offering our skills, these developments affect the ways the person is seen, the way psychological practice is understood and determines which goals are deemed worthy of mental health services and those that will be located on the periphery, available only to those with the resources to fund them themselves.

Despite this no matter how specialist we become, and how detailed our service's inclusion and exclusion criteria become, therapists work with a wide range of people that cross categories. We cannot avoid this; it's just the way people are. Problems exist however you group people. Group by gender and you quickly find debate about experiences that 'all' women or men are said to have. Group by mental health status and you struggle, too – do 'all' those diagnosed with the specific disorder experience the same concerns and triggers? No. Focusing on race and you wonder what it is that 'all' people of colour experience exactly like others? Even the experience of institutional and cultural racism varies in shape and form. To be a therapist means that you must be ready, willing and able to engage with diversity, even within the parameters of sameness.

Binary visions and individual care

To engage with the diversity of experience that clients bring and contexts create, and to do this ethically and effectively, therapists must consider the richness that diversity, and differing socio-political experiences brings. 'But to enhance or elaborate an understanding of our "selves" is only a part of the story. As psychotherapists we also seek to facilitate an awareness of the "other", of the potential reasoning and conditioning that produce the actions and motivations of the other or others with whom we interact' (Pearce, 2017, p. 29). And to do that, we need to consider the ugly underbelly of diversity – discrimination and oppression – and consider these much closer to home.

Therapists do not all hold the same cultural world views or political allegiances; we are a diverse bunch. That's partly what training, regulatory scrutiny of competences and professional socialisation is about – trying to manage our diversity. We have conservative psychologists and progressive, liberal ones. This became very evident during the process to establish a British Psychological Society Lesbian and Gay Psychology Section (which later became the BPS Psychology of Sexualities Section). As Sue Wilkinson has written:

> Three previous proposals had been turned down (in 1991, 1993, and 1994) by the BPS Scientific Affairs Board and/or Council on the grounds that the field was "too narrow" and "too political." Anti-lesbian and anti-gay correspondence was published in the BPS journal, *The Psychologist*, under

the heading, *"Are you normal?"* Members of the steering group were sent abusive hate mail by BPS members. The membership ballot which finally approved the formation of the new Section was notable for having more "anti" votes than ever before recorded in any parallel BPS ballot – 1988 voted in favour, and 1623 voted against the formation of the Section. (BPS PoS, undated)

This reminds us that just being a therapist does not mean we are all somehow naturally ethical affirmative practitioners, but that we must all work to develop and maintain reflective and mindfully affirmative, or ethically attuned, stances to the work we do. There is no choice in this, regardless of whether ethical and moral practice has been at the centre of a therapist's world view, whether you hold equality of opportunity as a key value and regardless of whether individual psychologists and psychotherapists natural stance leads them to understand psychological distress as a result of inequality, discrimination and oppression; to work as a therapist requires us to understand the impact of diversity on our clients and on ourselves (see BACP, 2012; BPS, 2008, 2009; UKCP, 2009; HCPC, 2015).

We also have to note legal expectation and the Equality Act (2010) requires us to pay attention to 'protected characteristics', many of which are the characteristics of difference upon which discrimination and oppression are targeted. These are age; disability; gender reassignment; marriage and civil partnership; pregnancy and maternity; race; religion or belief; sex; sexual orientation (Hepple, 2014). It is important to highlight this, as not only have individuals struggled but our theoretical bases have been problematic, as a short review of the field and its literature on working with minorities will demonstrate.

A problematic history of the professions …

The spectrum of abilities

While 'disability' services have long existed, services and relevant literature have sometimes been conceived of as rather a 'special' specialism, with many psychologists and psychotherapists having little, or no, contact with such experiences. It is not surprising, then, that the array of meanings associated with that term is only just receiving the wider attention it warrants.

One problem has been that the term 'disability' has allowed a field of diverse experiences and complex impacts to be seen almost as a singular, and specialist, issue. That a person is 'disabled' tells us very little about their experience and any difficulties or joys associated with it.

Another problem has been that by treating these experiences as something only specialists have awareness of, a perception of disability as a rare phenomenon has been fostered; we have come to see disability as something outside the norm, rather than the heterogeneous and widespread experience that it is (see Chapter 6).

Non-specialist therapists can struggle to find trustworthy literature in this area, which means that much practice has risked a reliance on ableist assumptions – oftentimes based on ignorance, fear and stereotypes (Reeve, 2000). When therapists do finally access some of the relevant material (see Hodges, 2013; Jones, 2013 among others) it becomes apparent that 'disability' and 'ableism' remain under-researched areas plagued by unhelpful assumptions of a binary split between normal and abnormal, able and disabled. They are also areas where service provision can be limited.

The gender binary

Former President Jimmy Carter explains that 'the mistreatment of women is the number one human right's abuse today' (Carter, 2015) leading to diminished physical and psychological health of individual women and our communities. Yet much psychological and psychotherapeutic literature has overlooked the negative impact that our gendered structures have. Our disciplines have developed and promoted models of gender as biologically derived and this has led us to assume that gender differences are set and 'natural'. This 'scientific' stance and professional status have bolstered social policies/ practices that have led to control of women and censored opportunities for all.

One of the key issues is that our fields consider gender as if it can be discussed in binary terms – men and/vs. women. But this is immediately problematic as it facilitates a view of men as all being similar and women being carbon copies of each other. It allows an essentialist vision of what 'women' feel, experience, want or need as distinct from what affects men (and vice versa). It overlooks the variety within these gendered categories, restricts opportunity and misses the similarities that exist for women and men.

These models have also tended to focus on the ways in which we construct the cisgendered person's experience, rather than helping us widen our understandings to encourage accurate reflection on *all* people's experiences of gender. More recently trans and gender fluid experience have received more attention (see Atnas et al., 2015; Richards and Barker, 2013) and this has proved useful in helping therapists recognise that gender is richer than our outdated visions would suggest. Binary understandings fail to capture the richness of gender and lead to hierarchies that foster discrimination and oppression.

Race

We have seen psychological and psychotherapeutic literature privileging some racial groups by writing as if race is not an issue – as if we can simply extrapolate experiences across cultures, from 'the majority' to 'everyone else'. This is a way of erasing a great deal of diverse experience, as well as some of the awful misuses of power that occur at personal and cultural levels. It has been argued that biased views are also evident, for example Jung has been accused of overt racism (see Adams, 1997).

One response to this has been to try to be 'colour-blind', to not focus on race or colour, to treat 'everybody the same'. While this may be well-intended and for some clients may feel satisfactory, there are problems associated with this stance – an obvious one is that when adopting such a position we are likely to overlook the powerful effects of racism (see Brantley, 1983). Phoenix (1987) characterised the impact of these stances as resulting in a position of 'normalised absence/pathologised presence' of people of colour. We overlook experience or, when it is powerful enough that it has to be considered, we tend to see it as a problem. This is obviously a significant issue for the professions as it means trainees and qualified practitioners alike are drawing on a limited theoretical and evidence base to deal with the damage done by racism and when trying not to replicate this damage in our therapeutic endeavours.

Sexual diversity

The psychotherapeutic literature has, and often still does, tend to look at the world through 'heterosexual eyes' (see Denman and de Vries, 1998; Kitzinger and Coyle, 1995; Malley and Tasker, 1999). This means that it frequently omits any attention to LGBT experience, or historically when it did focus on sexual minorities the focus would start with heterosexuality and implicitly ask, 'how is the LGBT experience different?' Other experiences of sexual diversity (e.g. asexual people's experiences, such sexual practices as BDSM, and non-traditional relationship structures such as polyamory) have seldom been considered (Richards and Barker, 2015). This is another example of 'normalised absence/pathologised presence'.

The ignoring of sexualities is evident across history and modalities with Jung only mentioning 'homosexuality' seventeen times in his *Complete Works* (see Hopcke, 1989); with psychoanalysis having promoted heterosexuality as the only healthy outcome (see O'Connor and Ryan, 1993); and with sex therapy, CBT and humanistic literatures appealing to a 'universal methodology' – meaning that practitioners learn the methods/develop the personal abilities correctly and roll these out in a universal fashion. A stance such as this, akin to being 'colour-blind' outlined above, fails to attend to issues of power and difference and is of no assistance in the therapist's attempts to attune to the experience of minorities (see Milton et al., 2010).

These are just three areas that illustrate the struggle that psychology and psychotherapy have had conceptualising difference and diversity over the years. Similar problems exist in relation to the diversity that exists in, and oppression that is exerted in relation to, different faiths, mental health status, wealth and poverty, and so forth. What is important to note is that it is a conceptual problem that underpins these historic and contemporary difficulties; they are an outcome of simplistic binary visions of difference, leading us to think that experience can be understood as *either* this *or* that, and after that it's a short hop, skip and a jump from considering what is more or less normative, to thinking, in essence, which experience is more right or wrong. These visions also suffer from the assumption that 'treating everybody the same' is the corrective to these problems.

So how is the field working to address these problems?

Conceptualising diversity: Additive approaches

Some literature discusses diversity by focusing on specific issues and experiences that are different from 'the norm'. This approach has had some advantages, allowing us to learn about different minority stressors. By utilising this perspective and adopting what Jordan-Zachary calls an 'additive model' (2007), the various differences a person has from a norm are 'added' together highlighting the degree of 'difference', giving an indication of the degree of stigma faced and allows individuals and policy makers to make plans accordingly. As my colleague Markus Bidell puts it, this helps measure the 'dose of discrimination'.

While it has some uses, the additive model is problematic, containing assumptions of sameness (or similarity) about those who were categorised and allowing simplistic visions to be developed as to what 'all gays' or 'all women' or 'all Asians' do, think, feel or cannot do.

The additive approach also risks accepting norms and overlooking issues of power. In the capitalist West, we tend to calibrate the norm as that of the white, wealthy, cisgendered, heterosexual male. Experiences different to this are deemed 'Other'. And 'different' and 'Other' are not value neutral concepts. 'Different' is usually seen as 'less good, or 'sub-optimal' and prone to misrepresentation through pathologisation. Where it is not seen as 'less good' it often leads to a different problematic, that of exoticisation.

Additive models mean that those in teaching, policy or health roles may focus on one 'issue' at a time; this is a long-voiced concern in therapeutic training where trainees, courses and accrediting/regulating bodies tick off lists of 'must-cover' topics. However well intended, this approach can *never* cover the number of positions facing discrimination, oppression and resultant trauma and means that other differences can be overlooked – for example, anti-racist work might overlook gender inequalities, women's groups may be oblivious to disability and so forth. Once this is recognised we can also see how groups then have to compete for limited resources, setting up conflict between oppressed groups and meaning that underlying factors fostering discrimination/oppression are overlooked.

Finally, a very important concern for therapists, is that additive models simply do not capture people's experience. Difference is *not* cut and dry; we aren't just black, *or* gay *or* with physical limitations. We inhabit several of these positions, and we live these experiences simultaneously. So, as examples, we cannot assume that two gay men will experience anything remotely similar when one is from the UK and the other from Russia – focusing on their sexual appetites or their maleness only goes someway to helping us understand their world; the experience of being a woman has to be understood in economic terms, too – the experience of the Manhattan socialite is markedly different to that of economically impoverished women in Khayelitsha; two experiences of race will be different if one is at the peak of fitness and the other has limitations due to a disability.

Conceptualising diversity: Intersectional approaches

A response to the complexity of difference has been an interest in more relational and intersectional models of understanding experience. These pay attention to the impact of different aspects of our experience, for example the impact of sexuality and race together (see das Nair and Thomas, 2012), race and disability (see Petersen, 2006), age and sexual identity (see Gibson and Hansen, 2012) and so forth. Intersectional visions have, at their core, a call to action. Intersectionality is a liberatory framework (Jordan-Zachery, 2007) and this is an issue that novice therapists must understand as they progress through training. Psychologists, psychotherapists and counsellors need to recognise that while quiet listening is important, a place for change – both individual and social – must also, at the very least, be considered. This is important as many therapists take seriously the idea that we facilitate and listen, but do not give advice or instruct.

What these relational frameworks call for, is a more sophisticated engagement than a binary of either be 'active or passive' in one's practice, 'direct or not'. Intersectional understandings mean that where we understand the practices that lead to discrimination, there is a moral and ethical requirement to work to limit these injustices. It's not enough to *understand* better; it is important to rethink and restructure oppressive systems so that a more just society and ways of engaging with people can be envisioned. Thus therapy's political potential is brought to the fore in intersectional and relational thinking.

In practice what can be seen? What can be said?

Therapists need to ask themselves how visible or invisible an experience is. A client may bring a story about racial abuse and in those circumstances race immediately becomes visible. But what about those presentations when race isn't mentioned but racial difference exists between a therapist and a client? Or even, when it doesn't? Just because client and therapist are of the same race doesn't mean that racial issues are not an important aspect of the client's being-in-the-world. Shared racial understandings can mean that some things are easy to conceptualise and others lie beyond that.

As noted above, understandings of diversity have tended to use binary perspectives, describing 'different' experience through comparisons. So women have been described as 'different to men', in apartheid South Africa people of colour were viewed as 'different to whites' and of course gender and sexually diverse folk are perceived through a heterosexual lens. This is not a neutral process, by seeing men, white people and heterosexuals as the norm, it leads to a sense of the 'Other' being different, less than, something abnormal, pathological or even unknowable. The binary tends to lead us to make hierarchies, to discriminate and oppress. This can also happen in therapeutic dialogue, risking an impeded attunement and limited impact of therapeutic potential.

When thinking about diversity, it is important to recognise that language *captures* and also *constructs* experience; it is a window into personal and political meaning. There are two different issues that are important to consider when considering language and the political dimension. First, what can language tell us about the client and ourselves, and secondly, what impact can it have on the therapeutic process.

Language: A window into the world of the Other

When listening to clients, therapists listen to both *what* is being said and to *how* it is said; as we do so we try to glean the meaning the words have for the individual and also the discourses adopted and the implications these have (Milton, 2016). The same words can mean very different things. A client distressed by their same sex attractions might demonstrate their internalised homophobia through the use of such statements as 'I hate being a fairy' or 'I don't want to be some butch lezzie'. However, you only have to attend a Pride march to see these terms used to indicate confidence and delight in being authentically oneself – recent examples include a banner reading 'Lezzies with Lovehandles' (reclaiming both sexuality and body shape) and 'Poofs, Queers, Faeries and Fags all welcome' on a sign on a bus.

Regardless of a therapist's assessment of good or bad taste, it is important to read the expression as meant and so therapists need to understand the political overtones of language and check whether pathologising terminology is being used to offer up a sense of self-hate or as an indication of pride. Of course, clients might also move between positions in their talk. Because of this, it is important that therapists develop a depth of understanding. Should we be too quick to accept the language as reclaimed and contextually appropriate, then a chance could be lost to understand the specific meanings and the use of language that has previously oppressed. In addition, as well as ascertaining whether some kind of negativity is being communicated (internalised homophobia for instance), or whether some kind of positive meaning (pride in the reclaiming and subverting of meaning) is evident, it is worth assessing the more complicated, but important possibility that both might be evident in the communication. This reminds us, once again, of the importance of getting beyond the simplistic binary approach.

Language: A therapeutic medium

Therapists should also be aware that language carries different meanings depending on who speaks (Ellis, 1997). A banner proclaiming that someone is Queer held aloft at a Pride celebration, will mean something very different to when that word is used by the playground bully. In 2016 we saw the trend of women calling themselves and their female friends 'bitches' and this meant something different to when those words were spoken by drunk men on the number 47 bus on a Friday night. One is empowering and the other is intimidating.

Therapists benefit from considering the meaning that the speaker's identity might have on what is said. They might even utilise reclaimed terminology themselves – maybe in service of the old therapeutic adage to 'use the client's language'. This might enhance a sense of attunement but might equally be a minefield – especially where the therapist is 'Other' to the client. For example, imagine the scenario should a male therapist ask his female client something along the lines of 'so which bitch are we talking about here?' The language of the therapist is telling as it communicates something about their relationship to diversity and their position within culture. Our position enables us to see some perspectives and blinds us to others and clients are often very aware of this.

Back to the binary

When we adopt binary perspectives, whether big P or small p, it becomes easy to construct things as self-standing, independent entities, allowing them to be compared and contrasted, and for hierarchies to be created. Once in a hierarchy, experiences and people are valued differently.

The notion of 'disability' is another useful example. 'Disability' is a concept that leads to assumptions about being *either* 'abled' or 'disabled' – 'do you have a disability or not?' is sometimes asked. Yet for many people disability is only significant in some contexts. For many people the experience of disability waxes and wanes; it is sometimes prominent and other times, something that recedes far into the background. Phenomenologically, it may in fact be the context that *creates* the sense of disability, because it is only when having to navigate poorly constructed stairways in buildings that a physical disability is experienced. Similarly it may be that the only time a sight related problem is experienced is when the person has to use websites that have no screen magnifier or screen reader technologies.

The binary can limit us so we understand the 'minority' experience as less than the norm. The comparison locates the less powerful Other as the one who is *lacking* something. Once a hierarchy is created those that are 'Othered' tend to come out worse. These normative views inform interpersonal, social and employment conditions as they become embedded in policy, legislation and practice and manifest in everything from salary scales to building structures (see Wilkinson and Pickett, 2010). Such conceptualisations and practices are not just inaccurate and unfair; they are at the heart of significant distress and suffering and are central to minority stress.

Minority stress

The concept of minority stress was 'originally applied to the stress those of a minority identity experience when their values conflict with the dominant culture's values' (see Whitman, 2015). The stress stems from negative events and from incongruent and *repeated* interactions with societal structures that target one's minority status; these oppressive practices and the stress experienced can also lead to maladaptive behaviours (see Whitman, 2015). Minority stress results in personal, psychological and social distress, both at the point of experiencing negativity and on an ongoing basis. Resultant difficulties can include mental health disorders (see King et al., 2008) and problems with accessing health care and social services (see Whitman, 2015), PTSD, violent behaviour, alcoholism and substance abuse, eating disorders and suicidal ideation (see King et al., 2008; Rivers, 2004). Of course, a great deal of social capital is also lost in this diminishing of the Other (Wilkinson and Pickett, 2010).

Binary perspectives and minority stress don't only manifest in overt negativity though; we also see this in, what might first appear as, positive reactions.

More 'positive' versions of Othering?
The stress of being exotic

Another use of the binary is where the 'Other' is exoticised. When this happens the minority can experience confusion: suddenly gay men are moved from 'fag' to 'fab', the person of colour is put on the sexual bucket list, and paralympians are referred to as 'super-human' rather than simply as the 'outstanding athletes' that they are. Trainee therapists might do the same thing when, in trying to extend their understanding of diversity, they foreground characteristics such as race, gender, sexuality or mental health status and request from their placement, a 'Muslim', 'black' or 'disabled' client. This is exoticisation under the rhetoric of competences and regulatory orthodoxy.

Being made exotic *might* be more benign than pathologisation, hate or aggression or *might* seem eminently more desirable, but it remains problematic nonetheless as Otherness is elevated to a key state of being, whether or not that is the person's own experience. Damage is done by the insistence on projecting a stereotype onto the person.

Exoticisation can be difficult to engage with. The person perceived as the minority may be aware that, the person responding to you in this way is trying to be '*nice*' and that they will be confused, and maybe hurt or insulted, if you call them on these practices. Secondly, as a minority you may be well aware that being 'fab' is a lot more fun than being seen negatively, but the stereotyping and pigeonholing limits imagined and actual possibilities for people. It is important that therapists get beyond this and recognise their overly positive assumptions as well as their negative ones.

Acceptability and fitting in

Another way in which current political mindsets are problematic systemically is where minority people experience 'conditional' acceptance. This is acceptance with a requirement to conform to a norm, to become the 'acceptable minority' (rather than the individual they may need, desire, deserve to be). We see this pressure on migrants where there is often a forceful and immediate pressure to 'assimilate' and become 'one of us' – learn fluent English, adopt Western dress codes, be quiet about your faith and so on (Rudmin, 2003, Ward, Bochner and Furnham, 2005). This pressure means that, in essence, an attempt is made to limit difference to just accent or skin colour. Another example is where lesbians and gay men are acceptable if they conform with sexist ways of being, so 'femme' lesbians get more praise than those who challenge the 'pretty little lady' stereotype, or acceptability for gay men can mean limiting ones 'deviation' from a gendered masculine stereotype to the choice of partner only. 'Be butch, be a lad, be a top. You may sleep with men but at least you aren't girly, you're still one of the lads', is how it goes. 'Don't even think about being femme or playing with drag.' These binary positions and the range of associated assumptions feed a splitting and pathologising process which is frequently seen in bullying, banter and everyday slights.

Hierarchies of the most oppressed

One insidious aspect of this disabling and disempowering system is the way in which those without power, and those who are discriminated against, can find themselves competing with each other for resources. In apartheid South Africa we saw it in terms of a racial hierarchy and of course it happens in relation to race, gender and sexuality too. The 2016 newspaper coverage of the UK government's resistance to offering PrEP (anti-HIV medication) to gay men quickly utilised comparisons with children's and elderly services. The implication being, that we should *either* treat gay men *or* other vulnerable groups. The discourse went further to imply that as children and cancer patients are 'innocents' they should receive the limited funding over 'promiscuous' gay men (Borland et al., 2016).

du Plock offers a more personal account of this to illustrate how it plays out in relationships. He wrote:

I recall explaining to my poor ignorant colleague that she could not possibly understand what it is like as a gay man to use public transport in some of the less salubrious areas of London. She countered that as a woman who used buses frequently she found my insistence on my special knowledge of threat and discrimination somewhat overdone. My reaction to this was to redouble my efforts to impress upon her that our two experiences were quite different and that the discrimination I experienced was the greater. (du Plock, 2014, pp. 150–151)

While such interactions may have meaning for the individuals involved, psychologists have to recognise that it is irrelevant whether one's experience of threat is more or less than another's – no group should have to face intimidation and the distress it creates.

At a broader socio-political level, this inter-minority competition can be seen as a deliberate political act; it also becomes a way of policing and managing difference. While pitting gay men's needs against those of children and the elderly in the PrEP debate, the eye is taken off those in power. It's all about the competition and not the decision-making processes in the political domain. From a social justice perspective this is problematic as it keeps the attention on the 'minority' person/population, allowing those with power to avoid reflection, responsibility and accountability for oppressive practices.

Diversity in the consulting room

As I mentioned earlier, no matter how tightly a service is run, and how stringent their inclusion/exclusion criteria, therapists still face diversity, day in and day out. So how do therapists engage with these differences? And what might we think they *should* do?

As shown earlier, therapists cannot simply rely on the body of knowledge in counselling, psychotherapy and applied psychology to guide them as some is still problematic. Therefore, it may be helpful to have some familiarity with sociological analyses, feminist and cross-cultural work and political theory (see Goodman et al., 2004; Eleftheriadou, 2003; Fanon, 1986). In addition, there are more recent, helpful contributions within a range of fields – including systemic, existential, psychodynamic and pluralistic approaches to psychology and therapeutic practice (see Dallos and Draper, 2015; Davies and Neal, 2000; Milton, 2014; O'Connor and Ryan, 1993; Samuels, 1993) – the key is for therapists to read critically in service of a holistic, pluralistic and biopsychosocial understanding of diversity.

Within these literatures we see that there are some key practices already advocated. For instance, it is generally understood that it is helpful to conceptualise clients' experiences *both* in relation to their private experience *and* in relation to social processes. This brings assessment and formulation into focus.

Assessment and formulation

Psychologists usually start a therapeutic relationship in the context of assessment and formulation. This is a collaborative process with the client and aims to develop a clear understanding of the presenting problem, the client's experiences and what type of intervention/approach might be helpful. While therapists could simply attend to the personal dimension, assessment and formulation allow therapists to pay full and deliberate attention to the personal *and* the social, and both the explicit *and* implicit communications, including that which is being communicated at a cultural/discursive level (see Langdridge, 2014; Strawbridge, 1994). As well as listening to family history and types of distress, therapists are able to consider how class, wealth, status, education level, or physical abilities might affect the experience, and question how they might impact the ways in which things can even be communicated? Do the genders of the therapeutic relationship make some things easier or more difficult to talk about – for either the client or the therapist? What about first or second language issues? How do these influence expression and comprehension? Do class-based differences aid or hinder the relationship and one's ability to attune to the needs of the other? These are important issues to be considering while also engaging with the client in the moment. Process becomes as useful a source of information as does the verbal content of a session.

The literature also argues that minority stress needs to be explored. A full understanding of an experience is not possible unless the person's world has been made familiar and the intersectional factors are understood. This means that assessment and formulation are enormously enhanced by an attuned knowledge of diverse populations. As mentioned previously, the 'colour-blind' (sexuality-blind, disability-blind, faith-blind or simply refusing to see difference) position potentially erases people's experiences. If we are to truly offer a useful therapeutic experience for clients it has to be attuned to the world in which they exist, not the one that we wish was available for them.

The process of assessment and formulation usually culminates in decisions about whether therapy might be helpful or whether some other intervention is more urgent – housing, dealing with benefit entitlements, physical safety and so on. If therapy is thought to be indicated, consideration is given to the therapeutic approach that might offer the client a chance of relief, change or learning. When the assessment points to external oppressive factors as well as personal responses, an approach open to this needs to be chosen. Considering the problems outlined in relation to traditional theory (and its associated training and practice), this might mean that the therapist is required to adjust their core model so as to take account of more specific and contextual factors. In doing so, therapy has to be recognised as going beyond manualised and stereotypical practice to a relationship tailored to the client's specific needs. The reader will see a variety of attempts to do this in the upcoming chapters.

Practice

One tricky area for therapists can be the translation of ideas to behaviours, the move from espoused theory to embodied practice. Therapists might understand cultural/personal experiences and even have swotted up on terminology, but it is important that they find a way of being comfortable speaking from/ to those positions. Our level of comfort (or discomfort) will be experienced by the client, and asking for the right information can be fruitless if one requests this in a problematic manner. This doesn't necessarily mean that a therapist is ever 100 per cent comfortable; it is unlikely that anyone is completely at ease discussing such powerful and personal aspects of difference. Indeed, for many people, sexism, racism and homophobia are all easier to ignore or deny than to talk about. This cannot be the same in the consulting room though. If we were to try and ignore such issues, then questions would be raised as to the point of therapy at all. So it is important that therapists find enough comfort to at least speak about difficult things. Once this has been managed, we may glean greater insight into the person and the world they exist in. The next step is to communicate the awareness gained.

Samuels (1993) proposed a 'plural interpretation' as being helpful – an everyday example might assist here. Imagine a therapist working with a woman who is concerned about her own shortcomings and who, almost as an aside, describes her male partner as being constantly critical of her looks and behaviours. One phase is for the therapist to recognise that this is a communication about multiple levels and become curious enough to track the different levels: to ask what is being said at the personal, familial and political levels; to listen to these and ask about them also. Should it then transpire that there is enough information for a therapist to formulate at different levels, a plural interpretation may develop along the lines of:

the experiences seem to relate to your own habits of negative thinking, seeking imperfections and ruminating on them ..., but at the same time they also seem to be aspects of relationships or a culture which expects female perfection by way of low weight, slimness and constant affability whether or not the circumstances facilitate it. Both seem relevant and I wonder which one seems to be more important to you?

Such interpretations aren't possible unless the therapist has paid attention to the socio-political dimension of the client's experience, is aware of the pressures that women are under to manage weight and body shape, and is also alert to the fact that the male eye, combined with male privilege to express an opinion, is a powerful constant in many cultures – and potentially in this client's relationship.

While a plural interpretation attends to both the personal and the political, it is also a democratic political act in itself, not overwriting the client experience with those of the expert. This might be especially relevant in this case should gender differences exist between therapist and client.

By using the notion of plural interpretation, readers might be forgiven for assuming that this section is primarily aimed at psychodynamic approaches. But, this is not the case. All approaches offer the client a different interpretation of their experience simply by virtue of the therapist offering their own, different understanding. Thus the logic underpinning this intervention is akin to existential and systemic ideas attending to, and formulating, the person in context. The phenomenologist, being aware of the notion of 'intentionality' asks about the world the client is describing, not just their description of self, and cognitive therapists evaluate the degree to which a client's automatic thoughts are 'realistic' or prone to catastrophising and thus offer their own interpretation of what is happening.

Having said this of course, it is true that assessment and formulation might lead an astute therapist to suggest a feminist group, work with an LGBT affirmative therapist or to match on the grounds of race or faith if that is important to the client. This can allow specific aspects of oppression to be confidently addressed. But a hope is that the better all therapists become at working with the intersection of the personal and the political, difference and diversity, such specialisms may eventually become less important.

At this point, it is time to move on to the stories of practice that aim to offer possibilities of thought and of engagement.

3

RACE

Racism inflicts enormous damage – on individual kids bullied in the playground to populations of entire countries being subject to segregation, slavery and genocide. We see the damage evidenced in medicine (see Kawachi et al., 2005; LaVeist, 2005), in the development of government policy (see Hepple et al., 2000), and in counselling, psychotherapy, applied psychology and mental health practice (Eleftheriadou, 2003; Lofthouse, 2010).

Racial minorities have to *more regularly* confront negativity, minority stress can be internalised and create difficulties in managing one's self image and emotions, and the stressors can be both overt or much more subtle. Let's consider a couple of overt and covert stressors that affect Taye in the next story.

Violence is a stressor that is all too prevalent. Some forms of violence are societal (think of our history of colonialism and slavery) and these seem to run throughout time and history and manifest across the world. Violence is also widespread at a person–person level – with opportunistic attacks on the street, in the playground and at sporting events. A 2013 UK government report noted an estimated 30,234 racially motivated hate crimes (ONS/MoJ, 2013) that included assault, rape, murder and bullying.

The *actual* rates of violence aren't necessarily the complete picture, as *threatened* violence and intimidation are also significant problems. Even when rates of violent crime are low and when individuals themselves do not experience actual attack, people are still alert to the *risk* of attack or negativity, and fearful of potential violence. People experience levels of anxiety, concern, avoidance and withdrawal as the possibility remains.

Race also factors into such societal mechanisms of control as the 'Stop and Search' legislation (or section 60 of the Criminal Justice and Public Order Act 1994) that gives police power to stop and search people. Analyses by the London School of Economics (LSE) and the Open Society Justice Initiative show that black people are consistently stopped and searched significantly more than white people (Hurrell, 2013; Townsend, 2012), racial differences in rates of incarceration are also telling (Blumstein, 1982). The impact of such policies on individuals varies but can be unsettling, as this awareness is internalised and the 'minority' person becomes alert to any signs of power and authority. Thus we hear of greater suspicion of the police; for some people there is a sense of defeatism, with ambition thwarted in the face of unreasonable and targeted hurdles. These factors can lead to personal and social difficulties and are impediments to people reaching their full potential.

Taye: Racial difference and questions of belonging

I

I meet Taye just before his seventeenth birthday. He arrives punctually for his appointment, dressed in inexpensive but trendy teenage clothes. Taye has been referred to the large London teaching hospital that I am on placement[1] with because his social worker feels that he would:

benefit from therapy as he is struggling in a range of areas, including with school, with friendships and with an upcoming transition from living in care at Foxdene to independent living.

As brief as it is, the referral alerts me to the fact that there is likely to be a history of family disruption, foster care being such a significant step for a family to take. I also wonder about Taye's wider interpersonal relationships.

After collecting Taye from the waiting room, I open the door of the consulting room and step aside, allowing him to enter the small dingy room. It has three old but comfortable seats and dim overhead lighting, with an additional lamp on the table. Taye stops in the middle of the room and looks at me expectantly.

'Make yourself comfortable', I say with a wave of my arm, trying to offer Taye as much freedom as circumstance allows.

'Where?'

'Wherever you prefer', I suggest.

This doesn't immediately result in Taye taking a seat though, and it highlights how unsure he is, as he stands there unable to choose.

'Anywhere is fine', I say. He still doesn't move. I point to one of the chairs and say, 'Maybe I'll sit here.'

Taye sits down in the chair opposite me, with the table and lamp between us. There is a brief silence before I ask him, 'So how can I help?' He looks at me with an almost imperceptible shrug. 'Didn't they tell you?'

'Who, your social worker?', I ask.

'Uh hmm', he nods while looking around the room. I can't tell if he is nervous or something else, annoyed maybe.

'Yes, I've had a referral and it sounds like you've had a bit of a tough time. Looks like you have a lot coming up too', I say. 'But that's all. It might be

---

[1] Like any other profession, psychotherapists have to start somewhere and that is usually under supervision in well-established psychological/psychotherapy services.

good to hear from you though, how things have been for you and what you make of it.'

'OK', he says.

Taye seems surprised, but not annoyed, I decide, as he smiles at me and takes a breath.

'Well I don't know how you can help but it's hard at the moment, ... it's shit really. I don't belong at the home; all the kids are younger than me and I am moving out soon. That should be good though. I don't like college much either. But it's more than that, I just feel bad all the time. Worried a lot. Bored as well. Like, there's nothing to do.'

I ask him what it is that he worries about, what shape and form these worries take. I want to get a sense of how severe they are. He describes the worrying, and as he does it seems that he tends to worry more when he is alone or when he is not distracted, but no matter how hard he tries, his worrying is happening more and more. 'And I am bored all the time too', he says.

I don't pick up on the boredom straight away; it's the worries that intrigue me (and I suspect will be of primary concern to my supervisor). They seem to be about how he *should* be, how others *might* see him, how he *will* be judged. I ask him who judges him and why? It transpires that there isn't anyone in particular, no specific person is out to judge him; he just knows that he is 'judge-able'. I have to think about this. As I do, I realise that this is not quite as illogical as I first assume. Our self–self relationship is distinct from our self–other relationship (and our self–world relationship too for that matter). Thus our self–self relationship may be coloured by dislike and judgement, while having no vision of a nasty, scrutinising, judging Other (Spinelli, 2014). On closer examination, of course, it could be linked to hypercritical discourses that abound culturally whenever someone feels different to the norm, but because these views are so frequent and normalised, we often fail to spot or understand their impact.

As we speak he tells me that sometimes he cannot sleep because of the worries going through his mind; that he will sit in class, be quiet and worry that others will tease him if they knew him. He also worries that people will judge him badly for being in care and living with 'a bunch of kids'. And he tells me that it is 'getting worse'.

'Worse?', I ask.

'Yes', he says. His head drops and his cheeks redden. 'I sometimes wonder whether it's worth it. I've started to wonder why I am even here. I've cut myself too', he says, with what I think is a sense of relief.

I ask, 'what's not worth it?' His head snaps up as he corrects me: 'I didn't say it's *not* worth it, but I wonder *whether* it's worth it. That's different.'

I see that and I agree with him. 'Yes, that is different.' I don't know whether to ask him about this important distinction or whether to ask him about the cutting he mentioned, so I revert to a simple 'Can you tell me more?'

Taye tells me how cutting offers some respite from this worry and effort. It takes his mind off things and calms him. This doesn't seem like 'self-harm' as training and supervision have suggested it might be; it seems more like self-management (of course, with some risk). While such distinctions may seem a bit pedantic to some, the psychotherapist's job is to understand the meaning of what is being spoken about, not just to obtain a stark behavioural outline. Meaning helps us understand the 'why' of behaviour as well as the 'what'. Once we understand what a behaviour means to the client, there is a much greater chance of the client clarifying the full range of options available to them and making the best choices they can.

'And you do this deliberately?', I ask, 'Or ...'

'No not at all', Taye says quickly. 'I ... it just seems to happen. I mean ... I know I'm doing it but it's not that I plan it; it's not like I think, "I'll do that when I get home". And it helps. But they don't like it.'

'Who doesn't?'

'The staff – they worry about the younger kids seeing it and getting upset. Actually I think they worry about themselves having to see it too.'

I am suddenly struck by this story being about people worrying about others, and not about him. I wonder if it is true that the staff are more concerned about the younger kids – not an irrelevant concern but surely it shouldn't be something that erases all concern for this young man. It seems similar to the things he worries about, prioritising what others are thinking, expecting negative judgement. There is very little attention paid to him by others or even by himself, to how he is doing, to what he needs.

This is our first session so as well as getting a sense of what his current experience is like I want to get a broader picture, of him over time, of what he is confident about as well as what he worries about, to get an idea of how he might have come to be the person he is. I am possibly too mindful of this though and so ask what seems to be a bit of a non sequitur: 'How did you come to live at Foxdene?'

Taye sighs and tells me about his background. He tells me that his father is absent and has been for a long time; he returned to Barbados years ago. While Taye received a few letters immediately after that, they stopped quite quickly. His mother has had a few relationships, which he describes as 'nothing too serious' and he has a younger half-sister, Leila. His mother hadn't married Jack, Leila's father, and is no longer involved with him. He sounds emotional though when he says, 'but he at least sees Leila, takes her out, buys her stuff'.

This is moving material and I almost forget that I have asked about Foxdene, but Taye returns to that.

'A couple of years ago mom got ill, couldn't work a lot, so they sacked her. We had no money, literally none. I had to look after her a bit. When she went into hospital they put a social worker on the case. They kept asking whether we could get family to help, but that's a joke, Mom *has* no other family and Vince is, that's my Dad, he's who knows where? Jack helped a bit but he wasn't going to clothe and feed me, was he? So the social worker suggested that I go into foster care for a bit. That was two years ago. Mom's a bit better but can still only work part time so I can't go home to live, so I've been at Foxdene for two years. They need the room so are moving me to independent living soon. But ... I want to; I don't fit in there.'

I listen to this as closely as I can and think I am piecing the story together quite well. My emerging formulation is:

Taye was born into a family that was already (probably) struggling with some discord and this culminated in the family breaking up a few years after he was born. As well as family instability, Taye has had to make sense of the fact that his father disappeared, physically and then from any contact at all. This is likely to have at least played on his mind, giving him cause to wonder what *he* did to cause his father to disappear.[2] The relationships that his mother went on to have meant that he met a number of people who were interested in his mother (and later his sister) but not in him. If anything he felt he was perceived as unnecessary, a problem, or an irritation, an arbitrary someone to be ignored.

More recently he has experienced the potential loss of his mother as she became unwell and while she has recovered he has felt left out and rejected, as Leila managed to stay with Mom while he had to be farmed out, made to live where he didn't fit in. This replicated a long-held sense of himself, in the family, in the care home and at school. This seems to have resulted in a lack of interest in self, a preoccupation of what others might want him to be and significant stress.

I discuss these early sessions with my supervisor who feels that my formulation is relevant enough but that it is a bit technical; it seems to be a little too

---

[2] While the break down of parental relationships is seldom about the children and more about the parents' strengths and abilities, limitations and compatibility, it's not unusual for children to assume that they are the cause of this. This may be a way of trying to limit the sense of rejection and being out of control. The child's theory may be incorrect but at least it makes the world a meaningful place.

theoretical. 'How do you *feel* about Taye?' he asks. It was this question that makes me realise that I have actually been quite churned up. I am very moved by hearing about how him being treated as irrelevant, disposable or unimportant *throughout* his life. This is not to say that his mother, father, Jack or anyone else actually thought or felt like this. Their own circumstances may quite reasonably explain why their investment in him was interrupted or partial. What my supervisor is asking me to work with is the client's experience and the meanings that they inhabit.

I also realise that I feel sorry that, even when he is alone, he is aware of and anxious about others ignoring him, judging him as unnecessary or not worth wanting to know. 'Keep an eye on that', my supervisor says, 'that may well affect the therapy'. At this stage I have not yet grasped how common it is that our core ways of being with others will also manifest in therapy. Psychotherapists must learn about and find ways to work with this otherwise, at best, it is an opportunity missed or, worse, we end up replicating some of the unhelpful patterns that are part and parcel of the client's difficulties. Different schools of therapy talk about this in different ways: psychoanalysis has theorised it in terms of transference and counter-transference; and humanistic therapies sometimes refer to it as parallel processes. Either way, the therapeutic relationship and its nuances and distortions are a vital part of assessment, formulation and the management of the therapy. This is true of 'personal' aspects of our character but also our socio-cultural positions and reactions to them. At this this point, though, I don't know how, or even whether, it will impact on our work.

II

As therapy progresses Taye starts to attend sessions with things he *wants* to talk about. In some respects he surprises me, tackling topics that I have assumed are the province of the twenty-something period of life, exploring what possible life he can have if people feel he isn't worthy; he is pondering whether and how to have friends and relationships when one is pretty sure that others won't be interested. Taye hasn't had the luxury of waiting till his cohort finds jobs and careers; for him, his place in the world has long been a question.

For my part, I enjoy working with Taye as it feels meaningful; we recognise the challenges he faces, gain some insight and despite facing a rather bleak vision of his circumstance he is enthused by thinking about independence, college courses, maybe apprenticeships, and other possibilities. He has ideas about what he might do and how he might go about it ... but as time progresses, we realise that ideas seem hard to enact; in fact he doesn't follow many of them up. Why put in an application if they are only going to turn you down? Why sign up for drama classes if no one is going to give you a part? Why bother to apply for a bursary as 'everyone knows' he won't be awarded it.

When we looked at these questions Taye quickly decides that it is an issue of courage or stamina – it is his fault; he knows what he wants to do but doesn't 'have the balls' to say it, or feels drained before he has the chance to put himself forward. This makes sense to him and provides grounds so as not to take or create an opportunity. If I had been listening I would have seen how our personal struggles are also linked to wider social dilemmas, in this case questions about masculinity and how men and boys are 'supposed' to be.

His potential inadequacy seems a 'possible' explanation and at first I go with it, start to think about how I support him, how he might learn about personal strength, how is it that people develop faith in trying.

This line of thought is useful enough but after a few weeks it becomes apparent that while it is important to think about his own contribution to this, we are overlooking some very real experiences he has had, and very real hurdles. The application is a long shot as the courses were indeed highly competitive; it's true that he might not get a leading part, but many others might not too; bursaries are rare and so he might not get that either. What is so apparent though is that these eventualities are always used to 'prove' his core view of himself, namely that he won't succeed and that is because of his perceived inadequacy. He cannot accept that he might not succeed for a range of other reasons too. The only thing that has impact is himself not fitting in, being the outsider. Spinelli (2014) notes the power and the consequence of the 'sedimented' self-concept. While none of us are completely capable of understanding our fluidity and our possibilities, there are often times when our struggle is due to a conviction we have about ourselves – a conviction that *feels* like a truth rather than an opinion and so becomes the basis around which we come to understand, orient ourselves and relate to others.

III

In the autumn Taye comes to one session and shows me fresh scratches on his arms. He talks, uninterrupted and with intensity, for over twenty minutes, recounting events of the previous weekend.

He had been at college on Friday and lingered after class, first with friends and then in the library. It was dark by the time he left and some boys were hanging around at the entrance. They are popular lads but also bullies, boys he normally kept his distance from. As he passed them he felt intimidated and self-conscious, thinking that they were talking and laughing about him. 'They wanted me to know they were laughing at me', he said. Taye hadn't been sure what to do; he didn't want to look 'soft', he said, but equally he didn't want any trouble. His attention to them meant he hesitated or looked at them for longer than they felt he 'should' and so more things were said to him. He didn't quite hear but it led to more laughter as he passed them and then he heard one of them say loudly, and clearly meant for him, 'that's right, keep walking, jog on back to where you come from'.

'And that's what I did', he says, 'I just walked on. I let them speak to me like that.' His shoulders sag; he shakes his head and seems aghast with himself. I feel angry as I listen to this, aware of the impact of bullying and xenophobia.[3]

Taye continues, 'I just left. Then I was walking across the Green and started to hear footsteps, I didn't look back though. I heard sniggering although I pretended I didn't. I acted as though everything was OK and carried on walking, but the footsteps kept coming. When I did look behind me, it was them; they laughed and shooed me on with their hands. One of them started to come forward, so I legged it. I just ran. I ran and ran. I just wanted to be away from them. I got as far as the main road and then ...', Taye pauses and rolls his eyes, '... then I bumped into two cops, who made me stop. They asked me all of these questions ... What is my name? What I was doing there? Why was I running? Where I was going? ... It was really annoying. I hadn't done anything except try to get away from those other guys. It was embarrassing too as those guys walked by and one even said "Evening Officer" as they passed. It's just not bloody fair.'

'You didn't tell the police why you were running? That it was to escape from those other boys?', I ask.

Taye looks at me with a strange expression on his face and I immediately feel stupid. He says, 'eh, No, ... They wouldn't listen and if they did I would get it later wouldn't I.'

We talk about the events a bit more and it transpires that Taye was 'used to it', being stopped by the police that is. It happens at least once a month, and

---

[3] The term 'xenophobia' is the fear of that which is perceived to be foreign or strange; it is a political term and not a recognised psychological phobia and can often be seen in negative attitudes towards other nationalities, where nationhood gets elevated to the key aspect of that person's being. Such public reactions intimidate and threaten the individual and can be a key factor in self-hatred, low self-esteem and psychological distress due to the minority stress it creates (see das Nair and Butler, 2012; Hatzenbuehler, 2009).

sometimes he is searched.[4] 'My face just fits', he said: 'Us brown skinned kids are a key ... what do you call it? ... Demographic', he said.

Clearly my world view – and my world – is very different to the one Taye has to navigate. My two questions have given away my vision of a trusting and righteous world, which doesn't tally with his experience. 'This isn't "just" xenophobia', I think, 'he's talking about racism'. As I realise this, I am surprised that he is so resigned to it; I am surprised that he feels so bad about *himself*, not the boys at college and not the police, why isn't he more pissed off with *them* rather than himself? I am overlooking the fact that, from a position of relative safety, it may well make sense that someone would – or should – protest intrusion by others. However, the frequency with which such events happen mean that Taye is 'used' to being on the receiving end of oppressive power. Thus racism both causes distress and exacerbates stress experienced from other factors. In addition, Taye's early experience means that he might be predisposed to accepting that he is the 'cause' of difficult experiences.

As I listen to Taye I try to shift from my own outrage and consider things from his perspective. The more I think about it, I start to see that these types of experience reaffirm his sense of not fitting in – anywhere. He can accept these events as they are congruent with his sedimented self-concept; as an outsider those with power, white youths, the police, bursary administrators and the like, remind him of his outsider-ness.

We have been working on this sense of not belonging for a while now, so Taye accepts it less than in the past; he is trying to reconcile this old 'truth' with his more critical, exploration. He talks about how bad he felt ... they weren't right to intimidate him (this is different) so *he* should have said something, *he* should have done something (this is familiar). My heart sinks a little as just as it seems that he recognises that others have agency and responsibility here too, he resorts to the tried-and-trusted vision of himself. If he were different, he would fit in and then they wouldn't act this way. He talks as if *he* is the problem and as if *he* is the only player with any reason to change. Other people always seem to get off scot-free.

Before I can comment on this, though, Taye comes to a slow halt. He looks at me tearfully and says, 'this is just so hard, ... so hard'. I feel for him and respond, 'Oh yes, I know. I know how hard it is.'

---

[4] This has occurred for a long time. Black people are stopped and searched significantly more than white people both in terms of absolute and relative numbers. Despite black and other ethnic minority populations being only 13 per cent of the UK population compared to the white population (87 per cent) in 2009 black people were 10.7 times more likely to be stopped than white people (see Hurrell, 2013; Office of National Statistics, 2011).

Taye's face changes as I speak. In reaction to my first sentence he seemed to ease slightly. But as I continued on, the relief changed to a look of incredulity. 'I don't think so', he says.

I open my mouth to respond but don't really have anything to say. 'Seriously, do *you* know? How? You didn't get told to go back to where you come from, did you? You don't get stopped on the street – do you? You don't have to sit there and wait and see whether the black kids will think you are black enough to join them, or the white kids think you are white enough to join them. You just fit in, don't you? You fit.'

He stops suddenly, looking worried. Anger and frustration have passed and now he reverts to worrying about the expression of his feelings. His outburst has put him at risk again, the other, this time it is me, might realise just how objectionable he is. But I don't get that, not at first.

A lot happens in that quiet moment: externally I just nod; internally I try to consider my racing thoughts and the accompanying range of emotions. I am surprised, embarrassed, annoyed and even a little hurt. Taye is challenging my, admittedly rather crass, overly simplistic platitude and recognising that my difference means I am unlikely to 'get' him. But I am trying to help him, can't he see that? Isn't that enough?

I know that I shouldn't try and overwrite his view, mustn't reject it out of hand. I have to try and see this as Taye sees it – I am older than him and am white. Fact. I have a job and that brings security and status – maybe not fact but it could do, at least this is what he sees or assumes. To him, it is clear; I experience a lot of privilege, and at some level I really can't argue with him. I am different, in some ways I face a completely different world with a different set of privileges and challenges.[5]

I struggle to accept this because, to me, that isn't the entire story. I am, in fact, also in a confusing transition myself, having just moved to the UK from the US for graduate school. I have grown up in South Africa as an 'immigrant' in an area hostile to us and have indeed heard those very words a multitude of

---

[5] There is a debate about whether therapists should work with specific differences (such as being of different races or age groups) and everything these contexts bring, or whether we should focus on how we are all different by virtue of simply being human. To my mind, there is no set answer. The decision is often one to be made in the moment; indeed such binary choices are themselves unhelpful, why should it be one or the other? It can also be important to consider our ontic responses to ontological factors, that is, in a world where racism is a frequent/constant factor, what is the client's experience, response, opportunity? (For more on these dilemmas and complexities, see du Plock, 2014; Langdridge; 2014.)

times. 'You are living off the fat of the land, fuck off back to where you came from' was said to me more than once.

I also experience discomfort around my own lived differences; in terms of gender, sexual identity, politics and more, I often feel that I don't fit in and I don't always know whether to voice my feelings or not. Even my professional role is less privileged than Taye imagines – unless in an existing post as a psychologist, social worker or psychiatrist, trainee psychotherapists tend to work for free while shouldering enormous expense and incurring great debt. I recognise the social markers that set us apart but it starts to become clear how complex this is.

During this quiet moment, my private responses are varied and powerful, including 'How dare he assume so much about me'. Thankfully I think this rather than try to justify or explain it to him. I know that trying to argue my way through this moment is unlikely to help and would be a psychological retaliation, pitting us against each other, competing for whom is most oppressed or discriminated against (see Chapter 2). Should that happen, it won't just be some random 'others' that are different to him; it could create a chasm between us.

I also recognise the issue of difference, that I am already Other; I have been from the beginning. What is new is just that it has come to the fore. I wonder whether my lack of attention to racial and other differences has been an attempt to deny the impact of insidious social reactions to difference, processes that seem so big and immutable, a way to avoid the guilt and shame of my privileged position, or is it maybe just one of the privileges that white people enjoy that we don't have to think about race much at all. My claim to know his experience when I couldn't *possibly* know it throws light on how Taye and I have to navigate very different worlds. That had been a foolish comment I realise. I might know something about differences, and not fitting in, and maybe also about some forms of being oppressed; maybe if I think about them properly they might be helpful, but … knowing his experience? That was definitely a claim too far.

So it turns out that my supervisor had been right in drawing my attention to the fact that Taye's experiences 'may affect therapy'; my supervisor didn't just mean as transference, but they affect us as real, lived differences too. My supervisor's comment has given me the chance to think ahead, to consider how I might respond if my intended connection fails to be felt, or what might I do if Taye feels that I don't care, or I can't 'get' him. I remember thinking of how important it will be to accept his view and of being explicit about this. We had also talked about how to confirm the possibility of relating even when there are gaps between us.

'You are right Taye; I don't know what it's like for you, not really. I think I know *something* about some of it, but it wasn't accurate to say that I know exactly how hard this is, precisely what it is to go through this.'

He looks at me and starts to say something. 'I didn't mean ...', but then he stops.

'Didn't mean what?', I ask. 'It's OK, part of this is about finding a way to say what's difficult.'

'I didn't mean to be rude.'

'I know you didn't', I say, 'and I don't think you were rude. You pointed to something that's hard to talk about, how we're different and it's important not to ignore that.'

He looks relieved and nods.

'But it's time to finish today. Maybe we can talk more about this next time', I say.

He nods, collects his things and says goodbye as he leaves.

The next session is not easy for Taye. He starts by saying, 'You said we should talk about something, but I don't know what it was.' In this way it is as if he takes some responsibility of drawing our attention back to difference but doesn't name it; indeed he leaves me to name it. In some ways I think that this isn't unusual, there is literature that notes how those with privilege or power tend to feel more confident about setting the parameters of such conversations; however, I am not sure about how I think the conversation should go. If I am too keen to speak and name things, or decide what is important, I am at risk of either setting an agenda that might not suit his need or I am at risk of walking into a bit of a trap, that is, stepping beyond what I know anything about ... again. So I limit my response to, 'I think we were at a point where we had become aware that there *are* some differences, and also the *appearance* of other differences, that might affect how people, and we, experience each other.'

My heart sinks a little. I have gone from simplistic oversimplifications to a clumsy elaboration. I clearly am not at ease in navigating these differences either.

Taye nods, 'Oh that's right, I remember.'

I ask him, 'Do you have any thoughts about it?'

'Not really', he says, 'I suppose you are right but I haven't really thought about it before. I know that you won't get everything I talk about, but then no one does. Why would you be different?' I get the feeling that Taye sees this through his lens of 'I am hard to understand' rather than 'It can be hard for people to understand other people's experience'.

Once again I feel a strong temptation to try and solve this, to create a comfortable balance, and comment in such a way that difference is eradicated and I can reassure him that I get everything he talks about. But that would be wrong. Luckily, supervision had prepped me beforehand. We had talked about the different meanings that moments like this might have. This isn't an experience with just one meaning, but several meanings simultaneously. It's a moment between Taye and I, but equally it is a moment related to much social difference and Othering. If handled well, it might help us reconnect, and it might help us shed light on the worlds in which we exist. Worlds where some have the luxury of obliviousness and others have to experience a preoccupation with, and elevation of, aspects of themselves an enormous portion of the time.

This session and the next few allow us to think about difference and its varieties. A sense of difference isn't uncommon in his day-to-day life; it is there in his history and present in the room too; he has noted my age, my ethnicity and my professional status/aspirations. As we talk about what he finds difficult, experiences he's had and his ambitions for the future, we inevitably come across other differences. None of these have to be discussed as stand-alone 'topics' but we touch on the way that race, age and being poor are also aspects of the experiences he's had. It means whenever he thinks that *he* is the problem, we can *also* acknowledge, for instance, that being poor affects how smartly he can dress and how that plays into acceptability and how someone fits in. We could look at how it isn't just his own anxiety at play when he worries whether the black kids would think he was black enough to join them, or whether white kids would think he was white enough to join them; it is also a theme around which much interpersonal relating occurs.

These discussions allow us to 'fact check', to think about the degree to which his experience might be a tangible reality in any specific circumstance and when it might be far from other people's minds; when it is a possibility, and when is it a reality requiring action? Does the girl he fancy really think 'but he isn't the same as me?' Or is she oblivious?

I take my own uncertainties back to supervision. I am alert to how I might say or do something to upset Taye. My supervisor is helpful saying, 'True you don't want to upset clients, but don't forget to think about what else this means, this is something similar to how this client experiences the world, he too is very nervous about upsetting others.' Recognising this helps me to accept the dilemma that I have since found always to be at the core of psychotherapy; the way we are in the world is both an aspect of our own choices and meaning-making, but it is also at least influenced by the lessons we have learnt from others over time.

As he had in earlier sessions, Taye accepts my observations and starts to pre-empt my comments and questions. It seems he is ready, emotionally, to be curious about the uncertainty that relating requires, rather than so quickly assuming that there is a key quality of his alone that eats away at all relationships and inevitably makes him 'the problem'.

IV

As a trainee, I have been quite taken by the literature on, and my therapist's practice in relation to, the 'frame', a concept in psychotherapy that refers to such aspects as length and regularity of sessions, the length of therapy, confidentiality, fees and so on. Some schools suggest there is one optimal frame (see Casement, 2002; Langs, 2004; Smith, 1991), while others have suggested that the more important aspects are the predictability and trustworthiness of the frame (see Spinelli, 2014; see also Chapter 9).

I have started, from the very beginning of this placement, to try and set up the frame as securely as possible, meaning that, among other things, set times are utilised and time boundaries are adhered to. Confidentiality and anonymity are fostered and as much as possible each therapy is separate to others – practically and psychologically. As well as the benefits the secure frame has for clients, it also means that I manage to schedule enough time between clients for me to stretch my legs, take a comfort break or have a cup of tea, and make notes. This means that I am refreshed and that clients do not have to bump into each other. But about ten months into Taye's therapy my plan doesn't quite work out. Taye arrives early for his session and the previous client is still there; she has lingered and I am struggling to get her to leave. It is Taye's arrival that brings her procrastination to an end and she passes him in the waiting room.

I see Taye for his session about ten minutes later at our scheduled start time. His first comment is to ask, 'Should I have stayed away? It's raining.' He is clearly uncomfortable and wants to know what he 'should' have done.

'No, it's fine', I say and don't think much more about it.

Taye is quiet for the next few minutes. When that becomes uncomfortable he makes short statements that don't require a response; they aren't questions or theme-laden stories, just comments such as 'Haven't got much to say' and 'Nothing has happened'.

Therapists eventually become more comfortable with silence, with pondering its meanings and developing a sense of when they might say something useful. At this stage for me, though, it feels new and so I retreat to a comment on the feel of the silence, noting that 'this feels like a difficult silence; it's different to some of those periods where you have been thinking quietly'.

Taye doesn't respond immediately, but clearly he takes this as a hint that he 'should' talk. After a few minutes Taye gives me a summary of his week and a light-hearted story about seeing a person whose umbrella had turned inside out. I am not sure what to make of this as it didn't seem particularly relevant to his usual concerns, nor to anything we have experienced. I become mindful of my tutor's wise words, however, that if a therapist has nothing to say, they shouldn't say anything. So, although I miss that Taye is now feeling a pressure to talk and to make it (or me?) feel OK, I at least don't compound things by saying anything more.

Then Taye suddenly changes tone and says: 'Oh I'll tell you what happened this week, and upset me. You know I have been thinking of doing a placement?'

I nod.

'I went to see the placement officer. I've been talking to her about doing the one with the photographer at a magazine and I'd decided I wanted to do that one. When I got there she was busy with another lad in my year, James. I was meant to see her at half past one but he didn't come out till twenty to two. I told her that I had decided to do that placement and she said I couldn't as she had sent James there instead. I was so disappointed.'

My heart sinks at this point. Partly because I feel his disappointment at being pipped at the post, but I also have a sense of what has happened with us. Communicative psychoanalysis offers a helpful theory about coded communications. It suggests that out of the myriad of events that happen to a person, our choice of telling stories about them is informed, unconsciously, by what is needed to be communicated to the person we are speaking to and that often what is most pressing is the management of the relationship we are in. Thus a patient might tell a story that is important in its own right, but it is told then and in that particular way as it also offers the therapist information about how they are being experienced in the moment (see Smith, 1991).

On this occasion the parallel is very clear – as in the placement interview he has come along to a scheduled meeting, relying on that person's input, and he arrives to see someone else receiving the attention and interest. I have to consider that him seeing me with another client feels like a disappointment to him, as if I am likely to value that person more, maybe offer *them* exactly what *he* needs. That seems clear and important.

I have another set of thoughts too, related to our recent discussions of difference. While I don't know James' racial background, here the previous client had been white. If that is a factor for him (and it might be as in his family his mother, Jack and Leila are all white and seem to have their needs attended to before his) it might be linked to *our* racial difference and anxieties about what is valued more. This seems less clear and I am not sure whether to voice this possibility or not.

Taye talks about the experience at college and expresses more than disappointment; he is surprised at how bad he feels, how resigned he is to it. He had wanted to say that this was unfair, that he had been told he could apply, but he didn't find the words and so accepted a different placement, this one in an art centre.

I realise that I need to empathise with what has happened but I also need to respond to the apparent concerns about therapy.

'That was a very difficult situation for you, wasn't it? And as well as it being about college, I wonder whether you are trying to shed light on something that happened here?' I am a bit slow in saying this and so before I move on I see that I have either piqued his curiosity or confused him.

Taye sits forward in his chair and says simply 'huh?'

'I wonder whether that story tells us a little bit about how you experienced it here today too. You come here, needing to get out of the unpleasant weather and while I let you in you see me with someone else and I wonder whether that unsettled you, reinforced your feeling that there's always someone else that's more important?'

I leave it there and wait to see his response, wondering whether it will confirm my theory or challenge it.

'You mean that white woman?', he asks.

I nod. Before I think of what to say next, he nods and says 'maybe ...' He smiles and says, 'I am pretty used to waiting for white people to finish. And James did get the best placement.'

I start to feel a little more confident, that we are actually unpacking something of the reality of his worlds, his family of origin, the world he lives in and maybe therapy too. In all he feels the need to be nice to the other, that he should foreground their needs and pleasures, both as a simple acceptance of that being the way the world works but also because that stops people recognising that they can reject him. I also start to think that while not necessarily an explicit aspect of his family life, he has come to learn that racial difference, his not being white, makes him vulnerable to rejection and increases the need to not give people reason to actively dislike him.

These key assumptions are put to the test through a set of new and novel opportunities – he starts the placement in January, which means being the newcomer, trying new things, some of which he is good at but he struggles with some of it. It allows him to try out asking for help, showing his vulnerability and because it is a busy centre, it also allows him to try out being what he calls 'pushy'. It was this, about six weeks later, that leads him to return to the time he had seen my other client. 'That had been weird', he says one day, 'I *know* you must have other patients but ... it didn't *occur* to me that you did. I didn't expect to have to see one. I think it confused me.' He surprises me then by asking. 'are all your other clients white?'

I am taken aback. Partly it is to do with the fact that therapists are warned about answering too many direct questions. There is logic to this, as therapists aren't there to talk about ourselves; we aren't there to act as model or to use patients to work through our own issues. However, in relation to a direct question, a question about my professional life, I didn't think it was an unreasonable one. 'Not everyone', I say.

Taye goes on to ask about the client and particularly why she had still been here that day. I tell him that I can't talk about clients themselves, as I am sure that he wouldn't want me talking to others about him. But I think it might be useful to talk about how he had felt and how he had responded, how he seems to have spotted that this woman was different to him. And not just because she was white, and a woman, but also whereas he usually arrives on time and leaves exactly at the scheduled end of the session, she hadn't done that and he couldn't understand that others might not.

His eyes widen as he laughs, 'I couldn't do that. I would be too scared to not leave. Refuse to leave! You wouldn't see me again!' He drops the smile and looks sad, and I feel sad.

'That's all it would take? Or you fear that's all it would take? One thing like that and I would end the therapy, send you away?'

Taye is crying. 'Yes ...', he says. A few moments later he says, 'Well no ..., maybe.' As he calms he looks at me again and says, 'I honestly don't know. I don't think you would do that, I really don't, but I expect you to, it's too risky to think you wouldn't.' And he sits back with a sigh.

'This helps us understand a lot I think', I say softly. 'You experience the world as saying you are just a hair's breadth from being abandoned, everybody is likely to dump, disown or reject you. Everyone else is more privileged and given more leeway. As we've talked about before I think this was the sense you made of your early experiences at home, and I think your attention to being different and not fitting in keeps that a reality for you now too.'

He thinks about this and asks, 'So is this my fault? You wouldn't get cross, you wouldn't see me as aggressive if I was pushy about things?'

I have to acknowledge, he has a point. 'Hmm ... I'm not saying that ... because we don't know do we? I'd hope I wouldn't do that, I don't think I would, but by us being involved in this tried-and-trusted way of doing things ... it's just, we haven't had a chance to look at it because you have been alert to that risk and made sure we didn't have to confront it. You have adopted a polite stance towards me ...

'Or subservient', he notes.

'Maybe ... And my part of this is that I overlooked it. I didn't spot the fact that it is also about how both our worlds work. I saw it as politeness not subservience.'

He thinks about this and agrees that there is something to it. 'Yes but ... what do I do? If I change it ... well I have been trying, haven't I? But if I change it too drastically, who knows what happens?'

'That's for us to think about some more and maybe for you to try out', I say.

V

Over the next few weeks it turns out that Taye likes the placement; it offers a lot more than he had realised and he is pleased with his new living arrangements too. When he had moved out of Foxdene he'd imagined a lodging arrangement whereas it was actually a small, self-contained flat in a building with an onsite manager and links to the social-work team should they be needed. He can be as independent or as linked in as he wants to be. Both possibilities are somewhat anxiety-provoking but also very exciting. In fact, Taye reports great enthusiasm and excitement almost to the exclusion of worry. The despair and boredom he had felt previously is diminished; they have taken up residence on the periphery of his daily life.

This isn't to say that the anxiety isn't still a factor; working with new colleagues and living in close proximity to other people means that there is plenty of uncertainty as to whether he will fit in, whether people will like him if he doesn't go out of his way to put them first and to keep his own essence hidden. But Taye manages to reorient himself towards the anxiety. When he feels it, instead of getting scared and retreating to his assumptions that he will be alone and have no one on his side, he starts to ask himself, 'What's this about?' 'Why now?' 'What's me trying to anticipate all the bad stuff and what is here and needs me to do something about it?'

I am pleased to see his curiosity develop, as it is one way in which Taye seems to feel more able to take hold of his life and engage with it more. By talking about life in therapy and thinking about it outside of sessions he finds a way to separate out fears and actions, to think before choosing options rather than just returning to his tried-and-trusted 'old' ways. The old stance isn't eradicated – I doubt it ever is for any of us – but it seems to be less frequently present and less powerful.

In particular Taye is able to separate out his fear of having 'aggressive' and 'over the top' reactions and recognises that he, like everyone else, has a range of feelings and reactions. We also explore the fact that sometimes the reactions of others have nothing to do with us, people have their own lives, their own fears and needs. At one point in this discussion Taye looks shocked and recognises that, as he puts it, 'it really isn't all about me, is it? By assuming I'll never fit in I have acted as if I am the centre of everything! Oh, I feel so stupid!'

In this final phase of therapy we also recognise that his learning and his development were not only achieved in therapy, but in the ways in which he tested things out and 'reality checked'. By being open to what actually happens, he starts to loosen the grip of what he had assumed *should* occur. At first he wasn't sure whether to trust some of the positive reactions he received – his mentor's enthusiasm for his work, smiles from people in his building, cheeky notes from a girl he fancies – these would all be enjoyed but at first doubted.

As Taye works through this different approach to people and to his assumptions, we see that he is a little disappointed when it becomes apparent that being different with new people, or with friends, was somewhat easier than it is with his family. He struggles to be more assertive with them, but this makes sense; his fear of rejection or not fitting in with his mother and sister have more significant consequences than with new friends or colleagues at placement. The latter would be temporary upsets, but if he upset his family he fears he really will be alone in the world. This is both a frequent and a logical fear considering how important family is to most of us. Very few people experience discord and separation without distress so it makes sense that it could also be an area of concern for Taye. But even here, the approach of slowing down, thinking about it, identifying ways in which he might experiment with his own needs, has some success. Taye is particularly pleased on one occasion when his mother calls to change the time for his visit because Leila wanted to go swimming; to change the time would mean he would have had to miss his placement so he said he couldn't do that and asked whether Leila might go swimming earlier in the day instead. He was delighted when his mother hardly reacted and said yes without a second thought.

Bringing therapy to an end is often a complicated and uncertain process, partly because our mental health is so dependent on the context and partly as the therapist really cannot be a mind reader. So decisions about ending therapy require discussions about how resilient the client feels alongside the evidence that they are – or are not – coping well with external factors. I've been seeing Taye for a year and I am confident that while we have not explored every single possible issue, he does seem a lot stronger – he sees himself as more authentic; he can catch himself when he starts to assume it is all about him when it isn't. He has also started to accept that the world is sometimes bad, and that he doesn't have to attribute all that to himself. I am particularly pleased when he muses one day that, 'I know what to do now when shit happens.' It seems that he is able both to look after himself but also to recognise and manage the inequality that we both know is part and parcel of the world. We talk and decide we will work towards ending in April.

We finish working together four months into his independent living; he has been feeling better for a sustained period of time and is feeling settled, has some good friendships and says he has started to like himself. He even reports enjoying writing his applications and auditions for drama courses. It feels right and he is looking forward to a new chapter in his life.

As I write up his discharge letter, I note that my formulation has changed a little.

Taye was born into a family that was already (probably) struggling with some family and cultural discord which culminated in the family breaking up a few years after he was born. As well as family instability, Taye had to make sense of the fact that his father disappeared, physically and then from any contact at all. As well as the masculine caregiver leaving, it was also that an aspect of his racial heritage was lost. This is likely to have at least played on his mind, giving him cause to wonder what *he* did to cause his father to disappear.

The relationships that his mother went on to have meant that he met a number of people who were interested in his mother (and later his sister) but not so much in him. If anything he felt he was perceived as unnecessary, a problem, or an irritation, an arbitrary someone to be ignored. He came to see himself as burdensome outsider, not understood and not desired, this was both a family and a cultural experience.

Later on Taye experienced the potential loss of his mother as she became unwell, and while she recovered he felt left out and rejected, as Leila managed to stay with Mom but he had to be 'farmed out', made to live where he didn't fit in. This replicated a long-held sense of himself that was active in the family, in the care home and at school. This manifests in a lack of interest in self, a preoccupation of what others might want him to be and stress associated with this. Experiences of being told to go back to where he came from and being stopped and searched also confirmed this 'outsider status'.

I am happy to note that over the course of the therapy Taye worked hard and reflected on personal and wider issues and managed to explore ways in which to clarify what might be nervous assumption and what was more objectively accurate. He has also gained in confidence, feeling that he can handle difficulties a lot more comfortably now.

On a more personal note, I feel the hole that Taye has left in my professional world. I think it is a good sign, as it shows that despite his worries, he has 'fitted in' well and would always have a place in my own history.

4

GENDER

Everybody is affected by gender, although people will not all experience it in the same way. Some of us are more conscious of it, of the joys or the challenges it offers, and some of us less so but no one escapes its impact completely. When we enter the world one of the first questions asked is, 'Is it a boy or a girl?' With the advent of technology this is often asked well before the child is born and everything we do is understood through the distinct lenses of boy or girl, man or woman.

While gender is often taken to be self-explanatory it is not. To help understand gender we consider the differences between 'sex', 'gender' and 'identity'.

The term 'sex' tends to refer to biology. Physiological characteristics that people use to understand sex include males having a penis, XY chromosomal pairing and significantly more testosterone than females. Females have a vagina, XX chromosomal pairing and produce more oestrogen than males. If many of our fairy tales, school and family stories and even birth certificates and legal statutes are to be believed – that is it. Nothing else exists. If it does it would – or 'should' – have been surgically or medically 'corrected'.

Gender is the social dimension where we are no longer talking of 'the male' or 'the female' but about concepts such as 'masculinity' and 'femininity'. These are attributes that society expects to see in men and women and they feed assumptions, such as men expected to be physically stronger than women (implying that *all* men are stronger than *all* women *all* of the time). These expectations can imprison us and create significant personal and interpersonal distress and trauma as will be seen in Amanda's story.

Gender identity refers to a person's subjective sense of their gender. For many the assumption is that those with a vagina *are* female, inevitably *feel* feminine and will *experience* themselves as 'a woman'. However, there is actually very little about gender that is inevitable; understandings are significantly different across cultures and times and gender identity is a very personal experience that may bear no resemblance to physiology. We will see this in Sam's story in Chapter 7.

While many societies have organised personal experiences, family structures and societal and political codes around a male/female binary, gender is much more complex and more interesting than these restricted assumptions allow us to recognise. It is important for therapists to stop and consider how accurate or inaccurate these visions are.

'Go on, be a good girl': Amanda and the oppression of gender

I

'My back's to the wall and I try to become as small as I can, as small as I possibly can, almost forcing myself into the cracks of the nursery wallpaper; I am desperate to hide between Little Bo Peep and Old Mother Hubbard. I try to squeeze myself into oblivion. As I do the world closes around me, the darkness is complete ... except for the lines of light that frame the door. It is stifling and I struggle to breath. No matter how much I try *not* to be there, danger approaches. My heart is pounding, I am desperate not to be seen or heard, although realistically I s'pose, my parents' fight is far too loud for them to hear my jerky breathing or my weeping. But I know it's coming, it always does. Soon I'll hear the sharp crack that is his fist on her jaw. Then silence. Then the door will slam and she'll drive away, tyres screeching as she flees. And I will be alone ... with him.'

'I must black out in terror for a bit but I come round with a start, it's his footsteps, I hear them coming up the stairs, slowly, methodically. He is muttering under his breath. I can't hear what he is saying but it doesn't matter, I know how this plays out. He is coming to me.'

At this point Amanda stops. She is crying and seems completely drained. She can't go on with the story, so all I can do is imagine. And I imagine the worst.

II

Let's go back a few months. Amanda was referred to our NHS psychotherapy service by her GP. The service was one that tended to receive referrals from people struggling with entrenched difficulties, and histories of relational trauma. Clients would commonly have experienced pharmacological therapy, counselling in primary care, or psychological therapy in secondary or tertiary services and sometimes all of these, before coming to us. It turned out that Amanda had also undergone ECT,[1] an increasingly controversial and rarely used physical intervention.

---

[1] Electroconvulsive therapy (ECT) is a physical treatment where electronic impulses are applied to the brain to disrupt depression and other conditions. In the UK the National Institute of Clinical Excellence state that ECT is 'used only to achieve rapid and short-term improvement of severe symptoms after an adequate trial of other treatment options has proven inadequate ineffective and/or when the condition is considered to be potentially life-threatening in individuals with severe depressive illness, catatonia or a prolonged or severe manic episode' (NICE, 2010). The guidance also suggests that, due to the lack of clarity about long-term effects, ECT not be seen as a regular treatment or as a 'maintenance therapy'.

As well as telling us about the ECT, the GP's letter explained that Amanda was referred at her own request, because of her history of very severe depression. It noted that while Amanda experienced the low mood characteristic of depression, problems sleeping, major shifts of appetite and very poor sense of self, she had never experienced thoughts of self-harm or suicide. The letter also noted that while Amanda had not been diagnosed as catatonic, 'at her worst' she had spent days in bed where time sped by without her knowing it. While managing, *just*, to keep on top of bills and debts, her life had periods where she seldom saw another person socially.

With this in mind, I am surprised to meet a warm, engaging woman who holds eye contact, is conversationally adept and seems to anticipate my questions and the areas I am curious about. Despite therapists' awareness that a referral report is only a snapshot of a person in their historical context, the variation in presentation can still come as a surprise. This may be to do with the fact that the written report creates an impression of the 'now', while drawing on difficulties and traumas that may have occurred back 'then', and 'then' may have been decades ago. Thus the therapist starts to empathise with an experience the client has previously had, as understood by a third party, rather than the person and their current lived experience. This is not necessarily a problem, as long as we are open to the fact that people move on, evolve and develop, that the map of a life changes and the person themselves always remains a unique and fluid person.

Amanda tells me of her work life, of how she is not in a relationship and how she is 'fine about that', and she fills me in on her childhood, saying that it was 'maybe not idyllic, but close [to that]'. I hear about her beautiful mother, how hardworking her father was and about how lucky they were to live in such a nice area, to go to good schools and to have holidays abroad. Amanda confirms much of the other factual material outlined in the referral too. Describing her depression, she explains it as an experience of 'being seduced into a state of nothingness, a bleak but effective removal of myself from the world'. Amanda seems to want to reassure me that she is not 'as bad' as before, that she is working and enjoying it and in many ways is 'much better'.

'But it's the dreams', she says. 'They are so vivid and powerful and it feels like the depression might be coming back.'

It is then that she recounts the dream to me and I start to get a sense of the awfulness that lurks in her shadows.

Throughout our conversation Amanda seems very attuned to the ebb and flow of the assessment and I speculate that this is testimony to her experience with GPs, psychiatry and other mental health professionals over the years. She seems so attuned to it that I think it is more than this though; she seems to know *what* I am curious about and *when* that curiosity arises, so I comment on it. She smiles and notes, 'It's just what women do', a telling comment that brings gender into the room very early on.

We schedule a second appointment to complete the assessment. Unfortunately I am ill on that day and ask the department secretary to reschedule for the following week, but the message doesn't get passed on, so Amanda arrives at the clinic only to have to turn away again. I meet with Amanda the following week. I apologise about not getting the message to her before she travelled all the way here and she is very gracious. 'Don't worry about it, it's fine. I wasn't doing anything and I even got some reading done on the bus', she says.

In this session Amanda tells me more about her history and the way it relates to the dream. She says that life is pretty much as described, the only blip in her childhood were these occasional fights between her parents and these are captured by the dream. It is at this point she briefly mentions her fear of her father, which she thinks is irrational, and her confusion in relation to her mother.

I asked Amanda about her parents' conflict and how she understands this? And how *had* she understood it? She doesn't skip a beat and offers a sympathetic reading of her parents' conflict; her father 'worked hard and "like most men" he found it hard to express himself, that explains how he occasionally shouted at those close to him ... well at Mum'.

She hesitates and then goes on to acknowledge that he also hit her mother. 'He shouldn't have done it I know, but it wasn't very often.' She seems to imply that this means it shouldn't worry her. Equally, she understands that 'after those rows Mum needed space, and she used that as a way to calm things down. It meant Dad and I could carry on as normal.'

Amanda has a script that allows her to understand these difficult and scary times without compromising her view of an almost idyllic childhood. Psychologically, she seems to have prioritised the love of both parents and focused on the tangible advantages that the family had enjoyed, the middle-class environment, schools and holidays over what she calls 'occasional upsets'. Her mother's disappearances were beneficent acts, protecting Amanda's relationship with her father.

Why would Amanda contort the picture so?, I wonder. But I am aware that it is equally relevant to ponder, 'well, why wouldn't she?' By focusing on this positive vision of her parents, she spares herself the reality of how scared, worried and distressed she really was. It has an internal logic; it sounds good in some ways, but I am concerned, emotion denied is seldom emotionally neutral and I wonder whether this is part of her experience of depression.

As we finish the assessment period Amanda and I reflect on our two meetings and consider what she might find helpful. We both feel that it will be useful to undertake a further period of therapy – outpatient this time – allowing her the space to consider the dreams and the questions they raise for her and to experience and reflect on the emotions that are still often overlooked. We are both mindful of her previous depression and don't want her to succumb to that again.

III

Amanda proves to be reflective, often prioritising the 'common sense' that she feels is so important to navigate life well. 'Common sense' means weighing things up, making choices based on evidence and prioritising the positive and ignoring the negative. 'People will inadvertently hurt us, but we shouldn't hold that against them.'

However, as I listen, something doesn't *feel* right. There is something inevitable to it; it feels almost scripted.

I wonder about my role in this – I feel seduced by the lure of logic and a common-sense approach to life, only to suddenly recognise that I also don't follow it, that I disagree with some of the implications. So yes, I accept it is useful to assess one's position, but I don't actually think that ever captures life's challenges; I accept that evidence is important but I think life is also more than that – what about awe, delight, excitement and more vital experiences? I accept that it can help to choose the positive but I am also worried about the fact that it is a situated choice; it doesn't necessarily remove the 'negative'. I also don't accept that relationships inevitably have to be damaging or violent. In fact I note that her friendships and her supervision of colleagues at work sound particularly sensitive and not at all harsh or hurtful. So I find myself in a state of fluid agreement, yes to some meanings and no to others – not that I share this.

From the very beginning Amanda is keen, and yet somewhat nervous, to start exploring the dream she says has brought her to therapy, and the questions she feels that it raises about the time in her life in which they are rooted. At first she is particularly curious about her mother, their relationship and what she terms 'the disappearances' – 'Where did she go? Why did she never take me with her? Why didn't *anyone* ever talk about these absences? It is as if I am the only one that noticed!' As these questions arise Amanda is torn, both wanting to ask them but also having a sense that somehow it isn't proper to ask them, that in fact she is being 'demanding or even naughty'.

The role of the therapist is seldom to give direct answers to the questions clients pose, after all how can we? We aren't there when these experiences happen. Even if we were we might still experience things differently. No, my role here is to witness and to confirm what I am hearing about. It seems particularly important to acknowledge how difficult the gaps in her knowledge are, to note that omissions and absences often mean that questions fester, simply because they are unable to be answered.

This can be a contested position with some disciplines, especially those rooted in a positivist epistemology and a faith in absolute truths, and the roles and responsibilities of experts, arguing that our studies and evidence bases mean we can have grounds to direct clients and answer questions categorically. On the other hand, the therapist is working with the subjective experience of a particular person experiencing complex contexts and processes of power and so their phenomenology is unique. Maybe the best we can do is navigate the tension between known generalities and the mysteries of specifics (for more on working with such complexity, see McNamee and Gergen, 2006).

I turn our attention to what she might know. 'Do you have *any* thoughts, theories or suspicions?', I ask.

Amanda is thoughtful for a bit and then tells me the things she *does not* think. 'I know she wasn't having an affair, she wouldn't have, she wasn't like that. I know she loved my father. Maybe she went to a friend's place … but whose? She had to go somewhere.'

There is a silence and Amanda repeats herself: 'She had to go somewhere …'

As I listen to her I think of a young Amanda hearing the disturbance, anticipating the screech of tyres and then the absence. Maybe young Amanda was even more confused than she currently is, maybe she fantasised that Mum didn't go anywhere, or maybe she just disappeared, or maybe she would one day.

The more she talks about 'the disappearances', the more Amanda comes to think that as well as curiosity, her mother's actions leave her feeling a number of other emotions. Maybe she has been scared, possibly angry or even jealous.

At this point Amanda's focus seems to be all on her mother, her actions and her intent are focused on. For several sessions, her mother's behaviour as part of a *sequence* of events, or a *reaction* to physical violence isn't considered at all.

Before commenting on this I have to acknowledge (to myself) that this irks me; it seems unfair on her mother and, anyway, how can she overlook her father's role in this? Especially when overt violence is involved. I have to be careful though. This seems to be meaningful to Amanda, part of her way of being in the world; right now she seems not to think in terms of sequences of events, not when thinking about her friends and their relationships, about work or about the way in which Londoners are bullish in their commute. So why would she be different in relation to her mother? In addition, the therapist's primary task is to help client's consider their experience and meaning making, so if this is what is meaningful to Amanda, then I should not force a different focus; I can think broadly *myself*, maybe even offer my observations but not *demand* that she see things differently.

As well as simply not wanting to be a therapist who is overly directive, in this case the material and the therapeutic process require that I think about the key theme, that is, a man who forced his will on a woman and a woman who could disappear for the greater good. As her male therapist, if I am too quick or too forceful with my views, I could, metaphorically, be replicating one of the family dynamics in therapy, an abusive one. Equally, say nothing and I might collude with a powerful, entrenched and well-worn vision of gender relations where women are responsible for the violence they endure. While psychodynamic theory helps us consider family relations in transference phenomena (see Hoglend, 2004; Langs, 1989; Smith, 2003), and other psychological literatures consider these issues and the possibility of 'parallel processes' (Cassoni, 2007; Clarkson, 2013; McLoed, 2003), it is also helpful to consider these ideas at a political level (see Milton, 2005; Samuels, 2006). One may want to avoid acting as if one is the 'father figure', but equally one may also want to avoid enacting the biased policing of gender relations.

So I wait ... and as I do I get to hear more about the raw emotion Amanda feels. She comes, at first, to hypothesise, and then to recall, the terror of abandonment she felt after her mother disappeared. She talks about a sense of guilt about this, her fear somehow making her demanding, or at least it would have done if she had voiced it. She also notes anger too. Anger confuses her as she remembers being angry on her mother's *return* rather than when she left. These emotions are all resisted at times, challenging as they do her vision of an idyllic childhood.

As she talks, Amanda seems slightly more familiar with these feelings and able to tolerate them a little better, allowing for deeper consideration. The terror of abandonment is initially powerful but an emotion that Amanda is able to accept relatively easily once it makes sense to her that 'surely, any little girl would miss and worry about her mum, No?'

Guilt is a little more difficult for her as she realises that she isn't actually guilty of anything in her parents' relationship *per se*, but she notes that 'like many girls, I didn't want to be a burden, I still don't. I wanted to love and be loved.' Being scared or being needy runs the risk in her mind, that she would be a burden to her parents precisely at the points in which they weren't coping. But once guilt is acknowledged, she comes to think of it as absurd and this seems to help her with the feelings when they arise.

It turns out that anger is a productive emotion for Amanda once she explores it. As she becomes more comfortable with the idea that she is, and may have been, angry, she starts to understand that maybe she wasn't angry *that* her mother returned, it was that the 'returnings' were simply the first opportunities she had to voice the anger about the abandonment and about being left all alone at home with her father.

Amanda is a fan of logic and 'common sense' and tries to use them to figure things out: 'I think Mum's rationale was not to involve me in their relationship. If she had taken me with her, away from home, I'd have been upset; and when we returned we would all have had to get reacquainted. By leaving me with Dad she protected our relationship, mine and his.'

'Maybe', I say, realising that Amanda was now talking about him more directly. 'So can you tell me about your relationship with your Dad?'

The question doesn't seem to pique her interest significantly as she simply says, 'it was good' and then she returns to the anger when Mum returned. Some psychoanalytically oriented theorists have illustrated how such seemingly everyday changes of focus might actually offer significant insight into the unconscious/unreflective feelings and thoughts a client might have (see Casement, 1992; Langs, 1989, Smith, 1991). In this case I had to ponder whether the return to 'anger' was her continued interest in that topic or whether it was an implicit communication about my attempt to change direction.

Shortly after this discussion Amanda comes to a session on the verge of tears, berating herself.

'I am so stupid, so stupid. I don't know why I have put up with it all; it's not fair, not fair at all.'

I'm not at all sure what she is referring to. 'What's happened?'

'It's work. Do you know that everyone gets paid more than me? Even those that I am supervising! I found out yesterday and it sickens me. I was angry, furious, but then I started to feel so negative. I felt disgusted, I thought I was going to be sick, so I had to run to the toilet. I shut myself in there for a bit to calm down. I asked my boss about it today and he confirmed it. Didn't ask why I was asking, what it meant or anything, just said "Yes". I couldn't believe it. I asked why and you know what he said?'

Obviously I have no way of knowing what he said so I simply shake my head.

'They just asked for more. That's it. They wouldn't start unless they were paid more so it was negotiated. I was stunned. Flabbergasted. It seems loyalty, diligence, hard-work, effort all mean nothing, absolutely sodding nothing at all. There's no point being good, you don't get rewarded; you need to demand, that's what they did, they just demanded. Be selfish, that's the lesson.'

She takes a break, breathing heavy, still filled with emotion.

'But why shouldn't they I suppose? Maybe that's what I should have done a long time ago', she says quietly, almost to herself.

As the session progresses and we explore these issues, Amanda raises her hands and stops. 'It's the same thing isn't it, being the bloody good girl again, the same issues in the dream are everywhere aren't they. It's like it contaminates my entire life.'

I see what she means, nod and note 'and that's the way you thought you'd get the world to be good to you in return'.

Her face reddens and she nods.

IV

It is a few weeks after this that Amanda knocks on my office door with great urgency. I jump at the sudden interruption, not expecting anyone (I usually collect clients from the waiting room) and I turn to see her. Something is different, she looks concerned, very much on edge. She looks at me as she takes off her coat and puts it on the spare chair and says: 'I had that dream again ... but there's more.'

'The dream', Amanda tells me, 'I hate it but I need to tell it again; I have to if I am ever going to get past it.'

'Sure', I say as I nod and gesture for her to continue.

'It starts the same way as always. I'm back there, my back to the wall trying to become as small as I can, forcing myself into the cracks in the wallpaper, trying to hide between those characters I used to love. I'm squeezing myself into nothing; the world is closing around me, it is so dark, and the door has that sinister backlight. I struggle to breathe as the danger approaches. I'm as desperate as I was back then, trying to disappear so as not to be a part of it all. But how do you escape your dream? I hear his fist on her jaw, that awful silence. Is she alive or dead? Then the door slams, a relief in some ways to know that she is alive but she drives away, leaving me there with him.'

'His footsteps scare me as they mark his approach, he is coming to me again.'

So far, there is nothing to say, it's a familiar recounting of the dream, although I am aware that the uncertainty as to whether Mum is alive or dead has not been voiced before. I am curious as to the function of this new specificity and also about the repetitive nature of the dream. Is it a desire to do it differently, to not have experienced this, or to have it be a story rather than a reality? But now isn't the time to become preoccupied with these questions. I wait to see what Amanda needs at this point. She takes a deep breath and continues.

'He stops outside my door, and he waits. Maybe he is listening or maybe he is trying to compose himself, I'm not sure. But when the door starts to open and the light extends a path through my bedroom, I freeze. I think I actually stop breathing for a while. I feign sleep, or at least I try to, but I don't fool him, my tear-streaked face must give it away. As he approaches me he asks in a soft voice "what's the matter Mandy?"'

Amanda stops, looks at me and says with venom in her voice. 'I *hate* being called Mandy. Always have ... and he bloody knew that, but it didn't matter to him.'

I don't need to say anything, as Amanda continues. This is good as I am aware of some strong feelings, 'Sadistic fuck!' is what I actually think, but I am very aware that it wouldn't be helpful to say something like this, so I take note of my own feelings as information, maybe they will help me understand what is new about this telling today.

'He comes to me and strokes my hair with his hand; it feels like an electric shock runs through me but I try not to react, but he feels it and he says "Go on, be a good girl" as he lifts me back onto the bed.'

My stomach turns as I hear this and I feel for the young girl that she was and for the traumatised adult that she is.

'He lies down on the bed besides me.' She is crying now.

'He cuddles up to me, lays his head on my chest and starts to suck his thumb. "Tell me a story Mandy", he says, "Tell me a story". I give in. I stroke his hair and start making something up. He likes stories, tales of silly animals and naughty boys, so that's the story I tell. I tell him about Cyril the squirrel, Billy the boar and boys who steal apples and let the ponies out of the stables. I talk until his breath evens out and he falls asleep. Then I lie there till the morning with his weight on my chest, a dead arm, scared that my beautiful mother has gone forever.'

Amanda slumps back into the chair, her face red, with streaks of mascara running down her cheeks. She releases an enormous sigh. But she seems calm now that she has finished describing the dream, the trip back through time. She even smiles at me. I smile in return.

'You OK?' I ask.

'Yes', she says. 'I feel a bit sick actually.'

She takes a moment. 'I'm not going to be sick though, but I definitely feel queasy. Maybe ... I think this is a good thing. I think I've ignored this for so long, it feels good to get it out. He scared me, he scared me a lot and yet I didn't realise it. I didn't know what he was going to do; I was always scared he would hit me like he hit Mum and so relieved that he didn't that I didn't think about what was actually happening.'

'So relief that you weren't hit, meant you didn't recognise ... what?', I ask.

'The disgust,' she said, her voice breaking as she said it. 'I was so scared but I was so disgusted as well. He shouldn't have been crawling onto my bed with me! At least not like that. He should've been looking after me, explaining that everything would be alright, reassuring me. Me! I was the child not him! Why couldn't he do that? He didn't you know, never once! He never once reassured me, told me it was OK, that Mum would be back, nothing!'

Amanda sits there, tears running down her face again; she is furious, not comprehending how her precious father could have put her, so deliberately and so forcefully into that role, making her make him feel better about his actions. After a while, it starts to feel calm again. So after a few more moments, I say: 'So you have felt anger and disgust. You have been upset but you also seem ... relieved.'

Amanda nods and takes a deep breath. 'I think so. I think I am.'

'Have you dreamt this before?', I ask wondering whether it is new or whether she has struggled to tell me about it.

'No', she said. 'First time. I sat bolt upright this morning. It was like the penny dropped. I felt sick but the penny dropped. He wasn't looking after me; he expected his good little girl to do the looking after. He could mess up and then expect me to make him feel better, no matter how bad I felt. He didn't console me, calm me down or even worry if I was comfortable sleeping with his heavy head on my arm all night!'

Her fury is undeniable and it has been important to connect with this; it has been lingering in the shadows for a long time.

Amanda returns to this anger in the following weeks, and sees that it gives rise to other emotions. She sometimes appears confused by this and asks me, sometimes repeatedly, 'Why is this so depressing? Why did I get depressed? Why am I getting so upset now, so distressed? OK he wasn't always as nice as I wish he was, but I wasn't raped or anything; he didn't molest me like so many women are. Compared to them this is nothing.'

The place of anger, and its expression, can be a complex issue in therapy. Clients fear it and are concerned about succumbing to painful and unhelpful feelings and they worry about the impact it has on others in their life. Therapists are cautious too. While the recognition and expression of one's feelings is generally taken to be important, contrary to some views, being angry for the sake of it may actually not help. Forcing a particular emotional experience can be counterproductive. This is, in part, because a person's own experience is usually multifaceted. So while anger is important, its relationship to sadness, guilt and fear, their intersections and meanings need attention too, sometimes *at the same time*. Anger underpinning depression can be a form of self-oppression, which the therapist needs to be aware of and work to avoid.

The type of questions Amanda is asking are a common response to distress, and psychotherapists often have to help clients make sense of their upset, especially when compared to others. It is a tempting logic, if I am not as hurt, traumatised or abused as someone else, then surely I shouldn't feel as bad as they do. It's a way to try and manage the pain while limiting the extent to which it is felt. It can also be a way of searching for a guide, a template for how one survives such painful experiences.

My role in this was not to decide *for* Amanda that her experience was more or less worthy of distress than anybody else's – that would have been 'leaping in' (see Heidegger, 2014). No, my role is to be with her as she adjusts to the fact that she feels it and to help her in her efforts to make sense of it, in its actuality. Neither denying its place in her life, nor assuming that it has to be present as painfully as this for all time. In light of this my responses are often limited to listening, accepting and at times clarifying her assumptions. Of course, a therapist may draw on all kinds of knowledge in their work with clients, psychotherapeutic models, developmental psychology, sociological and economic sciences and more, and so can be tempted into debating the 'facts' of the matter. While there is sometimes a place for this, there is plenty of research and client confirmation that, underpinning all therapies, a thoughtful, respectful and phenomenologically oriented stance is crucial (see Clarkson, 1995; Norcross, 2011; Norcross and Wampold, 2011).

Amanda continues to ask those questions regularly, almost verbatim and I find myself concerned about the way that they and the depression, upset and confusion seem to overshadow the other powerful experience she has had on first having the 'updated' dream – sickening disgust; I am concerned that this is also an important experience that is being erased and even overwritten with the type of thoughts a 'good girl' might have – nice, loving and contented thoughts. I can understand that this might be her attempt to avoid the reality she experiences, and deal with an easier experience. Yet I think her feelings are testament to abuse and trauma of a most hideous kind. For months and months Amanda witnessed (by way of sounds rather than sight) abuse and violence against her mother. It was frequent but unpredictable. It means she had to confront the reality of discord and violence in the house and the experience of abandonment and abject powerlessness – in isolation. Mum disappeared and Dad became needy and guilt-ridden and turned to his daughter to soothe his distress, to reward the abuser, or at least not to hold him responsible for his part in it. No one attended to her terror, her own desire to disappear, to become nothing. No one empathised with the fear, or the trauma, no one helped her understand that she too was angry and that there are healthy ways to engage with anger.

Once again I am having a different awareness to hers. But at this point I think she would be able to hear it and I will be able to change my perspective if she challenges it.

Amanda is still talking. 'Why did I get depressed? Why get so upset now, so bloody distressed? I am such a drama queen!'

I respond to her with my own set of questions. 'Well, why aren't you entitled to feel that way? Why should someone else's experience define what you feel? Are you assuming that if you feel anger or disgust that's all you can feel? Are you assuming that other feelings would be cast aside as anger has been for so long? Where are you expecting the disgust, the hope and the need for care to have gone?' No single question is more important; I am trying to show that there are a lot of other possible meanings available to us.

There is silence. Neither of us are used to me responding in this way, certainly not question after question like this. But it proves a useful quiet. Amanda is thinking, pondering these possibilities. After considering them for a while, she nods as she responds. 'Whether I want them or not, they aren't going anywhere are they? These feelings, they can't be denied, there's no point in pretending they aren't there. And ... I have just realised that sick feeling. I think it's the same as what happened at work. It's all the same thing.'

'OK', I say, 'so that feeling's not just about work, or buying presents or any of those other instances you feel it. It's all linked to you still trying to be the good girl. To have anything "not good", your fear, your anger, your disgust, makes you want to merge with the wallpaper. You're still trying to be the little girl that, like Mum, could disappear rather than be a burden, the good little girl who didn't demand anything of anyone.'

Amanda nods 'It's what I do ... everywhere; I would *never* burden anyone.'

'Not even me', I blurt out, 'I remember how accommodating you were when I was ill; nothing seemed to be too much trouble.'

Amanda nods again. 'I know, I know. You couldn't help being ill. Even if I wanted to push it I wouldn't. That could upset you, or people. If there's conflict, I'm convinced that there'll be trouble, that people will ... I don't know, fall apart in some way, or reject, ... abandon me.'

'So being depressed is safer than risking the wrath of, or rejection by, others. So before anyone else can censor you, you suppress your feelings and in doing so you experience the relief of conflict avoided, but you don't challenge the exploitation possible. So oppression seems to follow.'

'I think so', Amanda says quickly. 'Look at work ... by being so ... unassuming let's say, I've let myself be exploited. And why wouldn't they take advantage of that? It happens all the time doesn't it, to me and to a lot of women.'

I agree: 'I think so too, the pressures on you are such that you are expected to be nice and accommodating all the time. Your own struggle is reinforced at work and in all of those examples you gave.'

'And I knew that ... at least I think I knew that', Amanda says. 'That's why my depression is so seductive. Don't get me wrong it's not ... nice. But it is a way that keeps me ... maybe kept me, away from being a burden.'

She pauses for a moment before snapping her head up and looking me in the eye. 'So that's it then, unless I want to fade away to nothingness ... which I don't', she says, 'I need to be more present, risk people knowing what's right for me and what isn't. It's not about being good it's about being me.' She seems both pleased with this insight but also a little puzzled.

'I wonder what that's going to mean', she says as we end the session.

V

The impact of telling the dream fully, the meanings she takes from it, the ways in which these meanings impact so many different aspects of her life, and her recognition that she can tolerate her feelings a lot more now – are a signal to us that we are close to the end of therapy. It turns out that 'figuring out what "being more present" means' is what we spend the last few months of therapy exploring – in any and all areas that come up. This means that in some sessions Amanda is nervous, in others excited and in still others confused – what does '*not* being a good girl look like?' she would ask. 'Isn't it the same as being bad?' This is a core worry of hers. We consider whether it might be more subtle than that, less binary in fact.

The array of emotions Amanda experiences is different to earlier points in therapy as they now have some positive meaning, and spur her on to live life as fully as she can, whether that is joy or worry, excitement or sadness. We end therapy after nine months, with Amanda feeling more calm and confident in herself and about events that might follow. She seems realistic and pleased with her current (and potential) place in the world.

On my side, I think this has been a useful piece of work and I suspect that its brevity is partly to do with her understanding of the therapeutic process from before, her ability to use that to face the uncertainties of this therapy and the eventual recognition that she is only one part of this experience. Unpredictable and uncontrollable others are also a part of life.

I ponder the gendered aspect of our work. I suspect that recognition of the political, no matter how personally couched, has been important. Amanda has brought this aspect herself with an early comment that being good and compliant was 'what women do', and later on with the urgency she felt about 'being a good girl'. I have been in two minds as to whether it would be more useful to focus on her experiences, the ontic manifestations of gender in her world, or whether to bring in a more overt conversation about gender and its impact on society. As it turned out we did a little bit of both, but we primarily focused on her own struggles. I don't think a focused conversation about gender would have been anti-therapeutic, I just don't have the sense that it would have had more of an impact for her. When that happens, 'Big P' political discussions are absolutely appropriate. But for Amanda, reflecting on her place in the world has been wrapped up in being (or eventually not being) 'a good girl'. Unpicking her gendered knots and exploring her own possible ways of being have allowed Amanda greater freedom to be more authentic, to make and own her choices. And to be any kind of woman she decides to be. Politics by stealth is still political.

5

SEXUALITY

Like gender, sexuality has a lifelong impact on us, affecting us as individuals and in relation to friends and family; it is a cultural phenomenon that carries significant social meaning. The waxing and waning of desire and the choices available to us mean that sexuality can also be a very distinct experience – sometimes at the forefront of our awareness and at other times it is almost like a shadow just out of sight. Or as the French phenomenologist Merleau-Ponty notes, 'it spreads forth like an odour or a sound' (1996).

The term 'sexuality' itself is used in a variety of ways. First, to refer to one's sense of being a sexual person, of experiencing desire, of the urgency and assertiveness of those desires. Secondly, as 'sexual orientation', it focuses on our relational preferences and those a person is attracted to. Finally, as 'sexual identity', it is used to refer to the identities based upon those desires. In conversations or other descriptions we sometimes elevate our orientation (for example, heterosexual or same-sex orientation) to an identity (for example, 'straight' or gay, lesbian or bisexual) and this can be a form of individual concern, familial upset and social oppression as experienced by Kenny in this chapter.

As a child grows up they become aware of differences in attraction. For the child on a heterosexual trajectory, there may be no discomfort at all. For the outliers, those who feel Other, it is different. In his wonderful novel *Moffie* Andre Carl van der Merwe's nine-year-old protagonist notes, 'I am gay. Gay – this word and everything it stands for – is what I am at the age of nine, although I have not even heard of it yet. I know it, I feel it and, in secret, I start living it' (2006, p. 56). The non-heterosexual child knows that they are different to others, and to others' expectations of them and some degree of anxiety is almost inevitable, worrying that others will be surprised, and react negatively, punishing, or abandoning, them. In some families the child is even sent to therapy to be treated for their 'pathology'. That's a very damaging experience and it is only now that Malta and some US states have outlawed conversion therapy. In the UK we see movement towards this as well with professional organisations such as the BPS, the UKCP, the BACP and a raft of other organisations publishing their memo of understanding condemning such practices (NHS England, 2015).

'Can I ask if you are gay?' Kenny, toxic masculinity and homophobia

I

It's a bright spring day and the blossom outside my window tints my usually bland NHS consulting room a beautiful pink colour. Sarah, our receptionist, asks if I can take a call from Kenny.

'Kenny?' I ask.

'Yes', she says, 'the new referral from the health advisers; you asked me to send him an appointment for a couple of weeks' time.' Now I remember: 'Sure, put him through.' I hear the click and I say, 'Hello, Martin here'.

"ello, it's Kenny Duran'

'Yes, hi Kenny. How can I help?'

'Your letter asked me to confirm the appointment and yes, I can make it.'

'Ah, thank you. I'll make a note of that, and will see you ... on the 28th', I say as I check my Filofax, 'Thursday 28th at 4 pm.'

'Yeh ... and, um ...'

'Yes?' I could tell he wasn't finished.

'Yeh, ... um, ... can I ask, are you gay?'

This takes me a little by surprise. It's not that I object to such a question, in fact I understand that clients might find it meaningful to know something about their therapist. Indeed, while working in sexual health and genitourinary (GU) medicine this is not an unusual question at all. But if people want to know they tend to ask in person. As I didn't yet know Kenny, or what this would mean to him, I responded to him with, 'Why don't we talk about that when you are here?'

Psychotherapists and psychologists consider the impact of self-disclosure for several reasons, some of which mean it may need to be avoided. Technique is one issue. In a therapy where you are working with projection, it is often helpful to aim for as 'blank' a screen as possible (see Smith, 1999; Stolorow et al., 2014). It can also be helpful to limit self-disclosure with clients who are finding their issues difficult to think about, as they may try to focus on the therapist as a distraction. And of course there are therapist-centred reasons too, therapists need the separation so as to prioritise their understanding of the client. However, when self-disclosure is related to what Spinelli terms the 'we-focused' level of therapy, 'psychotherapist's disclosures may be both appropriate and beneficial to the client' (2001, p. 34).

As I think about all this, Kenny's reaction is simply to say, 'yeh, sweet. No problem. See you on the 28th' and he hangs up, leaving me to ponder his question. I make a note to have another look at the referral letter and see if there is anything to be gleaned from that before I meet him.

II

Having reread the referral, when I meet with Kenny, I know that he is a 24-year-old builder, recently diagnosed with gonorrhoea, for which he received antibiotic treatment. He tested clear on the other sexual health/HIV screens. During his contact with the health adviser, he described being anxious about the infection and disclosed how he is stressed and this is interfering with how he relates to his family, friends and to his boxing.

I collect Kenny from the waiting room and he chatters socially as we walk down the hallway. He comments on the weather (which 'is nice, it's turning out to be a lovely spring') and about the traffic (apparently 'it was pretty awful, but then when isn't it?'). I invite him into the room and before we sit down he says, 'It's good to see a gay fella.' I raise an eyebrow in surprise.

Therapists develop a bit of a 'poker face' as time goes on. It's not a technique *per se*, it comes from an awareness that whatever is said deserves thought before we assume that we understand what it means. However, I don't manage that face on this occasion; my surprise is evident. I have neither confirmed nor denied my own sexual identity. Before I have a chance to say anything, Kenny chuckles and says, 'A straight man would have said "No" straight away.' It is that cut and dry in his world. Straight people won't stand for being seen as gay.

I don't say anything about it at this point. There isn't much to say. So I just ask, 'So Kenny, what brings you here? How can I help?'

'It's the stress,' he said, 'that woman I saw first said it might be worth coming to talk to you about it. That maybe it would help?'

'OK, well fill me in', I say.

'Hmm ... s'hard to explain. There's nothing really to be stressed about, work is good, I like the lads I work with, boxing is going well, family is close and I get on with my brothers and they've both got new kids. Got some money, decent flat, you know. It's just that I get all wound up, I start to stress, and worry, sometimes I can't sleep. I end up avoiding people, for a long time, can't pick up the phone, don't wanna hang out or nothin'.'

I ask Kenny to elaborate and he tells me that he will worry, oftentimes about things that, in another state he doesn't notice at all. His sleep can be disrupted for a week or more, he's had problems getting to sleep, he might wake up with his heart pounding and then of course he'll be slow and sluggish at work or when training. And that doesn't do when up scaffolding or in the ring.

'And have you got any idea as to why this is happening Kenny? And why now?', I ask.

Kenny frowns, shakes his head, 'No'.

We sit quietly and then Kenny says, 'it's ... fucked up, its stupid. Don't get it at all. S'pose its worse when there's a party, weddings, or Christmas and all those kind of things. It's like I go all shy or get stage fright or something. When everyone gets together, I hate it. When we have big family meet-ups – and we do – everyone starts poking their nose into my business, or when work mates meet other friends. It's when there's big groups I think … it's when they all start asking questions.'

'Questions?', I ask.

'Yeh, you know, all that personal stuff, Emilio's married and got two kids now, Seb just got married last year and had a baby so now it's all eyes on me … "who you seeing, anyone special yet", wedding bells, all that shit. Or my mates asking if I am seeing anyone, whether I've shagged this bird or that one, they won't keep their noses out.'

I want to make sure I'm following, and I also want to see what style of intervention Kenny will find most helpful, so I make an observation based on an awareness of how families evolve over time. 'Now that your brothers are married and settled down might this anxiety … maybe, be something to do with your new place in the family? You've gone from being just *one* of the kids to ask about, and now you're the only one left for them to fret about, to worry if you are settling, if you are happy?'

'I s'pose, but I just hate it … How do I get them to stop?'

'Well, what have you tried so far?'

'Nuthin'. You don't tell Mum to shut the fuck up', he says and grins. 'She would smack me so hard I wouldn't see the back of yesterday.'

I get the point. 'And the others?'

'Um … I just try and get it over as fast as possible. I smile nicely, say as little as possible and then ask about them, I change the topic … sometimes …', his face reddens a bit as he says this, 'sometimes I just tell them what they wanna hear'.

'And sometimes that's too personal?', I ask.

'Yeh', he says, '… or it's just bullshit. My mates think I have been through half of the women in Peckham, my Mum thinks I am serious about this one girl – and I ain't, we're just mates. It's just, I never know what to say, so I join in and before I know it I have told them all a different story and then it's difficult remembering what I said to who, and trying to make sure they don't talk to each other to find out about the lies. Then I just stress and wanna leave or not see anyone. It's OK one-on-one though, that's cool.'

As the session comes to a close I realise that, like Kenny, I'm also a little confused, nowhere near having a sense of what's going on, of seeing the logic in his experience.

'Shall we meet again next week?', I ask. 'There's still more that I would like to know to help me get a grasp of what is going on.'

Kenny smiles. He seems pleased and nods as he says, 'Yeh that's cool. When?'

'Same time?'

He nods and picks up his things and starts to go. 'You haven't said whether you are gay', he says with his hand on the door handle, not the best time to open up a conversation.

'Well, if that's still important to you next week, ask me then', I say, as a penny starts to drop.

Kenny and I meet the following week and after the initial pleasantries, Kenny becomes quiet and more agitated than previously, fidgeting in his chair and scratching his arm and his head. He doesn't say anything so I ask, 'Shall we start by me seeing what I already know and maybe you can fill me in on what I missed or what else you think would be helpful for me to know?'

He nods.

'OK so ... I have the impression that in some ways life is good, work and sport are going well, you've got a good flat, enjoy your family, and have some good mates and you enjoy seeing people one-on-one.'

Kenny nods and adds, 'Yeh or in small groups, just the lads, or just me mum and dad, or just my brother and his family'.

'OK, and ... you find yourself getting stressed when those different groups come together, trying to remember what story you told each one so that they, so that what? So that they don't contradict each other?'

'Yeh, I spend *ages* planning how to avoid that, how to keep private stuff private ...' Kenny is blushing as he pauses at this point.

'OK, so privacy is important here. What "stuff" do you want to keep private?'

He looks awkward, 'um ... well ... dating, sex, that kind of stuff. And ...' At this point Kenny comes to a stop and looks uncomfortable. He fidgets more in his chair, and looks everywhere but at me.

I wait. And then wait some more. Then I ask, 'And ... ?'

'Ah shit, this is embarrassing man', he says. He takes a deep breath and says, 'there's something I didn't tell you last week'.

'OK'

'I didn't tell you everything. I didn't lie but I didn't tell you that one of the things that freaks me out most is ...' and again he comes to a stop.

'OK, so there's more about this than you told me, and ...'

'Yeh, well I think I am ... or I have, or I want to, no I mean I have ... ah fuck man are you going to make me say it?' He looks at me, and I see both fear and frustration.

'What? That you ...'

'Yeh, I think I am ... or I might be ... anyway. I've been having sex with guys. One-off hook-ups ... mainly ... Ah man.' He is quiet again but seems a little less agitated now.

At this point, I am aware, that like many people on the verge of coming out, Kenny is alert to the possibility of negative reactions, rejection and criticism. Just because we are in the consulting room, doesn't mean that he is completely sure that he will not face a homophobic response. I am mindful of this as I ask, 'And this is one of the things you haven't spoken to your family or your mates about?' He nods.

'OK, that makes sense; you're nervous when the topics turn to intimacy and this is very intimate, you don't want to talk about it at all really.'

He nods again.

'What do you think would happen if you *did* talk to them about it?'

Kenny's eyes widen and he retreats further back into his seat. 'Oh no, don't even think it! I am not saying anything to them. I'm not a faggot you know, not one of those queeny camp blokes! They don't need to know about this.'

I have heard the confusion he is experiencing, the conflicted way in which he talks about this aspect of his life and now the internalised homophobia and aversion to perceived femininity. While knowing that self-loathing is a factor of many anxious and depressive presentations, such homonegativity is hard to listen to; I have an urge to challenge it immediately; it can't do his sense of self any good, surely. However, I also understand that it is helping us understand his way of being and the world as he experiences it. So patience is important too. I am beginning to become clearer as to the meaning of his questions about my identity and maybe about how he found his way to the sexual health clinic in the first place. Come and talk to a gay man as a straight man won't accept it, come and focus on an infection rather than directly on sexuality.

'OK, sure. Let's not focus on doing anything, about saying anything to anyone right now. My question is more about your *thinking*, about helping me understand what you *think* will happen …'.

'It's not what I think, it's what will happen!', he snaps. I realise he has heard me doubt the reality he is facing.

'OK, fill me in, so far I've only heard about this warm family, the one you enjoy so much. Tell me what they'd be like if they knew about this.'

Kenny starts to tear up and his cheeks redden. 'I couldn't. It'd break Mum's heart, and Dad, he would … well he wouldn't stand for it. I'd never be able to see my nephews again either.'

At this point I feel conflicted myself. I am not in a position to know anything for certain, and I definitely shouldn't assume that I know anything about his family's responses. Homophobia and heteronormativity can be difficult terrain; on the one hand therapists might be sure that clients will have experienced these to some degree as, like sexism and racism, they are woven into our culture. While they are experienced individually they are supremely political, subject to regulation, policing and control. Yet we also know that a person's fear of the rejecting other may not equate to actual negativity. Some people surprise us by being far more understanding than imagined. Therapists can't know whether the family, work or sporting context is going to respond well or belittle, sanction or bully the client – these responses occur with distressing frequency and have disabling consequences (see Bagley and Tremblay, 2000; Diaz et al., 2001) and are fostered by toxic attacks on sexual minorities in newspapers, TV shows, pathologising legislation and the promotion of conversion therapies.

I am also aware that the negativity Kenny has shown so far is his own, and that he hasn't discussed it with his family or friends, so hasn't had the chance to test the waters. It is possibly more accurate to think that, at this point, rather than facing a homophobic family, he is facing uncertainty as to whether they *might* be antagonistic. Sure it is uncertainty fuelled by the reverence of the 'traditional' family, the man-talk at work, macho banter at the gym and the cultural negativity of the last decade. After all, its 1996, the Navy recently offered aversion therapy to a naval weapons engineer in an effort to make him heterosexual and the press are making a meal of the challenge to the unequal age of consent for gay men.

I try to find a way of pulling my thoughts together, without alarming him, without overstating anything, but still staying true to his experience.

'OK, maybe this helps us understand the anxiety you've been experiencing a bit better. We know that some of this is about anxiety in relation to *other* people, about *other* people's curiosity, that even if well meant, it feels so intrusive. But what you've highlighted today, is that it's not just any old irrelevant thing that people are curious about; it's something so personal; it's your intimate life and something that's a bit confusing for you too, at the moment. And maybe we could start there, trying to understand your own relationship to that.'

I am aware that anxieties about being known are often more intense when a person is unsure of how they understand, or feel about, themselves. This is complicated with aspects of 'self', such as sexuality, gender, faith and such like. Where these aspects of themselves are relevant to the presenting problem, the person can choose, although not without consequences, to engage or deny, to act or refrain, to live openly or adopt a façade. This is both an advantage and also a disadvantage, privacy may be gained but reassurance is missed. Until one is clearer on these issues it can be hard to confidently offer yourself to the world, and to gain support in clarifying your experiences. In relation to sexuality, people are isolated while exploring what same-sex attraction means; it can be hard to figure out might I feel 'straight' most of the time but desire someone of the same sex on occasion? Maybe I am gay but not yet in a context where I am able to live that way? Or maybe 'bisexual' is a more appropriate description of the desires experienced? These are all possibilities that it can be helpful to explore.

During the rest of the session, Kenny and I explore his feelings towards men and the sex he is having. He seems relieved to talk about it even if he struggles with what to say and how to phrase it. I learn that he has been having one-off encounters with men for a couple of years; that the need for contact and for sex is beginning to feel urgent. I hear how he 'likes it rough' and wants to explore that scene a little more.

We finish the session by discussing my formulation and what Kenny thinks would be useful.

The stress seems to make sense in relation you, in effect, carrying an intimate, personal and very powerful secret, a secret that even you aren't clear about how you feel. Sometimes you accept these feelings and sometimes you feel bad about them, very negative in fact; it's almost as if they challenge your sense of what type of man you can be.

In addition you are worried as to the effect it will have in other areas of your life – your family, work, boxing, your friends and possible relationships. So instead of feeling free to be yourself and explore this, you've adopted a state of being on "high alert", keeping people apart, trying to make sure you meet expectations, whether or not those expectations suit you. And if this isn't stressful enough, you are also reminded of, and threatened by, what you see around you with the negative talk, TV and press.

Kenny nods so I continue. 'It seems too early to decide on any one single "thing to do", so I suggest a time-limited therapy, to explore this further. It might result in you feeling clearer on what this all means to you, and that might be a better place to make some decisions about things.'

He nods again.

'How does that sound?'

Kenny asks, 'What does time-limited mean?'

'What about 12 sessions? That's three months of weekly meetings; it's often enough time to look at an issue from different perspectives, but still be manageable. What do you think?'

'Three months? OK, that's not too bad. I thought you were going to say there's no hope', he said with relief. 'I can manage that.'

The following week, the therapy starts.

III

The time-limited existential approach (see Strasser and Strasser, 1997) allows Kenny and I to explore how he sees and feels about himself, how he is in relation to others and his relationship to the wider world, including the clarification of his values and the ways in which they are congruent or clash with the values of others – an area that often leads to the experience of minority stress (see Chapter 2). Kenny has been good at spotting the conflicts that exist in all these areas.

In the early sessions, Kenny speaks clearly and movingly about the nature of his desires, whom he finds attractive and the type of intimacy he hopes for. At the same time it's clear that he struggles with this as, to him, being a gay man risks appearing feminine and he has no truck for the feminine, one day saying, 'I can't really be gay 'cos I'm not a fairy'. The conflation of sexual identity and gender is often something that has to be reconciled in the coming-out process (see Ellis, 2012). It is not necessarily easier for the LGBT person than it is for the culture at large (see Valdes, 1996).

There are other factors to his resistance too. It may be because the referral context was initially via sexual health/GU medicine, or it may be due to the wider public perception of same-sex sexuality being linked to HIV/AIDS, but Kenny sometimes veers between a sense of optimism about his same-sex attractions and a deep sadness and pessimism. At one point telling me softly, 'I can't do this. I can't be gay. I don't want to die young; this is fun but it's so fuckin' risky.'

The risks aren't only social in nature, they are a matter of life and death. These possibilities upset him terribly and need attention. But as we speak it becomes clear that it isn't factual material about HIV transmission and safer sex he needs, that was covered with the health adviser and he seems well informed and describes being able to negotiate safer sex in his hook-ups. So what does he need? His response to his upset is informative, some of the fear is about mortality but what he feels most strongly is that he shouldn't be crying, he should be 'more of a man' about it. It's his vision of masculinity that needs to be clarified.

His masculinity is important to him. Kenny tells me, 'I'm just a traditional bloke, just a regular fella. You know, I always thought that I would get married, settle down, be the breadwinner, have a nice house and a couple o' kids or more.' He smiles but only briefly. This is a difficult vision for him as his lack of sexual or romantic desire for women raises doubts as to the life he will lead. It also allows him to question how the world will see him.

As we progress, these personal dimensions open out and we are able to see that there are a number of assumptions and implications located in his relationships with others.

One conflict becomes very evident as we talk. He realises he is worried whether his family or mates will accept him as a gay man or accept his choice of partners. As soon as he thinks about this though, he has another thought.

'Why have I got to worry about them?', he asks. 'It's nothing to do with them … is it? I shouldn't have to give a shit if they like him or not', he says emphatically.

I wait a moment, in some respects, this does sound reasonable. Many of us ignore our authentic decision making by subjugating our responsibility and freedom to the will of the (sometimes imagined) other, thus failing to choose our pathway through life. We forget that choosing is living. But as he talks I also realise that he is constructing a view of himself as facing a challenge that no one else ever did. He seems to feel uniquely compromised.

'This worrying about people accepting someone you choose', I start.

'Yes.'

'Is this something that Sebastian or Emilio were spared?'

Kenny laughs, he is with, or maybe ahead of me. 'Alright, alright I will give you that one. No, my Mum was always dubious about who they were seeing and if I am honest, always moaning … No not moaning, but you could tell nobody was ever right for her boys. Never.'

He pauses and reflects: 'Fair point … if I want to take someone home, sure it might be a shock at first that I'm seeing a bloke, but no one is ever going to be good enough for her baby.' He groans and rolls his eyes. 'twenty-four and I am still a fuckin' baby!!'

It isn't just his family he worries about. He cannot imagine his mates at the gym being OK with boxing a gay man either.

'Why not?', I ask. 'What are you imagining? Fill me in.'

He ponders this for a while and then decides, 'I don't know which way it would go to be honest. Sometimes I think they would just give me the cold shoulder, freeze me out, refuse to spar with me, worry about getting AIDS and shit like that. We do bleed you know.'

I nod.

'Or', he says quickly, 'it might be that they just try to give it to me in sparring, really try and fuck me up'. He stops for a moment and smiles. 'But that's alright, that's what sparring's all about, no point pulling punches, if you can't handle sparring, what you gonna be like in the fight?', he asks.

'So it's more the first option you are worried about?'

Kenny shakes his head and has a puzzled look on his face. 'I don't think I'm that bothered actually … that's up to them.'

This seems helpful, Kenny is clarifying the fact that we seldom live lives where everybody appreciates or approves of us. We exist in relationships of different kinds, close and distant, those we cherish and those that we dislike. However, I am also aware that we need at least *some* good relationships with people in areas of life that are important to us.

It is helpful for Kenny, and maybe for anybody, to recognise that they do not need *complete* empathy and engagement from *all* others. To realise that you can withstand the stresses and strains of relating in the world is a boost to one's sense of robustness and resilience. This is not to say that homophobia shouldn't be addressed. It's a scourge, responsible for far too many deaths and constrained lives and should be challenged. But Kenny seems strengthen by imagining surviving if his gym mates aren't accepting. However, I am alert to the fact that it might still be hard for him. He likes 'being one of the lads', will he have to lose this? How would he experience such a loss? I wonder.

As we work through these personal and relational possibilities it becomes apparent that we are doing this alongside a cultural struggle with same-sex sexuality. I collect Kenny from the waiting room one afternoon and find myself acutely aware that the room is littered with red-top tabloids screaming about the dangers of HAART (highly active anti-retroviral treatment). Rather than reporting the huge step forward it is for the management of HIV/AIDS, the red-tops suggest that it is licence for 'homosexual promiscuity and disease', and this is accompanied by extreme moralising about decadent lifestyles that threatened to bring down 'decent' society. It's a reminder of the vicious and restrictive world we exist in.

The therapy has its own rhythm, open reflection on personal issues, and then a realisation of the interpersonal and cultural impacts these might have. Throughout the work we are recognising that as well as maybe having to face overt negativity from outside, he is also prone to his own negative assumptions. The phenomenological method proves particularly helpful with its three main principles being epoche (suspension of judgement), description (rather than immediate explanation) and horizontalisation (see Spinelli, 2005). These all help curtail (but not eliminate) the risk of bias and overdirection on my part, and allow Kenny a growing clarity and awareness of his experience and its many different and nuanced layers. Many issues raised are explored from different perspectives, with an aim of an increasing grasp of the fullest picture possible, a grasp that goes beyond simplistic binary assumptions of either being gay or straight, of either doing or not doing something; and we explore the way in which life calls for different decisions and a variety of actions at different times and in a range of contexts. It is this that allows him to say, 'I'm getting my head around some of this stuff. A lot of the time I can just ignore it, it shouldn't affect me.'

To me, this very personalised approach is helpful as it allows Kenny the chance to recognise that the contradictions and conflicts he experiences are both personal and also rooted in the world, an inevitable part of Being-in-the-world. Yes, they are his to sort out so that he lives as well as he can, but they are rooted in wider constructions of (toxic) masculinity and homonegativity.

These attitudes infuse much of the world so that most of us grow up affected to some degree, whether we be gay, straight or bi, male or female, young or old.

As is his style, towards the end of our seventh session, with only a couple of minutes to go, Kenny tells me that he has started seeing someone. Steve has become his regular fuck-buddy. He quickly tells me that this is good; random pick-ups have their place but this has more possibilities to it.

I feel bad but am aware of the time so say, 'Hmm, we are here again, aren't we. This seems important but we don't have enough time to look at it fully. We've run out of time for today, but maybe we can talk about this some more next week?', wondering about the emergence of important topics at the very end of a session.

Kenny grins, 'Yeh, of course. See ya next week', and he leaves the room.

IV

The relationship with Steve proves to be important. It is the first time that Kenny is able to navigate some of the most personal assumptions he has about himself, about relationships and about being a gay man. He likes Steve, takes pleasure in the fact that they share a similar sense of humour and appreciates the fact that through meeting regularly he gets to know Steve's body in a richer, more intimate manner than is possible with random hook-ups.

A couple of weeks later, however, Kenny is distraught. As his sobs subside I ask him to tell me what has happened.

'He doesn't want me', he says.

'Oh, I'm sorry to hear that it's over', I say, jumping to conclusions.

Kenny shakes his head and looks up. 'No ... It's not over, not unless I want it to be. But he doesn't *want* me. Not like that. Sex in secret is fine, but I wanted to take him out, like on a date. But he wouldn't even hear me out. Doesn't wanna be seen in public with me.' He stopped and the tears return.

'He said that?', I ask.

'Well no ... he's not a complete cunt.'

I am confused.

'He said ... but I don't believe him, that "it's not his thing". He doesn't *do* monogamy, dating and all that shit. For him it's about "fucking and freedom". What's that supposed to mean?', he asks. He is angry as well as upset.

So much comes together in this session – Kenny's 'traditional' vision of relationships, his surprise that LGBT people might construct relationships outside of the narrow heteronormative model he has never questioned, and uncertainty about himself. His initial, and very powerful, assumption is that he isn't good enough; he isn't loveable. He feels rejected as a gay man.

While these, and a range of other assumptions, are all useful to explore, to question and to challenge, this isn't easy for Kenny. He fears a return to the anxiety and stress that brought him to therapy in the first place. He is also, for the first time, experiencing unrequited desire, and the acute pain that this brings. Through it all Kenny asks, 'what does it mean that even gay guys don't "want" me?'

While being a shock to him, Kenny faces his fears head on. When he returns the following week he tells me how he has talked to his brother and sister-in-law about this and 'they are cool'. Not only has he 'come out' to Seb and Michelle, but he has discussed the fact that Steve didn't want to date him (he apparently spared them some of the details as to what Steve *did* want to do).

'How was that?', I ask.

'I was surprised to be honest. I hadn't planned on telling them much at all; it was at the weekend; I'd gone round for lunch, and after we'd eaten, littl'un was napping and they could tell I wasn't my usual self. They asked about it and I told them about being upset about someone I was seeing. Michelle said she didn't even know I was with anyone and asked who she was ... and at that point I just realised I could either lie again or I could try something different.'

He pauses and seems to ponder something. 'Actually it wasn't as deliberate as that. I said it before I thought about it. I just said, "it's not a girl this time".'

Kenny smiles. 'Michelle didn't miss a beat; she asked "so who is he?" Seb took a second or two but then he asked about it too. I told you they are nosy fuckers in my family. I told them they wouldn't know him. I said I was probably making more of it than it was, but they were cool. Seb said it didn't matter; it was hard when things didn't work out. Apparently Michelle hadn't been into him at first and he struggled then. I didn't know anything about that. I thought they were always into each other.'

As he talks, I notice that it is in an everyday manner. The 'coming out' he feared so much in anticipation seems to have been experienced as something much less dramatic. Of course LGBT people don't only come out once; they make decisions about this, time and time again depending on who they are with, what the context is and the expectations they have.

'So "coming out" was less of an event than you had imagined it to be? And Seb and Michelle responded in a way that you appreciated? That you needed, even?', I ask.

'Yeh, they did', Kenny replies. 'Actually, they were surprised that I'd worried about them, about Emilio and about Mum and Dad. Oh and do you know what? They reminded me that we have an aunt in Spain, Dad's sister, Aunt Gabriela, she's a lesbian. I'd completely forgotten about her. That's fucked up isn't it? I had forgotten about her completely. Why the hell would I do that?'

I have seen this often before and think of it as an understandable response to being under scrutiny and on guard. Risks are what you look for, to protect yourself and in doing so, safety and the positives can go unnoticed. 'Maybe you've been so focused on the risks and trying to protect yourself from them, the being on high alert thing, you haven't been looking for what could reassure you. Your attention was elsewhere.'

'Yeh maybe', he says softly.

V

Our final session is upon us before we know it and, unlike most of the sessions in which we've attempted to track his experience and sense of self in the different worlds he exists in, this session has a pre-determined focus. We review how he had initially felt, how he is now and his sense of how he might be in the upcoming weeks and months. I think we are both pleased that he is less anxious and is sleeping better. Kenny describes himself as 'out' to his family now, and to a couple of his best mates too. He tells me that he has decided not to rush telling his boss and work friends and wasn't saying anything at the gym – but then 'why do they even need to know', he asks? He has decided that he likes the arrangement with Steve enough and can live with them just being regular fuck-buddies but he is open to other possibilities if they come along.

As his therapist, I am aware that he has some challenges ahead, after all he is still immersed in a culture where the constraints on LGBT people are significant and the rules about how to be a man (or a woman) are fiercely monitored, implicitly and explicitly at all levels. But I feel confident that his approach to these difficulties will stand him in good stead.

Kenny and I meet again three months later for a follow-up session. As we talk, it seems that he is optimistic and is 'making progress', as he calls it. But Kenny also senses that he is still vulnerable to reacting to the negativity he hears on the street or in the press – sometimes with the familiar self-doubt and shame, but he is also interested in how he has started to feel annoyed and angry too. Whatever the response he is pleased that his reactions are less extreme now and he is delighted with the fact that he can talk to his family when he feels stressed. He and Emilio have even met in town at The Yard and enjoyed their time there. He tells me that 'It's Emilio's kind of place; he likes it, all the chrome, the shiny and expensive look. He even tried picking out dates for me.'

'How'd that go?', I asked with raised eyebrows and a slight smile.

'Uh uh', he said shaking his head. 'Love him, but I have to say my brother has lousy taste in men.' He laughs. I laugh too.

It is on this note that we end the session and the therapy, enjoying the fact that the personal and familial can be such a support when navigating the public and cultural minefield of gender and sexuality.

6

FAITH

Religion and faith are personal and yet highly social aspects of life. They are a source of meaning, guidance and offer comfort when disoriented, and can be a buffer against psychological distress (see Coyle and Lochner, 2011; Hannay, 1980; Jackson and Coyle, 2009), but they are also phenomena around which much Othering occurs. And this is not a recent issue, alongside other discourses, religious differences have long been used to justify persecution and to wage war (see the Crusades in the medieval period, the Northern Ireland 'troubles', both George Bush and Saddam Hussein invoking God in their actions in the Iraq War, religious terminology used by different groups in Syria, the invoking of religious freedoms in the persecution of LGBT people and so on). In the consulting room, the religious differences between a therapist and client may impact on the therapeutic relationship.

Religion is used by the media in a variety of ways, often focusing on *difference* between that of those of the perceived in-group and Others. For example, the religious allegiances of foreign terrorists are often made central, while the faith of 'home-grown' terrorists is seldom mentioned. Similarly, the press referred to former mayors Ken Livingstone and Boris Johnson as 'London Mayor', whereas it is common that Sadiq Khan is referred to as 'London's Muslim Mayor' or the 'first Muslim Mayor of a Major Western City' – whether or not the news is about faith-related issues.

What has this got to do with individual distress or therapeutic practice? Contrary to some contemporary visions faith can be directly related to psychological well-being and distress – loss of faith is often associated with depression and despair (see Wink et al., 2005); and of course if we consider difference and the ways this is used to 'Other' people, we can see how religion is another socio-political factor that can lead to discrimination, oppression and trauma, in turn producing anxiety, despair and social distress.

Another issue to consider is the fact that the psychological professions are often highly secular. When a secular therapist works with religious clients, two possibilities arise; most positively, therapists might bring less allegiance/prejudice to therapy. Alternatively, therapists may be ill-prepared to engage with the deep and powerful meanings that a client's faith holds for them, seeing it as an 'outside interest' rather than recognising the ways in which a person's faith is caught up in their way of being and view of the world. Either way, therapists benefit from reflection on their own position in relation to religion and the impact this has on their therapeutic work.

Neither mad, bad nor ill: Ravi, mental health and religious identity

I

It is too early, 5.30 am in fact, but Ravi decides he has to get up. He has tossed and turned all night, yet hasn't slept a wink. Lying here in bed isn't helping. In fact, the anxiety is getting worse, definitely worse than Monday or Tuesday nights. His head feels like it is in overdrive, physically whirring, flooded with fear, adrenaline coursing through his veins; it's almost too much to bear. 'What's happening to me?', he asks himself quietly. Shivering, he throws the bedclothes off and makes his way to the shower.

As the warm water cascades over him, Ravi starts to think. Not the panicky, worrying type of thinking of the last six hours; not the worrying about what will happen if the Tresslers don't like the tweaked design; or what his mother thinks of his move, or what he is going to do this coming weekend. Nor what he thinks of as ridiculous and unbecoming worrying, the fretting … actually worrying … about George Best. No this time he starts to think a little more clearly about all the worries he has been wrestling with, and realises they make no sense to him, in fact 'I'm just confused' he says out loud. 'Why the hell am I worrying about George Best? That's not going to affect me … none of these things matter'. He continues out loud, 'The Tresslers like the design, Mom's thrilled I have this flat … she encouraged me and … I'll figure something out for this weekend. So why can't I stop shaking and why do I feel as though I could cry myself out?' He slaps the wall as he turns off the water.

As Ravi dries himself his head starts to fill again. It's automatic. This time it's the upcoming Tory leadership election that infiltrates his mind, who will get in? 'Get a grip,' he says out loud. 'Just leave it, gonna go mad if I carry on like this.' He dresses quickly, grabs his sketchpad, his workbag and heads off, trying to outrace his anxiety and leave it all behind. 'Maybe some fresh air will take my mind off of all this rubbish', he says.

It is just after 6 am and still night dark; it is almost December after all, and Ravi heads off on foot. As he walks, his mind calms a little and he observes the contradictions of London; the shabby buildings of Shepherd's Bush, shrinking besides the ever-growing monolith that is soon to be the big, shiny, new mall. Once past the roundabout, weirdly quiet at this time of the morning, he enters the upmarket Notting Hill that borders the quirky and trendy Portobello Road. Ravi becomes preoccupied with the low light that is just beginning to infuse the day, creating interesting misty effects as it grows. He brings his sketch-book out – an extension of his senses, playing with the different shades of grey, interrupting his walk to sketch images of angles and textures. It also keeps people at a distance, a barrier between them and him; it stops anyone from catching his eye. His mind becomes quiet.

By the time he reaches Kensington Gardens, the morning (and his thinking) is brighter and he has almost forgotten about his sleepless night and his random, worried thoughts. Instead, he is entranced by the early morning sun, its reflections off the pond and the warm embrace of the plants. His perspective shifts and he has a different challenge, now trying to sketch light, the warmth of the golden hour. He finally stops, managing to take a moment to enjoy this urban oasis.

At 8.15 am it is time to compose himself, and to start the final walk down to the clinic and to pick up some breakfast on the way.

II

A little bit of background may be helpful here. I first met Ravi at the beginning of November 2005, and I found him to be a quiet, reserved man, quite tired looking and seemingly a little nervous. The initial couple of sessions helped me begin to grasp the nature of his difficulties and offered me a brief glimpse of his history.

Ravi described very strong and disabling anxiety – biologically it was interfering with his sleep and appetite, and it affected his friendships and social life too. Actually it impinged on a wide array of interpersonal relationships; he found it hard to be frank with friends, family and work. Ravi felt that people would – and did – treat him as if he were 'crazy, and they talk all soft and quiet'. He told me 'others act as if I am going to go berserk, as if I am mass murderer potential, and some think I'm ill and need a lie down, a cup of tea or a nice walk'. Ravi was experiencing that 'mad, bad or ill' perspective that corrupts many of our attempts to understand human distress (Milton et al., 2010). This created a dilemma; he found it stressful to keep his fears to himself, yet if he didn't censor them, or keep them from show (he thought) others judged him badly. This meant he struggled to be as open and honest as he might like to be.

As we spoke, Ravi appeared at a loss regarding the anxiety, why it manifests at this time, why it was so strong and why it took the forms it did – usually about things he knew he had no control over. As I asked about it, Ravi couldn't identify any event that 'caused' the anxiety; in fact he told me that things have been going very well. He enjoyed his work as a gardener, and had recently moved out of home and into a flat, which he was very pleased about. My question as to whether his new independence could be related to this experience of anxiety was answered with a straightforward 'No'.

Psychologists and other therapists recognise that it is important to understand a person's difficulties in the context of the life that is being, *and has been*, lived – so during those sessions I explored Ravi's history with him. I came to understand that this single thirty-year-old cisgender man was born into a Hindu family a few years after his mother and father migrated to the UK in the late 1960s. He was the youngest in the family with an elder brother and sister, both of whom were married. Almost as an afterthought, Ravi told me that there was one other sister but she had died before he was born, so he never met her. The family all live in the Shepherd's Bush area: 'Dad works, Mom doesn't, she never has, she is very traditional like that.' School was described as 'OK', but he told me that he had experienced some bullying in high school; however, he told me that 'didn't matter'; he ' had always liked doing things alone, like art and nature anyway'.

In the second assessment session, Ravi suddenly asked me my opinion. He told me that the psychiatrist he had previously seen suspected schizophrenia, and asked whether that 'has come back?' His question took me by surprise, as he hadn't mentioned anything of this nature in our first meeting and the letter from his GP hadn't mentioned anything of the kind either.

As we talked, Ravi told me that as a teenager he had received a tentative diagnosis of 'schizophrenia' but no doctors had 'called it that' since. Mainly the doctors called it 'anxiety'. As I listened to him, I realised how disabling these experiences were; they included periods of quite extreme and debilitating socially focused anxiety, always suspicious of others, sometimes feeling 'a bit paranoid'. Ravi told me he had seen psychologists in the past, too, both in primary care and in a CMHT (Community Mental Health Team) context, and that the 'step programme' had 'worked ... for a bit'. It seems that he and his previous therapists had undertaken some form of desensitisation but he voiced scepticism about this approach now that the anxiety was 'back'. He didn't think we should just 'redo the steps'; he had tried that on his own, and neither that, nor his faith, limited the worrying.

As Ravi mentioned his faith, I asked him about Hinduism. He looked a little confused at first and then said that he was happy to tell me about it, but pointed out that this was mainly his parents' faith, his brother and sister weren't followers and he himself was Buddhist, praying and meditating daily. He told me how Buddhism had been a revelation to him, a source of succour and inspiration, a vision of a way to live a good life. I had clearly made some assumptions there; why should the faith of the family be that of the individual?

At the end of the two assessment sessions, I sketched the beginnings of a formulation along the following lines and shared it with Ravi.

You were born into a family that had experienced a lot of change – your parents moving from India to forge a new life and then there was the establishment of the family. You were born soon after your sister died, and so were born into a distressing situation. As you grew up you were part of a family that was a little split, Dad and your remaining siblings, going out and making their way in the world, while Mom and to some degree you, were more firmly rooted in the house. It seems that for you, it might have felt that from very early on you had to confront a scary and threatening world. This, and then your later experiences at school, mean that your concern about the world was never fully overcome and at points of real stress you would withdraw and isolate yourself. Buddhism has been both calming and meaningful but you find that this isn't a panacea to your anxieties.

Ravi thought that this made sense and therefore he and I agreed that further therapy might be helpful – and that we shouldn't try to just replicate what had gone before. Ravi understood the theory and the practice of desensitisation but seemed to need, more than anything right now, help understanding the anxiety and assistance in adjusting to the fact that he was likely to experience fear and anxiety at times. He described knowing, intellectually, that life could not be without suffering; no one could escape it. Yet he also felt that somehow, emotionally, he couldn't accept the struggles *he* had, the things *he* was scared of and he couldn't countenance the gap between how he is and what he aspires to – to lead a moral life, mindful of thoughts and actions, developing wisdom and understanding as he did so. Instead he was sometimes fearful and desiring of relief.

I remember thinking that these didn't seem unusual or unreasonable dilemmas to have, but I did see the way they clashed with key tenets of his faith.

So that was our remit, time-limited therapy to explore the anxiety as much as manage it, to consider how one lives with such strong and difficult feelings rather than suggesting that some kind of miraculous, lifelong cure would be possible.

III

Our appointment is at 9.15 am and Ravi is early; he settles into our slightly gloomy, worn waiting room, with its array of leaflets, magazines and tabloids. As I walk down the hallway I see him working on his sketches. He seems engrossed.

Ravi jumps a little as I say, 'Good morning'.

'Oh morning', he says, snapping his pad shut, squeezing it into his bag and standing up – all in one clumsy movement.

Once in the consulting room Ravi starts to tell me about the last few nights and the problems he is having sleeping. He is particularly confused as to why George Best's demise is as upsetting as it is.

84

'I didn't really follow him, my Dad did, but I didn't. This worrying is definitely worse than it was on Monday or Tuesday night. My head's just on overdrive; it's too much.'

With drooping shoulders, he cups his head in his hands and asks, 'Why am I worrying about George Best?' He stops short, looks me in the eye and qualifies this. 'Oh I don't want anyone to die, but really, why should *he* affect me? Actually nothing I worry about should really get to me. My bosses like the new design. I don't really know anything about politics and elections ... Mom is happy I have the flat ... So why can't I stop shaking? Why do I feel as though I could just cry and cry and cry?'

As we confer, I too, experience some of the confusion; he is right, much of his night-time worries seem to be, on the face of it at least, unrelated to him. Maybe they *shouldn't* affect him, but they do.

As we talk, Ravi becomes exasperated and says, 'it hasn't been this bad since after 9/11'.

I am not sure exactly why, but this seems important. 'Tell me about that', I say.

'Er ... dunno', he says. 'I ... I just remember getting really worried back then, but I think everyone was, weren't they? Didn't everyone worry about that, everyone thought bombs were going to go off all over the place.'

I nod; I know I had felt that way.

'Well I just seemed to be scared all of the time, didn't want to go anywhere high, well not buildings anyway, trees were fine, but tall buildings? No. I couldn't sleep; every time I tried I had visions of people jumping out of the tower. It was horrible.'

I nod again. Of course Ravi's experience is his own, but I recognise it well. He is right, many people were affected by the atrocity, and not just those in the vicinity or those who actually lost loved ones. The impact was far-reaching, as it was designed to be. People felt scared and sickened. I had felt tortured by those very same images, of people in free fall, a tragic final, ultimately futile, grasp at life.

We talk about Ravi being right. This was a common experience; maybe we shouldn't worry too much about something that seems an understandable response to such a traumatic event.

'Yes, but not everyone got blamed for it did they?', he says.

'What do you mean?'

He takes a moment, then says, 'I might have imagined it but people watched me, you know. You could see they were worried; they pulled their children closer, got out of their seat on the tube. It was horrible, it was like an attack, a personal attack, was imminent.'

That must have been awful, but I am also struck by his doubt, that he might have imagined these responses. Had he been paranoid at this point in time?

'That is horrible, and it makes sense you would feel anxious. But what did you mean about you might have imagined it though?'

'Um ... don't know, really ... just didn't know if people *were* doing that, or why they would do that to me. It's not like I ever did anything. But I don't *think* I was imagining it.' He casts his mind back and then continues. 'No, I wasn't. I definitely had people ask pointed questions; they would say, "How can people do such a thing?" and then look straight at me; or I was asked, often actually, 'How does Islam allow that? They didn't ask anyone else and what do I know about Islam? Nothing! ... I don't blame anyone, but sometimes I couldn't handle it. Still can't.'

Of course not, and why should he? Ravi is describing a common, fear-based, reaction we saw after the 9/11 attacks. Fear interfering with thinking, race and faith getting conflated and fuelling projections, suddenly all black and brown folk assumed to be Muslim, and more than that, Muslims assumed to be terrorists, purveyors of death and destruction. People's fight-or-flight reactions seemed to come powerfully to the forefront, limiting clear thinking.

Then the penny drops, it is only four months since London suffered its own atrocity – the 7/7 attacks – and we are once again in the grip of intense cultural and existential anxieties: politicians are struggling to contain the practical and emotional needs of the population and a media fuelled narrative of the dangerous Other is flooding the front pages once again.

IV

This new awareness impacts on therapy. Both Ravi and I experience a more visceral awareness that his nocturnal ruminations are not actually the key problem; yes, they are distressing and sleeplessness can have powerful impacts, both physically and psychologically. But they are possibly better understood as manifestations of the bigger, more threatening and less manageable anxieties – ever-present threats to life and an ongoing Othering that is evident wherever he goes; people looking at him with uncertainty, the TV reminding us of the dangerous others and, here I feel both shame and frustration, safe places (like the clinic is meant to be) are contaminated by the negative, inflammatory press headlines that abound. It is a dilemma, and one that applied psychology, psychotherapy and counselling struggle with: how *does* one help a client feel calm, or maybe even good about oneself and one's place in the world when threat and rejection are so powerfully prevalent?

This awareness prompts Ravi to reflect on his faith again. He tells me: 'Buddhism's first noble truth, tells us that life is difficult, that it will throw up problems, and it is unlikely to be very different to that. Few people will ever get through life without experiencing anxiety or feeling low, without a sense of threat or isolation.'

As we talk, I suggest to Ravi that this possibly has *many* meanings and so far, in our discussions at least, I get the feeling that he tends to think of this situation exclusively in personal terms – as if *he alone* is under threat; it is just *he* that is misperceived; *he* who must single-handedly rise above this if he is to be true to his faith.

Traditionally, psychological and psychotherapeutic theory has offered assistance by helping clients recognise the ways in which their own thoughts, behaviours or relationships affect their experience. More recently, these fields have recognised the impact that the world has in constructing distress and therefore has been considering how we might engage with this fact. I have already mentioned plural interpretations in this book (see Chapter 2). In addition to that, we can learn from the decades of work that systemic and other therapists have offered, for example *encouraging irreverence towards theory* (Cecchin et al., 1992), so as to encourage the client to challenge beliefs about the necessity of specific forms of relationship, family structures and cultural forms; the usefulness of *understanding the problem as outside of the problem* (Bor et al., 1996), which can help clarify the ways in which reality is co-constructed in relationships, families and more contextually; and the *offering of socio-cultural interpretations* (Strawbridge, 1994) which highlights factors located in the 'external' world, thereby allowing that the experienced is influenced, constructed and sometimes caused by social and political factors.

Ravi nods and seems to understand me. Yes, he has a strong desire to be authentic, to be true to himself, yet he can see that this is affected by how others react to him. He struggles with the fact that his presence, and the voicing of his faith can appear counterproductive, in some situations they confirm his Otherness and risk making him the subject of difference and prone to misperception and projection. So, to counter this, he keeps himself to himself, shying away from others. Ravi can see that as well as these experiences being very personal, our emotional life is relational; it is related to ourselves, to other specific people and also to cultural events and world views.

Over the next couple of sessions, Ravi and I discuss his day-to-day anxieties through this adjusted lens, considering the ways in which he tries to navigate these external dilemmas. His preoccupation with celebrity deaths diminishes and he stops worrying about the Tory leadership now that David Cameron has taken the role. At work, as one project finishes the anxiety wanes, but he feels it more forcefully again when he has to go and meet with clients, talk to them about their hopes and present them with the plans or estimates. Interestingly, though, he considers these 'less worrying worries'. He sees them as 'typical' of him. These people are not an actual threat. He can feel nervous but 'lets it go' easily enough.

There is a break over the Christmas period and when Ravi and I meet again in early January he tells me he has started to avoid people again, limiting how much he goes out and is even avoiding the TV and the press. 'It's for the best', he tells me. 'I saw an old cover of the *Daily Express*, from just after the bombing and its headline screamed *"Bombers are all sponging asylum seekers"* and that's how people see me – as a wannabe bomber, or if not, a scrounger.' He had also realised that newspapers, either through ignorance or a wilful misrepresentation, use Indian people to illustrate 'Muslim terrorists' when it's very clear that the person is Sikh or Hindu. 'Or it would be clear if people bothered to look, they just see "foreign".'

As he shares these examples with me, I can see how powerfully they have affected him. He feels exposed and guilty, and he starts to flush and to shake. I am reminded that:

> when the breakdown of familiar structures appears to escalate, the world becomes threatening and 'unsafe'. What is safe is what is known, what can be predicted. So we seek to make the world safe, even if that means accepting a place of subordination in that world, as long as we have a place, a home that is predictable and more certain. (Pearce, 2017, p. 22)

Ravi tells me (again) that 'I am not a terrorist or an asylum seeker, so why do I get like this?' He is asking us to think about more than just objective facts, but to explore the power of the emotion too.

It's a crucial question and, theoretically, I ponder the notion of projection. While some psychotherapists consider it as an unconscious phantasy in which aspects of the self or an internal object are split off and attributed to another person, projection is also a cultural phenomenon (Smith, 1999). It has been suggested that intense cultural anxieties can also be split off and projected onto certain groups, usually minorities or those groups deemed Other (Samuels, 1993). Yes, maybe Ravi's history predisposed him (maybe) to anxieties about the world, but was he also absorbing interpersonal and cultural fears of aggression and annihilation from the events of the time? It can be hard not to as these projective anxieties are accompanied by behaviour and emotion that is intended to induce the recipient of the projection to feel and act in accordance with the projective phantasy (Smith, 1999). So, while Ravi may be questioning the personal aspect of this phenomenon, we cannot forget that it is happening within the context of a cultural process; his presence on the street is frequently being responded to 'as if' he is the violent aggressor; the looks, the movement, the pulling of children towards parents all communicate

88

this message. This, and the anti-Islamic press, political discourse and terrorist events themselves all carry meaning.

Maybe we need to recognise that these racist and Islamophobic responses are, in some respects, nothing to do with him – not in a way that he 'causes' anyway, so he has little control over them. Whether he is nice or nasty, vocal or quiet, public or private, the fear or the hate of the Other means that some see what they will and project aggression, threat and danger on to him independently of anything he has or has not done.

I emerge from my pondering, to try to put these thoughts into words, an amended formulation if you like.

Well, I wonder whether you kind of act like a sponge, absorbing all of these negative messages and assume they are about you. In one way you *know* that's not accurate or not right, but at another level, it feels too late; you have sucked them up and they weigh you down. Once this has happened, the emotions sort of make sense; you absorb all this anxiety about aggression, so you feel guilty about that; you pick up on all this fear, of violence and destruction, and not only do you feel your own anxiety but you feel it for others too. You then rely on withdrawal as the way to escape, and you have been doing this for a *long* time.

Ravi nods as I speak and says, 'But what do I do about it? I kind of know it's not right, that it's too much, but it gets to me.'

As is the case in much therapy, there is movement between understanding and acting, for the therapist from theory to practice. So our attention turns back to action, to what he might think and do differently; we consider practical changes, such as the timing of his prayer and meditation, food and exercise, the fact that he can lose himself in his sketching and we consider the content of some of the press head on. We reflect on the skills he learnt in the desensitisation programme and think of how he can structure his day to maximise the good experiences. Ravi is interested in these possibilities and seems to like thinking about living life rather than avoiding it, even if it might have to be a different response to life.

A couple of days later I drive past a demonstration outside the Danish Embassy in London. It is in response to the Jyllands-Posten Muhammed cartoons and has hit the headlines. Some commentators attempt to address the complex range of meanings involved, but much reporting has taken a lazy approach, rushing to conclusions, deciding that different parties are either in the right or in the wrong, that those who are upset are overly sensitive and those who approve are tasteless and blasphemous. As I reach Sloane Square I think about how difficult it is to judge meaning, especially when there are personal, interpersonal and cultural dimensions to it, when different faiths are involved and when identities are affected. As therapists we can't just think about any single issue in isolation; we need to consider the intersections between them as well.

At our next session, Ravi reports having felt a little anxiety this past week. 'It's not too bad', he says, 'but it is there'.

Before I can say anything, Ravi smiles at me and says, 'But this time I know it is a reaction to the protests, well not the protests themselves – I think I agree with them protesting, a bit of me wanted to go along and show support, but it's the media excitement that worries me. This time though I know that it's not about me even if people look at me as if it is. That doesn't make it right but it means I don't have to feel so overly involved.'

I nod and start to speak, but Ravi is on a roll and continues. 'I haven't thought of this before but I think I haven't understood some of the Buddha's teachings properly either. I've understood the third noble truth too simplistically. I assumed that because suffering can be overcome and happiness can be attained, I was … I don't know, "doing it wrong" maybe? I was overlooking that I was craving relief too much, so I wasn't learning to live each day at a time, I was *wanting* … wanting it to be different.'

As we continue, Ravi and I explore what possibilities these insights might allow.

'Well … if I am right, and I don't have to feel so involved, what do I do instead? How do I respond?', he asks me.

'Hmm, good question', I say not wanting to answer for him, 'What do you think?'

He smiles. 'OK, well, assuming I can actually do it, I could sleep more, be a bit more creative at work, I might even focus more on my art. If all this hate and fear is based on ignorance, it might be a good thing, to try and shed some new light onto events. I was thinking about signing up to do a course. Preema, my sister, showed me a good one, the idea being to be more focused on storytelling in your art, to show a different side to things. That might be good.'

I like this idea, but am surprised to feel some ambivalence. I am concerned that Ravi isn't completely comfortable with the notion of the world having an influence over our feelings yet and here he is trying to 'do something' socially and inherently politically. But I am also aware that, for him, it is a creative response, an outward-looking step. And also, I think, he is right; one of the problems behind the othering of people and discrimination against groups is a lack of awareness, invisibility and separation. Allport and Kramer found that greater awareness can limit fear of the other, and termed this the 'contact hypothesis' (1946). They argued that closer, meaningful, involvement between groups leads to diminished anxiety and less discriminatory behaviour. It seems that proximity, collaboration and interaction are ways in which we experience *people* rather than *groups* or labels. It is by meeting, knowing and enjoying people that we overcome separateness and enhance our relationships as individuals and as communities.

V

As we come to the end of therapy, I realise that I am a little nervous, and this is despite the fact that Ravi's more extreme symptomatology has eased significantly; he is not worrying about random things so much and he is sleeping again. The fact that he seems to be able to tolerate the anxiety he feels bodes well too. But, despite us having agreed that therapy was unlikely to be a cure-all, especially for the profound social ills that weigh so heavily on him, I still worry. He is likely to face racism and religious discrimination, to be misconstrued and misinterpreted whatever he does, and that will – or could – be a challenge for him. My colleagues and I have long wondered whether we are just metaphorically patching clients up only to send them back to the front line?

In our last few sessions, I try to address this anxiety by ensuring that we look towards the future too. Ravi is quite taken with imagining his potential self, himself as someone who can manage anxiety and have other, non-anxious responses. For my part, I ask him to consider how he might respond to hostility – whether that be aimed at him or simply the negativity that is so present 'out there' in the world.

'I just have to remember that often, it's not me that's the centre of this even if people look at me as if it is. Maybe I can see that the world has problems … and responsibilities too. And …' He pauses here. '… I also think it will be easier to ask for help … or maybe just talk to others about this. Preema understands this; she is the assertive one. I don't know why I haven't spoken to her about it more actually.'

This sounds like an eminently useful strategy and I am pleased he has at least identified ways in which he might garner support. It seems that Ravi has been able to reframe some of these issues as contextual and traumatising rather than inexplicable and his fault and responsibility. And to do this within the framework of his faith too.

In our last session, we are wrapping things up when Ravi says, with a twinkle in his eye, 'And what are you going to do?'

I am not sure what he means and I start to talk about discharge letters and re-referral protocols but he interrupts me.

'No I don't mean that', he says. "What can you do … here?'

It is clear that I am not with him so Ravi says, 'You could do me, well everyone that comes here, a favour and sort that waiting room out. Some of those papers are not helpful, you know. I know that rubbish is out there but to have to see it when you come here ... if I wasn't affected before I came in, it could set you off, you know.'

I am sure that I blush. I know what he is talking about and have long struggled with keeping these hateful headlines out of the clinic. No sooner have I, or my colleagues, picked them up and thrown them out, we find another. I assure him I do try and I will continue to try. Then we say goodbye.

As Ravi leaves I have rather an odd feeling; I am pleased that he could voice appreciation for our work but I also feel unsettled. I ponder it for a while and then I decide that maybe this is how it should be. Ravi's final comments are about the world, the world that he is going back out into and he has left me, very powerfully, with some insight about it. The ever-present Islamophobia affects us all; it is persistent, hard to tackle and creeps into even the safest of spaces. He has left me with a greater sense of the importance of being constantly vigilant and, in a way, reached out with a comradely call, not to give up in the face of frustration but to keep up the fight myself.

7

NON-BINARY GENDER

In Chapter 4 we saw the ways in which gender creates particular lenses through which we scrutinise and police behaviour and experience. We saw how that can lead to gender-based assumptions that affect the way that individuals can be in the world. Amanda's story gave us the chance to consider gender-related factors *within* the binary understanding of gender. But these are not the only ways in which gender manifests itself or can be experienced.

This chapter explores Sam's experience, a client for whom the gender binary, being thought about as 'either' male 'or' female is nonsensical, failing as it does to capture their experience. Despite us knowing that many gender-diverse children are born every year, they are born into a world that fails to recognise, understand or accept them; they are born into a struggle, into a fight. A fight to find a way to know themselves, and fight to have their voice heard and their experience recognised or honoured. This occurs at all levels, interpersonally, in the family and community and within our cultural institutions, resulting in distress and difficulty, some of which is brought to therapy. Qualitative research into the experience of trans people, has revealed descriptions of anxiety, isolation and social exclusion (see Atnas et al., 2015, 2016). At the cultural level, we see medicine's response to children born with, what are deemed, 'ambiguous genitalia' often being to encourage surgical intervention to bring the body into line with either a distinctly 'male' or 'female' morphology (see Kitzinger, 1999) and this is legally facilitated by birth certificates for binary-based declarations of sex in most countries. At school, parents are consulted when children show gender 'incongruent' behaviours, interventions are made to encourage 'normal' gender development or referrals to psychiatric or psychological services are made. We also see trans people being murdered in the UK (and the USA), we know that 48 per cent of trans people attempt suicide and that half of Britain's 28,000 trans students consider leaving their course (see Jones, 2015).

These experiences feed into a traumatising culture with far-reaching personal and social impacts. Trans, non-binary and gender-fluid experience is clearly both personal and political.

Beyond the binary: Sam and gender

I

'My anger is righteous. It is quite reasonable to be angry in the face of injustice, the misuse of power and the refusal to listen. I don't know why my friends suggested I see you for 'anger management', that's not what I want nor what I need. *I* think it's a good idea to see you because I do want some help thinking about managing stress effectively; I need to think about looking after myself, being strong enough to face all the crap out there.'

A statement like this is not *quite* what I had expected just a few minutes into an assessment session.[1] It was also not what I had been told to expect when accepting the six-month locum job at the college to offer sabbatical cover. I have been primed to expect high rates of anxiety, a preponderance of difficult relationships to food and a regular call for support as students transition from school to further education. As my first client, Sam doesn't seem to fit this profile at all. Sam is quite clear, explicit in what is wanted and not at all anxious. Sam is confident and has conviction; the statement feels neither equivocal nor transitory.

'OK, fill me in then Sam; how can I help?'

Sam tells me that despite the fact that college 'and everything' is going well, 'it won't always be like this, will it? I need to think about how to manage this messed up world, manage the stress, so full of expectation and prejudice, that doesn't want people to be people, just cogs in the machine.'

'True enough', I think as I embed myself in the task of assessment and ask Sam to elaborate what 'stress' might mean? What stresses have been experienced in the past and what is envisioned? And what does 'cog in the machine' mean?

I quite enjoy the assessment session. Sam and I talk about past experiences, present practices and future ambitions. I hear about the family, how Dad,

---

[1] While different settings have different views on the nature of 'assessment', in my view the first encounter between a client and a therapist is always exploratory, with both participants assessing what possibilities the encounter may offer the client. In addition to this, applied psychologists and psychotherapists attempt, at an early stage, to get as clear an idea as possible as to the nature of any difficulties, the experiences the client may have had and the way in which the two are related. Assessment also allows the pair to consider whether therapy might be the most helpful intervention or whether a different form of help might be better suited to their needs. The context really only affects the manner and style of the assessment, not the need to undertake some kind of thoughtful assessment at the beginning of the work together.

Steve, is a teacher, Mum, Felicia, is a designer and then there is Jacob, Sam's brother, older by two years. School gets a bit of a mixed review; overall it seems that it was 'fine', some fun with mates but not really challenging enough intellectually or creatively; 'to be honest, it was a bit boring actually', Sam says. Despite that, both the family and the school sound like places that offer love, support and challenge.

Sam tells me of some minor teasing early at school but that didn't last long; friends were protective but it was a talent with words that nipped it in the bud. 'I *can* be a bit vicious, with my tongue. I don't suffer fools gladly and I let people know. Or if it's not politic, I moan at my mates or at home. Maybe that's why they think I have an anger problem.' Sam looks quizzical at this point.

Sam seems bright, very creative and strongly guided by a vision of a fair and just society, with the right for people to be respected as they are. I am impressed with this' it's not all seventeen year olds that are so eloquent about these values. While working hard on a number of courses Sam seems to have realised that it is photography that calls forth the most passion: 'They tell us it's all about light and dark but actually I love the spaces in between, where its neither portrait nor landscape, but populated space and people in context. That's where the stories lie, where the clashes come to light, where the discomfort can be explored.' A career as a photojournalist is of interest right now.

As well as being guided by what Sam is interested in talking about, I also run through some of the key issues that all therapists consider on first meeting a new client. I am told that there is no suicidality; in fact Sam is quite definite about it: 'As if! I am only just getting started, why would I finish it now?' It is a rhetorical question though as Sam continues: 'although you shouldn't be negative about those that do; they have a right you know.' I hear Sam finds alcohol to be 'an over-rated drug, hangovers just prove that you are basically poisoning yourself, it's a toxic reaction', smoking is 'a mug's game' and when I ask about other drugs I am told that 'cocaine is a bit of a Gen-X stereotype, don't you think?' Sam has tried cannabis and says that 'while it was OK, I can't say it did very much; it's an occasional beer or glass of wine and that's it really'.

As I think about the session it occurs to me that Sam would be an unusual referral in many public sector settings, where a declared problem and a focus on 'diagnostic criteria' is becoming increasingly rigid. This is often presented as a reaction to 'the evidence base' but it is also used as a way to limit demand for an increasingly stretched and underfunded mental health workforce. Another worrying aspect of this phenomenon is the privileging and strengthening of a medicalised understanding of people and their experiences; it constructs health and illness as distinct personal phenomena rather than the reactions to difficult and distressing events in the world (see Fletcher, 2012).

With Sam, I am not being asked to 'deal' with a crisis, there is no need to force a particular 'disorder' and no 'problem' to get preoccupied with. The rejection of the reductionistic notion of 'anger management' seems sound to me – indeed, I often wonder why we fetishise the 'management' of anger more than we might 'manage' any other emotion. In Sam's case there is no sign of anger transforming itself into antagonism or leading to altercations or fights. The request for therapy feels more like a process of personal reflection and challenge is being requested, something more akin to the facilitation of a developmental process, helping this young person orientate themselves to the world they know exists out there. If anything it is an opportunity to offer the type of therapy that so many psychologists and psychotherapists avail themselves of (albeit briefly). It is this that leads me to offer Sam sessions on an open-ended basis during the time I am at the college, that is, therapy for up to six months.

In the first couple of weeks of therapy, Sam is active in thinking about a number of issues; preparation for exams and assignments gets some attention, there is some reflection on what career would suit and how to approach it, and some pondering of whether to apply for university or to start looking for apprenticeships or entry level jobs. While thinking about these headline issues I get to see a thoughtful approach to life, an awareness of possibilities among the wave of uncertainty being faced. I also hear about likes (the colour purple, Twitter, and black-and-white photography) and dislikes (the screams of foxes mating, Jacob's interest in shooting, The X Factor and formulaic music) and I hear about the rough and tumble of friendships. I am aware though that I frequently get picked up because my reflections and interpretations are frequently seen as too 'black and white'. Sam tells me explicitly 'the world isn't all either-or you know; there's a lot in between.'

II

It's three weeks into therapy and as Sam arrives I hear a snippet of McFly, although I can't tell which song as the iPod is quickly turned off. Sam is in a foul mood; it seems to be something between fury and agitated despair – energy comes and goes, moving through periods of acerbic attacks to a defeatist questioning of whether it is possible to understand the world.

'So what happened Sam?', I ask.

'These!', says Sam showing me some beautifully painted nails.

'Your nails?' I suspect my face gives away that I have *no idea* how the nails are linked to this very different mood.

That's the first 'mistake'. My blank face, my questioning, is read (quite rightly) as being poorly attuned to Sam's experience.

'Oh not you too.'

Sam goes quiet and the head drops. I have the feeling that I have done something horrible but am not yet clear about it, so I'm at a loss as to how to understand it or how to respond. If this occurred at home I might simply ask my family, 'Is it something I said?' but that's a bit redundant here as Sam has already indicated that it is. The nails are clearly a lot more meaningful than I have imagined.

As I struggle with this, Sam sighs. 'It's just all happened today. There were some odd looks on the bus this morning because of these! There was other stuff, lot of rubbish in the paper, that got under my skin and then there was Rachel. I don't normally do my nails, but I thought I would try these out; I just felt like it. I showed them to her and she said, "Oh they are so pretty, you should do that all the time". "All the time", I ask you. I thought she got it but clearly she doesn't!'

I am being offered more information but am still not seeing the thread of meaning.

'And that's the painful part, you thought she would understand but she doesn't', I say. As I do, I am very aware that this sums up the dilemma between us as well. It is clear that Sam feels I should understand, but I am at a loss.

'I thought I was over all that not being understood', Sam says. 'I worried about things for years, was worried Steve and Felicia wouldn't get me, would get all weird and avoidant or forceful, or that school would be awful when kids got preoccupied with fashion and dating and all that, but generally people have been alright. It's just all come at once today I suppose.'

As Sam finishes explaining, I still am not exactly sure of the meaning of all these incidents and why they are as upsetting as they are. This is not to say I assume they should not be upsetting; I am just acutely aware that I am not following. So, I have a dilemma: try and bluff it out or be direct and 'admit' that I am unsure. The former seems a bit ethically dubious, the latter a little risky.

'I'm sorry Sam, I can see how upsetting things have been today, but I have a feeling that like Rachel, I am not getting it. I am sorry about that, can you fill me in?' Such a direct admission, a form of self-disclosure, can be considered differently by the various therapeutic schools. It might be seen as nothing more than a statement of fact, it could be seen as a weakness in the authority of the therapist and for others it's a key aspect of the therapeutic relationship, being an observation on the process that the client and therapist are involved in, offering insight into the type of tangles that the client is likely to get into in their wider interpersonal encounters. I also see such statements as having a political dimension to them, the levelling of the field a little so as to democratise the relationship.

I brace myself – for what I am not sure. I am half expecting that sharp tongue to tear shreds out of me, but I am also worried that Sam will walk out or at least not come back again.

There is a pause, then Sam exhales and the shoulders drop a little.

'Well, thank you for saying sorry. I don't blame you really, as you haven't known me long and there's probably a lot that you don't know about me.' Sam takes a deep breath and tells me explicitly, 'I am just so tired of having to come out to everyone, explain what it's like to be non-binary. To live with this constant pressure, even my mates "forget". Rachel would prefer it if I was more girly more of the time. She thinks she's being all "liberal" and stuff, but it misses the point.'

I am relieved that we seem to have survived a disconnect, a potential rupture, and I am much clearer that Sam is facing a very different set of dilemmas than I have imagined. Sam isn't just preparing for a cut-throat world where for instance jobs are in short demand, where it's hard to get into university or the intricacies of navigating first love; for Sam there is also the daily need to steel oneself for entry into a world that tends to think of people in 'either-or' terms, whether its seeing race in terms of black or white, physicality in terms of abled or disabled, and gender solely in terms of male or female. Even the increased attention to trans experience can sometimes complicate things, as people assume the trans experience to be a move from 'one' sex to 'the' other. Seen this way trans status sheds no light on being non-binary, which can straddle or is beyond either of these experiences.

I have to admit to some concern too. While I have long read and been concerned about gender as it is played out in contemporary culture, know that gender is an area of such powerful (and constant) scrutiny and policing from pre-birth throughout life, and have tried to challenge that, I am aware that this is all rather a cerebral perspective. I also live, and have been trained to live, in a binary framework. Unless I have '*reason*' to think about gender, I have the luxury of forgetting it; as a cisgender man I seldom think about people using 'he' and 'his' as pronouns, for me they fit. Is this why maybe I overlooked Sam's cues, when dressed in 'male' clothes I simply assumed 'he' would be comfortable with being called 'he', not just in the moment, but as a permanent form of address. It seems that there are times when that is acceptable to Sam, when it does capture an experience of self – but I am reminded today that it isn't a static fact. Sometimes Sam feels differently, sometimes 'she' would be better, or in Sam's own words 'to be honest its best to stay with e/em/eir, they fit more of the time than "he" or "she" does'. Sam is referring to 'Spivak pronouns', introduced by Michael Spivak in his maths textbooks of the 1990s (Spivak, 1990).

I also become aware of another dilemma, for me that is. We therapists are trained to be alert to the ways in which clients impact us, oftentimes thinking of it as a client's attempt to try to *control* their therapists, sometimes as a way to avoid looking at painful issues or perhaps as a way to secure some kind of relational gain. Might this be a case here? Is Sam telling me what I can and cannot say, what I should and shouldn't even think? Or is this simply a request to respect Sam's self-definition. As I ponder this, I realise I have dived straight back into the binary – it doesn't have to be one or the other. It might be both or neither of these.

After this Sam brings more of emself to therapy, not just thoughts and discussions about the frustrations of a binary experience, but e also outlines preferred pronouns, is more relaxed about clothing and make-up as well. Working with Sam is always interesting, e certainly keeps me alert and on my toes. One minute we discuss the possibilities of photography, how it seems to hold such promise, opening up a world of curious exploration, challenging us by showing that things aren't the way we think they are; the next Sam talks about fear and nervousness, worrying about the new Anti-Terrorism Crime and Security Act and the press speculation about it allowing a British version of Guantanamo Bay. 'That's not right. You can't lock people up without knowing the truth; you can't just assume people are bad!' Sam's reflections on the 'real world' are interesting and seem helpful – but they are not the traditional material of psychotherapy. There I go again, questioning whether it is either right or wrong, wondering whether, if it's not as expected, it's a problem. It seems the binary is very tempting and the political is just as meaningful an aspect of a client's conversation as anything else.

Although we wouldn't advocate it, therapists are sometimes, unconsciously, tempted to overwrite client's experiences so that the external world is nothing more than a symbol of the more important 'internal' world. So I was not surprised that my supervisor encouraged me to talk to Sam about 'black-and-white' thinking, rather than about photography per se; to think about rigidities of the persecutory self rather than to talk too much about legal rights and wrongs. In fact it was quite important to be reminded of these valid ideas. However, I was most uncomfortable when a colleague suggested that these interests of Sam were distractions from the 'real problem'. When I asked what they were referring to, my colleague blurted out 'gender dysphoria of course' and promptly advised a referral to the Gender Clinic – the work changing from a developmental process to a psychiatric issue in the time it takes to say two small words.

While pondering some of these theoretical and practice-related issues, I try hard to remain phenomenologically oriented, to take a client-centred perspective and primarily to work with the range of meanings that seemed pertinent to Sam. Eir own curiosity and exploration of a wide range of issues seems helpful, allowing the consideration of desires and realities, possibilities and constraints, authenticity and strategic decision making about options faced.

Curiosity and enthusiasm are pleasant to engage with, the recognition of constraints and resistance is less comfortable. It is hard to see Sam ponder these social problems knowing that e is well aware of the possible confusion and opprobrium that might have to be faced when living authentically.

III

It is about four months into therapy when Sam comes to a session and it is evident that eir confidence has taken a knock. Sam is feeling defeated and anxious. Once again it seems not to be a reaction to any single issue, but to several challenges, slights and aggressions, all coming at once while away on a photography weekend organised by the college.

'I just wonder whether it's going to work ... maybe it's not. You know what it's like? It's like living a secret, no matter how open you are. You can't *not* be a secret; it's weird. People just *won't* see it, they can't, or they refuse to. So they push you back into the binary all the time, when there's no need ... no need at all. We were out at night shooting an industrial area. It was nothing special; I was thinking about what images I wanted to get. As we were getting in the van, my mate Leroy said, "you need to shave if you are trying to look like a girl!"' Sam looks incensed at this point.

'I wasn't "trying" to look like anything. Being a boy or a girl wasn't relevant then. Having my gear ready, making sure I hadn't forgotten batteries, trying to plot which angles were going to have the best light ... that's all I was thinking about. I didn't know what to say. I think I just looked blank and asked, "what the fuck are you talking about?" He knew he was talking shit, he just said, "Oh nothing, forget it, didn't mean anything". And that's the problem, he can get away with saying "it doesn't mean anything" but I can't. Even when I try I can't. People look and you can see they want to talk about *that* and not the camera, or the project. And Rachel didn't say anything, no one did. It's not that I want others to fight my battles but is it really all up to me? That's like saying only black people have to worry about racism!'

'I asked Steve and Felicia about that and they fudged it. Their best advice was "try not to flaunt it" ... I got so pissed off with them too. I know they worry and just want the best for me, but "flaunt it"! Is that how they see me?'

Sam has a horrible dilemma here. E was hurt, e felt misunderstood and e was railing against the notion of having to hide away, be something inauthentic for the sake of an easy life. I know that this is reality. I too have felt some of the desires that eir parents had voiced. The world is a risky place, quick to wound and slow to comfort. So hiding away, being closeted, silencing oneself can seem sensible ways of avoiding trouble, of looking after yourself, but this isn't the whole case. Sam continues.

'Oh and I feel like, there is just so much of it. "Questions about surgery ..."
Really? Is fluidity so hard to understand? Don't they see that for those who are
trans and happy with the binary that's one thing, but that's not going to help
me now, is it!' Sam looks both angry and tired.

'Then there's the preoccupation with who they imagine I want to sleep
with – they just don't get it, for me it's not "boy or girl", or "cock or cunt" as
Leroy calls it', Sam blushes as e says this. 'I wish they would try nice vs. nasty,
good vs. bad, if I have to think in polarities! That explains it more for me.
So much more. But no, I don't need people to find me dates thank you very
much, I am perfectly able to speak to people thank you very much.'

I see Sam's courageous attempt to live honestly and authentically. I also
note that gender-fluid people are subject to significant prurient intrusive questioning about sex, love and romance. It is a form of *Othering* by way of exoticisation, seldom leading to enhanced awareness on the part of the inquisitor,
more likely to ridicule and tease. However, I am further aware that Sam is
seventeen and, whether by way of biological reality or narrative norm, it's an
age where sexual curiosity is a major currency.

'It's a lot isn't it', I say, 'a lot to have to manage and you are right; its messed
up that you have to carry all this.'

'I know, I know', says Sam. 'I am getting better at "playing" it ... playing
people maybe, or just playing the game. I get treated differently depending on
what I look like or how I act. Butch up a bit and people listen, be more femme
and I see more of the back of people's heads as they listen to other people. One
or the other is fine; it's the middle ground that confuses them.'

As with all clients, as we talk I try to offer Sam my effort, my understanding and care. I want Sam to understand that I know eir position is difficult,
with expectations encroaching from all directions, weighing heavy on those
young shoulders. I cannot remove the complexity, nor can I single-handedly
banish the faulty thinking, problematic policy and shitty support that Sam has
to endure. What I can do, both psychologically (and politically) is to listen to
Sam's experience, see the meaning within it, accept the fact that social reality
is a powerful and active influence upon us all and consider the ways to engage
with this, some will be ways in the consulting room, some will be outside of
therapy. As Rogers noted all those years ago, people have within themselves
vast resources for self-understanding, for altering their self-concepts, attitudes,
and behaviours. These can be tapped in the presence of a climate of facilitative
psychological attitudes, that is, unconditional positive regard (when truly felt,
not when forced) (see Rogers, 1966).

As we consider Sam's experiences, we spend time looking at the existential
concept of Being-in-the-world, which is very helpful for thinking about rela-
tionality. Sam is not an automaton, not a self-contained entity. Not only will

e be affected by the world but e has the chance to shape it. Together Sam and I consider the various responses that are available to eir – directly challenging micro-aggressions, ignoring them, being selective over who e engages with and about what e choses to tackle. We try to go beyond a polarised vision of just the closet *or* being exposed, hiding or shouting all the time. These are not the only positions to adopt, indeed to assume so would be another case of being hoodwinked by the binary. Movement between polarities is an option, holding conflicting possibilities is another. These are somewhat technical ideas, but Sam takes them and is using them as e navigates the landscape, in discussions with Steve and Felicia, with friends and when choosing college projects.

As the weeks go by Sam discusses events and experiences and so these ideas became much more real; Sam has talked to Steve and Felicia and they are all aware that living authentically is very different to 'flaunting it'. This has helped Sam 'let go' of some guardedness with them, trusting that their intent is not related to gender but a sign of their care for em; Sam talks about having had a 'relaxed' conversation with Rachel, not just telling her what she 'should' or 'shouldn't' think or say, but rather explaining eirs experience and was delighted that she was able to think about how she might best respond when e needs support; Sam also recognizes that e is more able to accept that the world is sometimes 'clueless' and while this can be deliberate, it can also be for other reasons – maybe others haven't had the chance to consider these issues. Sam talks about the way that choice is an issue, that it is not possible to tackle all of the binary-based micro (and major) aggressions in one go. Sometimes e might tackle it directly, sometimes in eirs art and sometimes let it go.

I am pleased. Sam seems to be *feeling* OK about these interactions; they are not just internet memes being quoted. Sam is finding a way in which to challenge without ending up as the exoticised solo crusader. E is attentive to eir social and relational needs as well as the expectations and needs of others. In some ways, I am surprised remembering that Sam is only seventeen. Eir approach to the world seems to be both a courageous and a mature way of being that many of us struggle with regardless of age.

IV

Time passes and my colleague's six-month sabbatical is almost up. As I prepare to leave the college my notes indicate that my colleague had been right, overall there has been a regular flow of encounters focused on those issues known to bedevil college students – anxiety, relationships to food and transition from school to further education. The level of distress was higher than many imagine, with student counselling sometimes being seen as an easier job than working in adult mental health. It is a mistake to think that, and increasingly so as mental health services become more rigid about their inclusion criteria. Like primary care, student counselling services are engaging with a much wider range of difficulties than was perhaps originally imagined – they have to, there is nowhere else to go.

The overall experience has been good, and I will look back fondly at this period. I will perhaps reflect most fondly about my work with Sam. I am confident that Sam has benefited from therapy, becoming more resilient and prepared, with experience of shaping eir network so that it is very supportive.

But it's not just Sam that has been affected by the work; I have too. While still prone to binary thinking, my way of being with difference is far less cerebral. I have less reliance on the 'this-or-that' way of thinking and take great delight in the opportunities that more fluid experience and non-binary perspectives offer us. Reliance on rigid categories is often a nonsense, simply adopted out of habit and a position of unrecognised privilege and power.

My final task at the college is to write up a short document, offering my thoughts on the service provided and suggestions for development. Suggestions about space, time and resources are welcomed, but I feel these are somewhat expected: which therapeutic service in the land is not feeling the weight of referrals and the struggle to meet the need?

On this occasion, my true contribution is two fold – I suggest different wording on intake forms; this will allow greater inclusivity in a number of areas – for example, allowing for more than 'M' or 'F' in respect of gender, suggesting that 'gay' and straight' be complemented by L, B and T as well, and the possibility of using self-descriptors for race as well as those normally taken from the census categories.

I also propose some CPD training for the staff (therapeutic and otherwise) around issues of difference and more inclusive ways to understand it and to engage with it. I look forward to hearing back about that one and maybe returning to contribute in this manner. This is a professional – and political – intervention that therapists can be well placed to offer. When we hear from clients about their struggles, and see it too, it behoves us to take all of the actions that we can to create facilitative and socially inclusive environments for all our sakes. And it's not just the gender binary that is a problem; race, sexuality and disability and many other aspects of our lives are also affected by this limited way of seeing the world and each other. In our profession the emotional/mental health binary categories frequently fail to capture experience. So I have taken to heart Sam's sage advice: 'It's not a case of being confident or nervous, optimistic or depressed – you can feel both you know.' And I think e is right: 'that's OK.'

8

DISABILITY

The concept of 'disability' can be difficult for people to understand, partly because the term is used so broadly as to be phenomenologically meaningless; the term is applied to an enormous range of different conditions and diagnoses, despite the fact that two people's experiences may have almost nothing in common; for example, blindness won't be experienced at all similarly to that of mobility issues, or systemic organic disease. When trying to understand 'disability', we have to recognise that experiences vary in nature and they differ in relation to their genetic, developmental or traumatic origins or those that might be age-related. Some disabilities are visible whereas other, equally challenging conditions, may not be evident to others. This is the case for Rhonda who you will meet shortly.

Another problem is that our use of binary concepts means we tend to think of people as *either* abled *or* disabled, often extended to 'normal' and 'abnormal'. This leads to insidious ableist assumptions that bedevil understandings and practices, professionally and socially. Many developmental and psychotherapeutic theories, for instance, are based on normative assumptions about what people can and cannot do, and what is 'better' and what is 'lesser'. And intended or not, we then create the binary oppositions of the 'normate' and the 'disabled' (Hodges, 2013). A range of different understandings does exist, the medical model considers disability as pathology – while social and other models recognise disability as the result of a disabling society. In UK legal terms the concept of 'disability' recognises that a person experiences limitations arising from particular physical, mental or psychological impairments and these are understood to be long-lasting, for at least twelve months (Lockwood et al., 2012).

Disability is therefore, a unique and subjective experience. As well as the different impacts that disabilities may have, therapists must consider the various possible emotional consequences: some people may experience fear and panic, as if they are the only person in the world experiencing this, others may experience nothing of the sort.

Social and cultural assumptions of able-bodiedness (as a norm) are very prevalent and can impair our grasp of subjective experience too. Such assumptions are not always clear, being embedded in theory, and becoming active practices through policy, all of which can create significant distress and difficulty. Therapists might need to intervene in practical and pragmatic ways too, if we are going to tackle the political triggers of disability-related distress.

Politics of the unseen: Rhonda and hidden disability

I

My first impression of Rhonda is a difficult one, not 'bad' per se, but I feel a little distant; it's hard to get a feel for her. At first I am confused about this; is it me? Am I having a bad day? I don't think so; I'm sitting in my comfortable consulting room in the quaint GP building in a small picturesque suburb in London's commuter belt. The sun is out – although it's not too hot – birds are singing and my commute was easy. So I'm in a good mood and I would have thought I would be open and receptive today.

Rhonda is forty years old and the GP suggested she see me in relation to 'anxiety and depression'. Rhonda is different to how I had imagined an anxious forty-year-old woman to be. In appearance, she seems closer to sixty to me; her skin is bad, her hair is a little unkempt and unwashed and she smells. There I've said it. I am not proud of myself for being so aware of this but there is a strong smell of nicotine that overlays a staleness emanating from her. I force myself not to open the window here and now.

I put that aside as best I can though as Rhonda is here for a reason and I ask her about that: 'How can I help?'

Rhonda shrugs and says, 'The doctor says it might help' and then she stops.

'OK', I say, 'tell me what the problem is'.

'Depressed … and worried', she says as she hands me the *Hospital Anxiety and Depression Scale* (HADS) that the GP had asked her to complete. The scores do indeed suggest that she is experiencing what we call depression.

This rather stilted to-and-fro is the style of the first part of our assessment meeting. It becomes clear, very quickly, that Rhonda is unlikely to say very much spontaneously and that if I am going to get a picture of her experience I am going to have to seek out information.

As I take a more active approach to the assessment, I find out that Rhonda has a number of physical issues, including a lifelong struggle with asthma, and that she now has a more severe problem she refers to by its medical abbreviation – COPD (chronic obstructive pulmonary disease). 'COPD describes a group of lung conditions that make it difficult to empty air out of the lungs because your airways have been narrowed' (British Lung Foundation, 2017). Although it is not a visible disability, it is a chronic, progressive and disabling condition, limiting mobility, causing appetite to wax and wane and Rhonda can no longer be very active outside of the house. But because there are no external physical scars or markers, and no chairs, sticks or breathing apparatus at this point, people do not necessarily understand the challenges she faces. She feels that they see her as lazy rather than limited, a deadbeat rather than disabled.

Rhonda, understandably, finds the illness distressing and gets depressed about the disease and the limitations it places on her. Despite it being such a clear stressor, Rhonda finds her depression confusing and tells me that she is not sure why she is depressed and that she wishes she could pull herself out of it.

'The anxiety is not a problem at the moment', Rhonda tells me. I ask more about it and she says, 'it's an occasional thing, usually when I feel ill or need help or when I have to deal with the DSS'.

'DSS' is an abbreviation for the forerunner of the government's Department for Work and Pensions and I establish that Rhonda receives a range of benefits that allow her to eat, heat her flat and to manage difficulties she has getting to the shops and back, difficulties created by her breathing problems.

'It's not the fullest of pictures', I think to myself, but it seems to me that the depression and the anxiety aren't actually that mysterious; wouldn't any of us feel sad and down at the loss of freedom that such an illness brings? And wouldn't anyone get more anxious when ill? And when dealing with the uncertainty that bureaucracy creates? I suspect the GP is right, a brief period of therapy might be useful. But ... I am still bothered by my initial reaction and by the clinical to-and-fro style of our encounter. These can of course, simply be experienced as personal idiosyncrasies, but therapists need to keep an open mind as such reactions can be indicative of a range of other meanings and processes.

There is also an ethical quandary here as I am pretty sure that Rhonda will return if I ask her to, but I have no sense of her having found the session useful or whether she will take anything from it; I wonder whether she might simply do as she is told? If that's the case, I am less sure of what to suggest; there's not much point in the therapist thinking that meeting and talking is meaningful if clients themselves don't, and I am yet to get any sense of investment from Rhonda. So I suggest a second session, as a way of extending the assessment, maybe getting a richer understanding, and who knows, maybe Rhonda will be different next time?

II

It's the following week and Rhonda and I are exploring a few issues, in a little more depth. This is still being led by my interests though, as Rhonda is once again, quiet, responsive but not very forthcoming.

As I ask about Rhonda's past, I start to piece together a bit more of a picture of her upbringing and development. Rhonda had bad asthma as a child and as a teenager too and was often reliant on inhalers and other medications. This meant she was 'excused' sports and PE for much of her schooling. This may have been sensible physically but I can't help but wonder what impact this had on her socially and to her sense of self, always being the one who stands out by virtue of her limitations. I ask about her friends and social life and she confirms that she has indeed felt an outsider a lot of the time and has been treated as such too. Her peers would either ignore and minimise her difficulties, or joke and tease her about her wheezing, performing a horrible mimicry of her more severe attacks.

'So I stopped caring about them', she said, although in doing so Rhonda isolated herself. The only respite was when boys became interested in her and she speaks ruefully about this. 'Nothing puts boys off, not even wheezy me, not when there's a blow-job in the offing', she says in a rare moment of spontaneity. 'That got their attention.'

Her honesty surprises me and I see her smile fade away as quickly as it had formed; she explains about becoming pregnant at sixteen, and her family's embarrassment about this. She dropped out of school, had the baby and had him adopted.

Rhonda proceeds with her history, telling me that she was married in her early twenties and had a second child, but they lost him to heart problems when he was aged just four. She was twenty-nine at the time. Her husband left soon after this, taking all of their finances with him, and, as they were no longer a family, she lost the house they were living in.

It's a horrible story, but I start to feel cut-off as I listen to this account of three decades of isolation, scorn and attack, the loss of two children, a husband and any financial security she had had.

'This cut-off-ness, what's that about?' I wonder if my sense of being cut-off is related to the way in which she describes these events? They are delivered in a flat, monotone voice, and when I think about it I realise that this must cover all kinds of emotion – lost hope, sadness, anger, being overwhelmed and maybe more. And it is this that I start to want to know more about – the lack of emotion I am seeing and hearing. No emotion in the telling of the story, nor in her history itself. It is all rather detached and fatalistic.

I ask Rhonda about her family, how did *they* respond to everything she is telling me about? Her illness, her exclusion, what seemed like bullying to me, the pregnancy and so forth? Rhonda looks at me with confusion at first, and then says, 'They helped; they always do.'

'OK ... But that's not really what I was asking', I think.

I push a little more: 'I wonder how they responded emotionally? Were they angry about the teasing? Did you feel they understood the asthma, or pitied you? Those kind of things?' I tail off as Rhonda's face remains confused.

'No', she says as she shakes her head. 'As I say, they were supportive, they always are. They looked after me when I needed it. They still do.'

Rhonda tells me how her brother has gone on to do well with his own plumbing business in Brighton and her sister is thought to have 'married well'. Both sometimes help but she seldom asks now, worrying that they pity her and are embarrassed by her being 'the runt' of the family.

This second session is helpful, to me at least; it's giving me a greater sense of the possible roots of her propensity to depression and anxiety. I now think that the COPD is, of course, a stressor that cannot be overlooked, as might the medications be. But so is a history of being ridiculed, diminished and poorly attended to. It seems that she learnt early on that she is not someone of value, that she may as well keep people at bay; it's safer than letting them in to tease or take advantage. Taking this into account, and the fact that Rhonda is not seeking a long reflective approach to her difficulties, I suggest a standard six-week time-limited therapy in the context of primary care.

Rhonda agrees and we meet for the following six weeks. During these meetings we discuss her depression and the anxiety, we talk about when these experiences occur, what they might be related to, what triggers them and how she might think about them so that they are less debilitating. Although she is not 'enthusiastic' about it Rhonda starts to keep a journal and recognises that she could capitalise on some of the things that she enjoys and this in itself seems to make a difference in her day-to-day experience.

My sense is that the therapy goes well-ish – I add the qualifier as the work never really shakes the slightly cut-off feel that bothers me; but Rhonda is compliant and when I get her to do the HADS again at the end of the six weeks, her scores are down and she is happy to end. As we say goodbye, I assume that that is all the contact I will have with Rhonda.

III

It's about six months later when I receive an urgent call from the GP, who tells me that Rhonda is having panic attacks, and that as well as being distressing, they create problems for her breathing and physical health. I call Rhonda and offer her an appointment for later in the week.

Meeting with Rhonda this time is a little different to previously. This time she is more actively distressed in the moment; I see fear and I see panic first-hand. In other ways, things are similar to before, as she is confused by the level of emotion and can't understand why she is so anxious all the time.

'Maybe start by telling me what has happened recently', I suggest.

Rhonda replies, 'Well nothing much has changed'.

'Nothing?'

Rhonda tells me that the end of last year was uneventful and gives me a summary of events; Christmas and New Year passed 'OK'; she had seen her brother and his family on Boxing Day and seen her parents at her sister's place on the 28th. 'There were no arguments, it was all OK.' I ask about her medication, being aware that steroid treatment can lead quickly to heightened and sometimes extreme anxiety, but no, there had been no change in her medication. I start to see why she might be confused as to the anxiety manifesting right now.

'And anything coming up?', I ask, mindful of the fact that anxiety is oftentimes a future-oriented experience, when we are caught up in what might happen or what we think we are powerless to avoid.

Rhonda shrugs her shoulders and shakes her head. She tells me that there's nothing on the horizon, she isn't going anywhere and there is nothing happening this year. It's a puzzle, but a very frightening one.

I wonder if it is that, an emptiness, that's the problem? But I also remember a comment made months ago; I have an echo of her explaining that the reason she wasn't feeling any anxiety when we had met previously was because 'it usually happens when [she] feels ill or needy or when [she] has to deal with the DSS'. So I wonder whether her current panic might be related to the recent press coverage of draconian changes being proposed by government, alongside a ramping up of discourse about 'chavs', 'scroungers' and 'cheats' in our media.

I temper my thoughts and ask, 'And how are things financially and with your benefits?'

Rhonda's eyes widen and she says loudly, 'I worry about that, I really do. I've finally had my letter saying that my benefits are safe this year. *This year*!!! This year is almost up. So what happens in April? I have to have another assessment? And they say that they might "invite me in to discuss my health with an officer" of some kind', her hands indicating air quotes as she talks. 'What do they think? That I'm going to recover from this? I wish; oh I so wish!' With this Rhonda breaks into a prolonged period of hacking coughing. She has to sit back and stop talking.

If her response to my question is anything to go by, it seems that Rhonda's anxiety has spiked as she approaches a fresh round of externally triggered scrutiny and assessments. I could make a more personal interpretation about her being prone to worrying, focusing on this too much, and catastrophising about something that hasn't happened yet. That *might* be helpful, but I am aware that this isn't just some unique idiosyncrasy of hers. Like many people in the UK, Rhonda experiences a dilemma, on the one hand appreciating the support of the benefits system and the NHS, on the other being subject to considerable scrutiny, monitoring and judgement on a regular basis. She has no control over this; it is a political process and constantly in the media. It is hard to imagine that this *wouldn't* play on her mind. It's not just some arbitrary, meaningless task; a lot rests on this: food on the table, being able to get to town and back, being able to stay warm during the plummeting winter temperatures – these are all reliant on sustaining an income and as she cannot work, it is her benefits that do this. So, instead of focusing on her own approach to the world or her style of thinking at this point, I try to put the worries into context.

'Rhonda, I know you say that you don't understand the anxiety, but might it not be to do with this assessment, the uncertainty you feel, the fact that it's a recurrent experience and that you fear loss and everything that comes with it?' Rhonda nods and says, 'I suppose so'.

As we proceed with the exploration of what triggered this period of distress, more information is offered, some about the past. The focus on scrutiny and assessment has reminded Rhonda of the judgements made at school, at work and in her family. She tells me that she worked hard at school but didn't do very well as she missed so much due to her ill health. After school she had a series of jobs, working hard before and after she was married. Some of these jobs she liked, and some she didn't. She tells me that she enjoyed working in 'office junior'-type roles, organising and supporting different teams and managers. But she tells me she also worked in retail and in hotels, liking the flexibility that these offered.

Rhonda found it hard to keep the jobs for very long, as she would often need to take time off, or she would miss out on full-time posts because management knew that other candidates would be 'more reliable' than she was able to be. And now, as April approaches, Rhonda has to endure more scrutiny and more judgement.

'And how was that?', I ask her, 'how was it to feel that you would often lose out, others would be picked over you?'

'Um, don't know … you get used to it I suppose.'

I go to speak, but Rhonda continues.

'No, if I am honest, I didn't like it; it made me angry at times. Just when I liked the job, was getting on with people, I would have another episode of this. They would be all sympathetic for a while but after it happened two or three times, they would stop asking. Offer the shifts to someone else … I don't blame them but I would get cross, and embarrassed, so I would leave.'

'And what would you, or do you, do with the anger?'

'Do with it?' She looks quizzical, maybe confused even. 'Nothing much; what can you do? It's … it is what it is.'

And that is it, as far as Rhonda is concerned. Life is scary and depressing. You try your hardest and then simply accept what comes your way. She has come to expect life to be a struggle, both physically, which it definitely is, and socially. Her story is one of others getting more, enjoying the breaks and benefiting from life's bounty. She seems to have accepted that this is the case in terms of the health and social care system as well, that she is a burden to 'good, hard working people' and that while support will be offered if she asks for it, it will be begrudgingly given; people don't really grasp how difficult her life can be, a common experience when your disability is a hidden one.

As Rhonda has been speaking I have remembered my original impression of her. For the psychologist or psychotherapist, these personal and intuitive responses can be quite telling, as – whether flattering or offensive – they are like clues to the detective; they are meaningful aspects of the therapeutic encounter, reflecting both personal and socio-political biases.

So what can this impact possibly tell me now?

It occurs to me that maybe these differences between her and others mean that she often comes out worse in life's relational rough and tumble: her body isn't working as well as she wishes (although people can't necessarily see this); her physical and intellectual confidence is low and that leads to a negative view of herself. More than this, she has internalised this view so that her expectations are low and her readiness to demand is limited. I consider the possibility that Rhonda fails to look after herself; she doesn't feel it is worth cleaning herself up when she has leaves the safety of the private realm to transition to the social world. This has become the fabric of her being, so much so that this is how she presents to others, including me in our first session. I was polite in my approach, but there was part of me that was tuned in to her expectations that I wouldn't care and would only offer help begrudgingly. The fact that she smoked while suffering such a disability also prompts confusion and reaction in the helper. If she doesn't look after herself, why should anyone else? We are not immune from the moralistic and paternalistic discourse that abounds.

As the new round of assessments approaches she is feeling low in confidence, expects that others (including the anonymous state system) will not want to assist if it can get away without doing so, and so fears the removal of all support and the difficulties that this will create for her.

IV

Where a client chooses, or a service imposes, time-limited restrictions on therapy, I am often reminded of my former supervisor Freddie Strasser's concept of 'modules' of therapy. Freddie and Alison Strasser developed a time-limited version of existential therapy (Strasser and Strasser, 1997) in which they note the usefulness of separate periods of therapy and the ability to build upon work that has previously been undertaken. It is in this spirit that Rhonda and I work together for another 'module' of therapy, this time looking at the anxious 'side' of her difficulties.

As we work Rhonda and I explore her assumptions about herself and see that she feels she is vulnerable, both physically and materially; she perceives herself as uninteresting and having little to contribute and this gives rise to an anxiety about her ability to cope with the challenges her illness and disability present. We also consider the realities of the assessment process and recognise the fact that many people find the system arduous, uncertain and stressful. We also question her expectation that she should not be affected by it.

As we explore this we realise that, although she often overlooks it, Rhonda does sometimes feel angry about this too. But she has assumed one shouldn't be angry, rather than considering that anger is just as valid a feeling as any other.

'If you accept that this system does make you cross ... what does that tell you?', I ask midway through therapy.

'It tells me ... oh, I'm not sure', she says and stops.

'OK then. What if it were someone else who was angry, how would you understand that?', I ask.

'Oh ... Oh, OK, well ...' Rhonda thinks for a minute and when she is ready she sits up and starts talking: 'I would tell them they have every right to be angry, this system is ridiculous; they expect YOU to do all kinds of things but they don't play by the same rules, they lose your stuff, the forms themselves are like writing a book, then they take forever to make a judgement. Did you see they always get it wrong too?'

Rhonda looks at me. She is referring to recent reports of how frequently people have been declared fit in Work Capacity Assessments, often when blatantly unable to look after themselves or in some cases just days before their death (see Butler, 2015).

'Yes, I know they sometimes get it wrong', I say, before asking about her again, 'So what about your anger ...? '

'Right, well I suppose it's OK to be angry?' Her statement feels more like a question. 'This is really difficult isn't it. My anger also tells me that I shouldn't worry about being angry; I should maybe accept that I am rather than fight it' – and she smiles as she says this.

'OK. And I wonder what seeing it that way might mean for how you seek support?'

'Oh ...' she pauses and frowns as she thinks. 'Oh, you mean if it is really a difficult thing to have to go through, maybe I shouldn't feel so bad about getting help?'

'Well, that's something that's certainly worth thinking about, isn't it', I say. 'Part of the depression seemed to be about you judging yourself for needing help, wasn't it. And it looks as though part of the anxiety is about you refusing to ask for help or for limiting who you ask for help. Then that means you feel unable to cope on your own.'

'Oh, I never thought of it that way', Rhonda says. 'So will you write to them for me, as my psychologist?', she asks.

I feel a little ambushed here. Not that her request isn't perfectly in line with our understanding of her difficulty, but her direct request was not expected. And of course it also means that I am now invited out of that rather neutral role of the therapist, to put my money where my mouth is, so to speak. I am invited to act rather than just think, to actively and publicly support her, to participate in the politics of her existence. It's a perfectly appropriate professional role but one that psychologists frequently are spared, working as we do to empower our clients and alongside social workers and medics who tend to take on this role.

'Um ... let me have a look at the forms and see what they ask for. Bring them along next time and we can see whether it would be helpful for me to write', I say. I want time to think about this, but I am nervous as I do not want to appear to offer help begrudgingly, a state that Rhonda is very well attuned to.

'OK, I'll do that next time', she says as we bring the session to a close.

Before I leave for the day I catch Rhonda's GP and discuss the upcoming assessment, to which she rolls her eyes. 'Again?', she says almost under her breath. 'This seems cruel you know, Rhonda clearly can't work and, her condition is such that it will not improve a great deal ... but anyway. No, I don't think you can complete it but it would be helpful if you write separately, so I can append it, to comment on the psychological perspective – and the impact of this bloody process.'

'OK, I will see what I can do', I say as I head out of the door.

Rhonda starts the next session by giving me the forms and has already put a post-it note on the relevant section. I can see immediately why I may not formally be the one to complete this form, the perspective of registered *medical* practitioners is clearly privileged, with a GMC number required. The form is clear though and they ask for a description of the conditions the client is experiencing, an assessment of the impact of these difficulties and an opinion as to whether the client is able to work now, or whether they will be able to in the foreseeable future. With the GP's expert advice on the trajectory of the COPD, its disabling impact and prognosis on record, it certainly seems appropriate to contribute a psychological perspective as both Rhonda and the GP are requesting.

'That seems fine Rhonda', I say. 'I won't write on the form itself, that's for your GP to complete, but I can write a separate letter.'

Rhonda nods.

'Are you happy for me to comment on anything we have talked about?', I ask, being mindful that one implication of writing in support of a client is that confidentiality is, by definition, breached. 'That's fine', she says with no anxiety apparent at all. I am alert, however, as the breaching of confidentiality, even if statutorily required and with permission given, can still mean something to clients. Permission doesn't obviate the fact that it is a breach of confidence and that it is paternalistic, with two (or more) 'authorities' talking *about* the client, rather than the client being in control.

Over the course of the week I write the letter, and provide the GP and Rhonda with a copy. Rhonda thanks me and then we return to the focus she has brought this week. She wants to think about how to be if she is called in for the interview. This means we get a chance to talk not just about her assumptions about her health and about help seeking, but also about the way she actually behaves with people.

The final couple of sessions of the therapy seem to be helpful for Rhonda; she tells me that she is sleeping better and worrying a lot less. I get her to repeat the HADS form as is expected by the practice, and this adds to what Rhonda has been saying and my own impression of her lowered distress.

In some ways I think that the therapy has been helped by thinking about the actuality of the assessment procedure and by me participating in a way that goes beyond the consulting room. It seems to have allowed us to deepen the therapeutic relationship somewhat; Rhonda seems to be more trusting and I feel more invested.

A few months later I get a note from Rhonda saying that the assessors have sent her a letter much more quickly this time, confirming her entitlements for a period of three years and noting that the assessment would not be undertaken again until that time and that this is a huge relief. She is feeling good, no significant anxiety at all, and no depression. It seems a change in the external world can be as important as a change in an individual's perspective and interpretation.

9

OTHERING AND THE ENVIRONMENT

One of the most urgent political issues of our time is our care for the environment and this has become a focus in consulting rooms. Our stance towards the environment, like our stance to race, gender, disability and so many other forms of difference, is subject to Othering and the limitations of a binary view. This stance damages our relationship with nature and has done, and is doing, extraordinary damage to people too. By taking power and believing we have dominion over all others, we cut off, and have only an instrumental view of the world. It is this dissociated perspective that means we fail to see the planet as the single functioning ecosystem it is, and instead see it as a 'thing' that can, apparently forever, take our abuse with no untoward consequences.

This is a problem. This view of (assumed) power operates in a similar way to practices around gender, sexuality and disability (with one group being powerful and the other much less so). In the same way that earlier chapters have illustrated how outdated binary visions are problematic, so it is with the planet. Othering constructs a distinction between 'us' and 'them' – and what greater 'Other' than the non-human world? We know that when it comes to issues of competition, aggression, scarcity and power, we tend to act in favour of 'us' and to the disadvantage of the 'Other', seldom taking responsibility for this; the same way that it can be very uncomfortable if we accept that we were knowingly going to treat defenceless people in an aggressive manner, so it is with animals or the environment.

Even if brutalising the planet and extinguishing thousands of species was not a moral issue, we do *ourselves* no favours, in fact we hurt ourselves enormously, but we avoid recognising this. Writers and conservationists are desperately showing the damage that is done spiritually (Griffiths, 2006), imaginatively (Macfarlane, 2007), physically and psychologically (Louv, 2006; Rust and Totton, 2012). In counselling psychology and psychotherapy Rust and Totton (2012) and Jordan (2015) have considered the ways in which access to, or dissociation from, nature is linked to much human well-being or distress. This is the type of struggle we see Monique being engaged with in this chapter.

Monique: The guilt of living while the planet dies

I

'We're standing there on the top of the koppie, looking out over that vast savannah, coffee in one hand, rusk in the other. The binoculars are safely stowed in the Land Rover alongside my camera. I can do without those; I am immersed in the plains, the blue skies above me, brown soil beneath my feet and green grasses spread for miles before me ... I am struck by how vast it is here, so big ... enormous ... Non, even that's the wrong way to say it, it's not "it" at all; that suggests it's a thing separate from other things and I don't think it is. It's as if there is nothing else, it just runs as far as the eye can see.'

She looks briefly to her left and continues. 'I hear Jean say, "Wildebeest ... wildebeest." He repeats himself again and again, and I see why, it's like the world is suddenly filled with them, there's nothing more to say really. How do you sum that up? Can you tell someone else in a way that makes them understand just what it is like? Non, you can't; it's physical, you are captured by this space, the smell feels thick and sensual, the earthy aromas of the approaching rains and the animals themselves. You can taste the air. And there's the sound as well ... it has substance to it, it fills the air, there is honking and calling and pounding as waves upon waves of wildebeest and zebra thunder past us, big ones, little ones, all on a single mission.'

Spreading her arm in a wide arc, she indicates the view spread out before her and returns to her place on the koppie. 'The migration is the main attraction this morning but there are more than just the stampeding hordes too, somewhere out there, there are many others. We met a cheetah this morning, there's a lion pride on a kill just a few miles away – we can't see them from here, but the circling vultures give them away – and we watched some travelling hyena first thing, but right now, or then ... it was more complete; there is more of a sense of being part of something so much bigger than any one single thing; it is so much bigger than me. And it was showing itself to me, calling me in. I belong. That's the wonderful thing. It shows just how insignificant I am, we are. And that's not a bad thing ... oh, non, non, non, it reminds me that there's more to life than me, me, me. We think it's all about us ... but it's not.'

'I don't feel like I usually do, I am full ... of something; I don't know what. Excitement possibly, but I don't think that's quite accurate; it's calmer than that ... delight maybe. Perhaps that's the right word ...'

Monique is awash with reverie; she inhabits it yet she shares it too. Her visceral, embodied memory of her most recent trip, this time to the Masai Mara, is compellingly vivid. And I love it, the images and feelings conjured up are indeed delightful and she has a knack, a skill of bringing these experiences to life and including me in them. There is wildness at the core of Monique, an empathy with place and its inhabitants and a deep commitment to them.

II

When I first met Monique I was not expecting to have wilderness-related experiences, to be transported in such a powerful fashion, to enjoy her descriptions as much as I do, nor to hear and learn so much about the natural world. Why would I? I work in London and see people who live here. Monique presents as a very chic Parisienne, a successful architect, now living a busy life here in London. I also found her to be a bit imperious, slightly intimidating and more than a little depressed.

Monique approached me and described her desire to start psychotherapy as related to a confusing despair. She had tried to make sense of it herself but it simply seemed beyond her.

'I've tried to think about why I feel like this, but I don't get it – I struggle to sleep sometimes – why? I feel so down that I just want to fade away? *Pourquoi*? Why is that? My appetite comes and goes, but I go off food very quickly; I am also so picky at work, the bits I like I am 100% into, but the mundane, boring stuff, the management and reporting … it kills me; I cannot muster any enthusiasm for it. I sometimes get really angry too.' She takes a breath and continues: 'but the worst bit, is this dullness, this pointlessness I feel, this….Oh, I don't even know how to describe it, this emptiness maybe.'

She pauses for a short while and then says, 'I just don't get it because I have a great relationship, my job is wonderfully creative and I have very good friends. I know that you psychotherapists often put it down to repressed childhood trauma but I've thought about it long and hard and I really don't think I was neglected or abused as a child. In fact it's quite the opposite; I'm very spoiled and very privileged. You are going to have your work cut out trying to help me.'

The recognition of wealth and privilege (or the absence of these) can be an important factor in understanding a client. We know that the stresses of poverty are clearly linked to distress, and are impediments to health, educational achievement and employment and social mobility (see Hamilton, 2004 Ludwig et al., 2001; McClelland, 2000; Pickett and Pearl, 2001). However, this does not necessarily mean that wealth and privilege are *guarantees* of happiness and contentment, nor are they perfect barriers to discrimination. Sometimes the recognition of wealth itself can be a stressor and inhibit a person's development. (For interesting work of the psychological impact of wealth and privilege, see Duffell, 2000, 2012; Schavarien, 2015.)

I feel a little taken aback by Monique's statement. On the one hand it seems that she has great support, is well versed in psychotherapy, has insight into her current and earlier experiences, and is already well invested in trying to understand herself. This is important, as while much contemporary thinking surrounds the investigative and expert role of the therapist, we should not overlook the fact that clients often approach therapy with curiosity about their distress. They will have thought about it before finding their way to a therapist. They may have spoken to family and friends, tried writing it down in a journal or in poetry. The view of clients as exclusively needy, disempowered or passive is a mistake and says a lot about a political stance of the therapist.

As well as this array of theoretical ideas, I'm curious about my response to Monique. Alongside the facts she is telling me I have a sense of being subordinate to a parent, older sibling or boss, someone seductive yet also rejecting. This gives rise to an enthusiasm to work with her, but a powerful sense that I will probably fall short in some way. As I make my notes later that day I ponder 'imperiousness' and what it might come to mean, maybe as a form of power, or as a defence. I also make a note about her saying how hard it is going to be to help her. Is she suggesting a view of therapy where it would be my job to magic up clarity out of nowhere? If so we could be off to a problematic start. The psychologist or psychotherapist must navigate a bit of a tightrope in their relationship with a client. On the one hand they must own the fact that they have access to knowledge, skill and ability that may be of assistance. Equally, psychotherapy is not like a medical intervention or an instruction manual. Despite what some policy seems to suggest psychotherapy doesn't really work if we intend to do things 'to' clients. The skilled psychotherapist must forge a relationship wherein the contributions of both client and therapist are sought and utilised.

In the next few sessions, I learn that Monique is in her mid-thirties and moved to London after university. She tells me that she enjoys working in the practice and has become close friends with Justin, the partner and his husband Ahmed. She lives close to work and so walks most days, and as she lives near Hyde Park she adores running in the crisp early mornings. 'It's like the city just falls away. Its where I can feel alive.'

Monique also tells me that she could have been a 'trust fund baby' and that her family do not understand why she put herself 'through such a demanding training and ... oh *quelle horreur*, why I even have a job', she laughs as she says this. 'I think the family's charitable foundation was my father's only professional expectation of me. The fact that I work and chair the foundation too comes as a surprise. But it's not the only surprise' and she smiles.

I am intrigued and she notices. '*Ah oui*, I am a woman of mystery as far as my family is concerned', she says enigmatically. I wonder silently whether she is also referring to the mystery that she is to herself. I am still mindful of the description of her, so far unsuccessful, attempts to make sense of the despair she is experiencing. But Monique tells me that her parents were surprised when she told them about her poly relationship and how happy it makes her. 'Surprised but not upset; it's very French after all', she says. Despite there being a norm of seeing relationships as dyadic – husband and wife, husband and husband, wife and wife, two living together in a relationship and so on, it is important to note that other relationship forms exist. While triadic relationships are often understood as a main couple with one of them being 'unfaithful' or having an affair, or several, there are also relationship forms where several people coexist in a relationship clearly, consensually and transparently. (For more information on this, see Barker, 2005, 2014.)

Monique continues: 'I think it's just the legal thing that bothers them really; my father thinks of it as two claimants should anything go wrong. They actually love my Jean, my father has even taken him hunting', she says, 'and no one got shot, which is a good sign'. She smiles again. 'We are not a triad exactly, although Siobhan, Jean and I have shared some times together. I understand that Jean loves us both – and Siobhan understands that too and this suits me perfectly.'

One of the key stages of the therapeutic process is the assessment stage as it allows one to get a feel for the landscape of the person's world and the way in which they navigate it. It can be helpful to want to know about the client's early, as well as contemporary, life and the significant relationships in both. Despite the caricatures that abound, this does not mean that everything is laid at the feet of any particular relationship. All relationships are unique, moulded as they are by the participants and the contexts in which they are experienced. So when a client discloses a relationship that might be considered 'non-traditional' the therapist simply has to hear it, empathise and identify with it. It may prove to be important, or it may not. Assumptions about monogamy and heteronormativity can be particularly dangerous when the therapist fails to think critically about them (see McGeorge and Stone Carlson, 2011; Moon, 2011).

After commenting on her relationship, Monique stops to look at me, her gaze sure and steady. I suspect that she wants to see my reaction; am I going to be surprised as she says her parents were? On the one hand, why would I be? I have only just met her; I have no sense of her that this might confirm or contradict. But of course, Monique has just described a form of relationship that runs counter to much contemporary expectation; in the capitalist West we tend to construct romantic relationships as dyadic, monogamous and lifelong. We haven't just seen dyadic relationships as a common form of relationship; we have laden them with religious and moral values. We have transformed them from a possibility to an expected norm.

The fact that relationship forms are not apolitical has oftentimes been overlooked and so have the capitalist and patriarchal systems that underpin and rely on the nuclear family system. This has often not been recognised and we have come to take the modern dyadic and now nuclear family as 'normal' when it is anything but (see also Barker, 2014; Richards and Barker, 2015; Richards, 2010). So Monique would be watching me for my reaction, whether this proved to be meaningful to her despair or not.

'So you surprise them with your professional *and* your personal life', is all I say.

Monique nods and continues: 'And my ethics too …' She pauses and looks quizzical: 'if you want to call it that. I think they see me as more liberal than they are. My family has a long history of hunting, both for … pleasure and also in relation to business. I, on the other hand, hate it and won't have anything to do with it; I work against it when I can. I don't think my father expected our foundation to support so many human and animals' rights charities. He doesn't object though, he even uses this as evidence of the family having a moral high ground, but it does create some difficulties sometimes.'

I can see this. Credibility must be skilfully managed when advocating two different sides of the same issue, particularly when family and business are wrapped up in one entity. Is this enough to create such despair I wonder? I don't know yet but it is hard to think of corporate clashes being the basis of what sounds like a powerful *existential* experience. Or, I wonder, is the despair symbolic of something within the family? Can her description help me make sense of my feeling of being called, but most likely failing, to assist her? These were questions I would mull over and need to consider as we went forwards.

Our early sessions are typical of most therapies, where information offering and gathering occurs, where each of us tries to understand what Monique's life is like – now and in the past. By exploring these we have the chance to consider what might meaningfully shed some light on her current experience of 'despair' and its characteristic depression, low mood, boredom and sometimes apathy and lifelessness.

In these sessions, as we explore the family, I hear about Monique having spent a lot of time with her mother both at home in the apartment in Paris and on her grandfather's estate in the south where they always spent at least some of the summer. The farm is where she played with puppies and kittens and where they spent mornings taking long walks before swimming in the river all afternoon. I hear how the family are great hosts, often having impressive parties. She tells me of her experiences of travel at an early age, holidays in Mauritius and the Maldives, shopping in Miami and New York. Once her brother and sister came along it became a busier family too.

During these sessions I am struck by the conscientiousness of her descriptions and can see why she feels that it is hard to make sense of this despair. Unlike some clients she does not bring overt experiences of neglect or abuse. Monique offers information regarding some of the obvious stereotypes that we therapists are supposed to focus on – yes, her father was more absent than her mother, but she saw him at home most days and when they travelled to Grandpa's farm they spent whole days together. If he travelled down a few days or a week later, he would be there, and available, for them. She loved spending time with him, walking for miles as he told her stories of his travels and of places he had been.

Therapy seems to progress as well as one might expect. Monique is working hard, thinking about her experience, being open with me and trusting me with information – granted, at times it feels a bit 'informational' but it isn't *without* feeling.

We have been working for a few months as the summer break comes upon us. At the start of therapy we had discussed the importance of regular sessions and the need to try and time holidays so as to coincide with therapeutic breaks. Monique saw the point of this, but it is seldom completely possible and on this occasion it means I am away for three weeks and Monique is going to miss a further week as she will be travelling abroad to see the progress that some of her foundation's projects have made, so it is September before we reconvene.

III

September arrives and I look forward to seeing Monique. However, when we reconvene, she looks different: drained, low in energy and depressed. Thoughts race through my head: 'Is this about the break?' Clients are often resentful of therapists' absences as they can, at some level, be experienced as abandonment, so it is always important to consider the therapeutic relationship when such a strong change is experienced.

I also wonder what her trip has been like, maybe the projects have disappointed her; or maybe it's the family, maybe there have been some problems; or maybe work has gone wrong. Although I am worried, I restrain myself and don't pry about anything too specific as I want to see how Monique will be and what she will tell me. I am also aware that my reaction here is reminiscent of Monique's own questioning of her despair.

The first half an hour feels slow, effortful and somewhat bland. As well as wanting to know 'why', I am also wondering whether I am missing the significance of something in the blandness? Or is it me? Am I maybe expecting something more, and being demanding of her? While therapists shouldn't overstate their role in a client's experience, it is important that it is not overlooked either; it often sheds light on the ways in which a client relates to others in their world.

The feel of the session seems not to be shifting at all so I decide to at least offer her my observation.

'You seem a bit down today, did anything happen that's not been mentioned yet?', I ask.

'Non ... I don't think so', she said, 'but yes, something is up, I felt alright before I got here and I do feel ... flat and shitty now. Well, I didn't feel alright, I haven't felt right since I got back from Madagascar, but I felt ... better than this ... definitely.'

So it seems that Monique has gotten in touch with *something*, that much is clear. So we think about this for a while – feeling good while away, feeling low on return and then increasingly sluggish and 'shitty' as therapy approaches.

Monique says, 'It's not about you, I don't think. While I was in Madagascar I remember thinking how excited I was to tell you about this. I think this feeling, this ... shitty bleeugh feeling ... is about what I have to do here. I have to feel what I feel, and think about it.'

It certainly feels like more than post-holiday blues. Many of us experience those; we leave the relaxing, stress-free break, where we shake off the shackles of everyday expectation, where we eat differently, take leisurely exercise as we swim, walk and maybe feel the sun on our skin. It can be a hard transition to return to the regularity – or maybe monotony – of our urban lives, what we might think of as normality. We shift from a more relaxed, sensually mediated response to the world to one that is now more covered up both by clothes and by urban busy-ness, our lives characterised by stress and demand. But it isn't just this; it worsened as she approached her session.

'Some degree of this feeling isn't unusual', Monique tells me, 'especially if I've been somewhere remote. A weekend in Edinburgh or Madrid won't do this to me, nor will a week in New York; it's something to do with truly getting away. It's because I've been to Madagascar.' As she says this, her face reddens, she drops her head and starts to cry. 'I miss it so much.'

It is time to end the session though and she is both upset and disappointed. 'We must talk about this next time', she sighs and I agree.

In the next session Monique wastes no time in telling me about the Madagascar trip, and the two projects she is involved in. It is only the second time she had visited them and this is, for all intents and purposes, business. One is a women's co-op and the other was known as Lemurien SOS. She is proud of them both but she is most pleased with the fact that they dovetail – assistance to people and to wildlife.

'This is the only way conservation can truly make a difference. If it is piecemeal, it can't work. Separate the forest from opportunities for people and you end up with hardship and the forest is ravaged. Join them up and you help the entire system', she says and with that she burst into a smile. It is a bright smile and I realise that it has been a while since I have seen this.

The pleasure is related to the accomplishment and the promise it shows, and it is more than work; there is something more profound for her. She tells me that 'just being there, it brings out a different side to me, I feel alive. Oh, we had the most amazing hike though the humid forests of Mantadia. You enter this living, breathing ecosystem. You can almost tell it's making oxygen ... or I might have done if I'd stopped to think. We hiked though it and before you know it, you lose track of time or place or effort. I felt consumed by a hauntingly beautiful soundtrack too – it was the indris singing. That was mesmerising.'

She looks up and indicates size and location with her hands as she says, 'the indris remind me of pandas but they are no relation, they are enormous lemurs, huge black-and-white animals that watched us from high up in the trees with as much interest as we watched them. Oh, yes and we saw the most special sight, a family of champagne-coloured diademed sifakas. Mom, Dad and the most adorable baby. We stood there for ages, maybe an hour I think. The baby can only have been a few days old, but it was making its way in the world, from Mom to Dad and back again. I almost wept, I was so moved.'

I can tell; I am moved just by listening to her. At this point, Monique changes tone and looks at me directly. 'Maybe that's the problem. I only feel whole, true to myself when I'm there. It's so powerful; it's like I belong there. I miss it.'

This is helpful – the content of what Monique is saying is informative but it also tells us about the way she is, her way-of-being – this is something about what she thinks, what she feels, emotionally and physically. We now have a grasp on something we have not paid too much attention to before, the part of her that can, and *does*, feel vital and alive.

Importantly, it isn't a case of paying attention to *either* her despair *or* her vitality, it doesn't mean we should switch attention *from* her urban life *to* her way of being in the wilds. It is important to utilise her own view, that to make a contribution to something both aspects need to be considered, to make different aspects dovetail if at all possible. What seems the important thing to consider is the relationship *between* the states she is experiencing. She isn't just one aspect or the other. Having said that, she is experiencing herself as a divided self, not fully complete in one place or the other.

The divided self is a concept that highlights the problem when we view ourselves (or others) as single, standalone entities, either feeling this *or* that, or even being one thing *or* another, when actually we are contradictions and paradoxes. This concept is outlined in *The Divided Self* (Laing, 1990; see also van Deurzen, 1998, 2015). And right here, in the UK, in London, the division feels irreconcilable to Monique. It is a dilemma she seems unable to resolve; how can a person be a successful, socially skilled urbanite while also being a sensuous, ecologically attuned creature[1] who comes to life when part of a greater whole, alongside other animals, in a wider landscape. This is quite an insight for her and it is the first of several that impact her powerfully.

'Oh, that's it, that's what happens. I want to ... non ... I *need* to live in both of those worlds ...', she frowns as she pauses, 'but I need to live in them simultaneously. I am not happy if I only have access to the one. I'm not even me if I'm only in the one.'

She looks shocked and her voice is pained when she continues: 'but I'm never going to live in the wilds full time. Yet being in the city is suffocating; I have some fun, yes, but it's so stifling. I must do both. But how?' and with that she begins to cry, a chasm has appeared out of the clarity.

As she considers this, Monique's tone changes and a panic creeps into her voice and her posture. She looks at me: 'I can't feel good just living here, but I can't ... I can't move out there! I don't have the skills; I can support projects but I couldn't *actually* run a study in the Mara or the forests of Madagascar. I couldn't run those projects in town either! Who do I think I am, fly me in and we will change the world? Ha! Such hubris, such arrogance! Oh, what am I thinking?'

I haven't seen her so self-critical before. Yes, she is often reflective and will frequently identify her impractical, illogical assumptions but this is strong. This feels aggressive. I wonder whether this is the depression talking? I have plenty of colleagues who would think about it this way, because on a conscious level her statements could easily be disputed. She is a conservationist, supporting actual projects that seem to be making very real differences. If anyone is doing their bit and making a real difference, it is her.

'I'm never going to manage to live in a way that suits me. I already can't get my carbon footprint down – even the trips to check the projects mean jumping on a plane, and that's without me travelling for work, the family, for holidays or even simply to get my fix of wilderness! To have that, I pollute! I want to feel alive, but if I live, the planet dies. This is impossible!' Monique sinks back heavily into the seat aghast.

---

[1] I use the word 'creature' cautiously. I am aware that for some readers it might smack of a tabloid-style exoticisation of women, especially (but not only) relevant when the therapist and client are of different genders. However, in this context, what is important to consider is not just her place in the human world but also in the natural and animal world, where she sits alongside other creatures, no more or no less than them, coexisting.

Of course, Monique is not alone in these difficulties. We are seeing increasing interest into the environmental despair that clients are bringing to therapy (see Jordan, 2015; Rust, 2008a, 2008b; Totton, 2011). While we might expect conservationists, naturalists and other environmentalists to feel it particularly strongly as they face the reality directly every day, we see it in the everyday dilemmas faced by all kinds of urban dwellers. We hear about the strong feelings that recycling generates, how guilty people feel when they buy 'their' second car, anxiety about health risks from pollution and when clients' sleep is contaminated by dreams of global collapse and systemic poisoning. While governments play with climate change agreements, people are becoming increasingly anxious. Traditionally psychotherapists may have limited their understandings of these concerns to a symbolic representation of the client's inner world but as Harold Searles noted with concern, in much psychiatric and psychological thinking

the non human environment is [...] considered entirely irrelevant to human personality development and to the development of psychiatric illness, as though life were lived out in a vacuum – as though the human race were alone in the universe, pursuing individual and collective destinies in a homogeneous matrix of nothingness, a background devoid of form, colour and substance. (Searles, 1960, p. 3)

IV

The next few months of therapy are difficult for Monique. She had started therapy with some optimism, but now she believes her dilemma is irreconcilable – and that isn't something she wants to entertain, let alone accept.

I, on the other hand, am reminded of my feelings in the early part of therapy, where we had seen, or I had felt, a premonition of this. I went back to my notes to try and see whether there were any clues. I find that unsettling statement from our first meeting: '*I am very spoiled and very privileged. You are going to have your work cut out trying to help me.*' In some ways Monique warned us that this situation might evolve. I start to mull Monique's experience over and take it to supervision.

While the public may not be aware, psychologists and other psychological therapists don't only have supervision when training; it is deemed good practice throughout our careers. 'Supervision' in this context does not imply relative rank, but it applies to a process whereby reflection on practice is facilitated. It may have different foci over time, often reflecting on the process between the client and the therapist, but can also be used to develop knowledge, enhance skills or be a forum for self-care.

As we talk about these feelings and my sense of Monique, my supervisor notes the risk of limiting the dilemma to the practical – getting preoccupied with how Monique might straddle these places? How might she have wilderness experiences in fast-paced London? How can she do the impossible? Or how might she adjust to the loss?

'But maybe it's time', my supervisor says, 'to explore working outdoors with this client? You understand the importance of nature for us all – and for this client in particular – maybe you should raise it with Monique?'

'Great point', I think, wondering why hadn't I thought about this before.

My supervisor's observation strikes a chord – reminding me that the practical bits are not the entire work. Right now, it is less about fixing an unsolvable problem, but more about exploring and understanding it, what it means and responding to her distress as it is manifest. Doing therapy in a more natural frame is worth considering as it might suit Monique. Indoor work means that we sit in the room remembering her experience of the natural world, talking about these experiences, rather than taking advantage of the nature that is on our doorstep. No wonder she struggles to stay in touch with that vital part. It also occurs to me that she drives through the park to get to me, seeing it briefly and then leaving it behind. In some ways coming to therapy is a reminder of what she cannot have. It is a tease.

So I need to do a couple of things. First, I have to trust that clarity will bring possibility – either for change or maybe for acceptance, and I need to stop trying to figure it all out *for* her. Supervision has also reminded me that the therapist never sorts the problem out in isolation. Even in the most psycho-educational methods of therapy, involved, curious clients use the experience to help themselves. This does not underplay the commitment and effort of the therapist. That is also a crucial aspect of effective psychotherapy.

This isn't a new lesson for me; I have simply got caught up in the emotional pull of the work and I have started to feel that I want to sort this. And why wouldn't I? Seeing someone bogged down in despair, guilt and images of a decaying planet is not at all comfortable; in fact it is decidedly unpleasant.

I have time after supervision and so instead of driving through the park, this time I stop, walk, enjoy the clear autumn sun and watch the deer. As I do I think about the possibility of working outdoors. I am aware that such a change makes a lot of sense but it is also important to consider whether there are any downsides to it. Might it be related to the urge to 'do something' for instance? I need to think it through properly, to make sure that I cover the possible flight to health as well as consider any benefits it might offer.

I think about changing the frame without imagining I have to, without it meaning I am taking over. As we saw in Chapter 3, the frame is a concept in psychotherapy that refers to such aspects of therapy as length and regularity of sessions (fifty minutes for many therapists, once, twice or more times a week at set times), the length of therapy (short or long term), confidentiality, fees and so forth. The frame impacts on the nature of the work that can be done. When considering adjustments to the frame I am aware that some schools suggest there is one optimal frame which requires steadfast holding to regular space, time, in a sound-proofed and confidential location (see Casement, 2002; Langs, 1989; Smith, 1999), while others have suggested that the exact shape and form adopted can be more flexible. From this perspective the more important aspects are the predictability and trustworthiness of the frame (see Spinelli, 2014). While different understandings of the frame exist, the consensus is, that once agreed, the frame needs to be respected, and breaks and amendments need to be taken seriously. Where the frame is trustworthy, a stronger therapeutic alliance is likely to develop, whereas a poorly held frame compromises the therapeutic process.

I remind myself that, should a change seem useful to me, I can have a discussion with Monique and allow for indoor *or* outdoor work, and maybe by doing it this way any decision will actually be more democratic. This is important politically and, more than that, it seems useful in terms of the formulation we were working with. Therapeutically I need to avoid trying to take over and fix Monique much as a part of her would like that; and to not take over will allow us to reflect upon the limits of our power – this is a theme embedded in the work, as is the experience of struggling with, and of not resolving, issues.

Much of my to-ing and fro-ing on these issues is a result of recognising what is known as a possible 'transference' issue. Psychodynamic thinking helps us understand the ways in which an interaction can be a replication of past historical relationships and I am mindful of the idyllic way in which Monique describes her long country walks with her father. I have to consider whether I am trying to create something along those lines.

I am also mindful of more recent ecopsychological thinking that reminds us that transference and countertransference occurs in relation to place (see Devine-Wright, 2009; Morgan, 2010). While considering both possibilities I am sure that any father-transference type phenomena can be discussed and explored if it is relevant, but that we should not overlook, or avoid capitalising on, Monique's lifelong experience of positive psychological states when in nature.

My ponderings come easily and fluidly as I walk and this helps me decide that I am happy to discuss the current frame with Monique and to explore whether a shift to the outdoors might be a useful adjunct to our work.

As the management of the frame is a key responsibility of the therapist I introduce the possibility of working outdoors as Monique is settling down for our next session. I say: 'I've been thinking about what we've been talking about these last few weeks, and I've been wondering about a possible change.'

'What change?', she asks, seeming anxious.

'About where we do this. I had an idea and wanted to see what you feel about it. We don't have to change anything but I have a sense it might … maybe could be helpful.'

Monique relaxes a little and nods, 'OK'.

'It occurred to me that much of what is important at the moment is how you are with nature, how important this is to you. And I am wondering whether it might be helpful, for a period anyway, to have these sessions in the park.'

'How would that work?', she asks.

'That we can decide together. In essence though we would do the same work but instead of here, we might walk as we talk, or depending on how you feel, we might find somewhere quiet to sit.'

Monique takes a few moments and thinks about what I have said. 'I think that would be helpful', she says. 'Sometimes coming here, watching you watching me, it gets really difficult … I don't know why, but it does.'

'It might still', I say smiling softly. 'I don't want to suggest that therapy is necessarily any *easier* when walking outdoors instead of sitting looking at each other, but it seems important, considering how you experience nature.'

Monique and I discuss the possible change and agree that we will check in again next session and see what her thoughts are then. We also discuss what the ground rules for therapy would be if we were outside. I reiterate that the purpose of therapy remains the same and we keep the same time slot. We discuss interruptions that seldom occur in the consulting room; there is the possibility of being approached by others, we might be jumped on by dogs, have apologetic owners commenting, passers-by acknowledging us and there is always the weather to contend with. There is also a chance that we might be approached by people one of us knows. We have to decide whether we will utilise this opportunity in all weathers or revert to indoor work in the face of rain and storms. We consider, in principle, the ways in which Monique would want us to deal with these and I confirm that I would also take my lead from her. (For more on the management of the frame in outdoor work, see Jordan, 2015.)

We start working outdoors two weeks later and after an initial adjustment, finding out the pace of walk that is conducive to thinking (it isn't a hike after all), and getting used to the rhythm of looking ahead and looking to the side, the occasional bumping against each other as one does walking alongside someone, we find a stride that seems to work.

Working in this way helps *me* immediately; it limits the time I give to the tyranny of the practical, to assessing whether Monique's ideas are helpful or not, sensible or not, feasible or not. It also helps me become aware of when I can or cannot feel and understand anything about the emotional tenor of her experience.

As we walk I become aware of Monique's pleasure in the breeze and the light, the space before us and in movement. I watch to see whether this might distract from the work; maybe enjoyment will push despair to the periphery, risking turning it from work to pleasure, helping avoid important feelings. But this doesn't happen. As we work this way, Monique still experiences the despair as is clear one day as we say our goodbyes: 'This is great', she says, 'but even here I have to leave and go back to work; I have to get my head into regulations and the politics of planning. It's so pointless, so painful.'

As we continue to work, we find that alongside despair is a great deal of fear. Fear of what we have already done to the planet and what we might still be capable of doing. Monique stops and looks around. 'We think of this as "nature"', she says, 'but look, it's all controlled and managed by us – this length grass isn't just because of the deer, this is mown! And they cull these beautiful animals. This is a caricature of nature. Can we stop ourselves? Will we find a way to do that before it's too late?'

I don't answer. I don't have an answer.

As Monique explores her fears she becomes more aware of a heavy sense of responsibility. It is a state that makes sense to her. 'If we don't take responsibility, who will? Those of us who are aware, who know something about this have to work really hard to make up for all those that don't … won't … or can't. AAGGHH!' She is frustrated and I can feel it. She almost shouts as she continues: 'And in my position I have *no* excuses!'

I see logic in this, but struggle with it too. Just because we want to be responsible, are we able to be responsible for everything? No, not always. We can do what we can, but we can't make others act differently. And Monique knows this too I am sure. But I'm not here to argue the logic with her, so instead I try to bring some clarity to her dilemma. A key part of psychotherapy is the attempt to offer clarity, to distinguish habit from potentiality and the important from the merely expected. This is done differently in different approaches, but interpretation, clarification, empathy and challenge might all prompt such insight. The idea is to facilitate greater personal awareness, not to superimpose the therapist's (or the State's) preferred vision.

I say: 'This is part of why it's so hard, isn't it? You're damned if you do and damned if you don't. You feel like you *have* to take responsibility and compensate for what we are all doing to the environment, because if you don't, who will? Yet you know, quite clearly, that in some ways this is an impossible task.

This means that while your efforts are helpful, you don't feel that. You don't feel the relief or comfort from what you do because you are wrapped up in the amount of awfulness that exists. This responsibility is evident even when you are in nature, but put you back in London and … the need, the lack of responsibility and the apathy is so stark for you. It's all you see.'

Monique takes something from this. 'So I am being responsible, alone, for what I am not responsible for. I have to fix something I can't fix alone.' She looks pained as she tries to figure this out. Both seem true to her, but it is becoming clearer that she can't fix this, but equally, she is not sure that she can bear for it to go unfixed.

Over the next few weeks Monique's response to this is instructive. She starts to think that some of the feeling underlying this drive to responsibility is guilt. But guilt is something she doesn't like; she can't bear to feel the guilt so she drives herself to fix the world. Yet when she thinks of the guilt, some of it seems reasonable. 'I probably can "do better". I sometimes use hire cars when the tube would be fine, some of the renovations in my apartment are completely unnecessary and I fly … a lot. My lifestyle *makes* me guilty.'

Insight is helpful and it doesn't take Monique more than a couple of weeks to make some changes, projects are cancelled or amended, the use of the car is halved and she becomes even more efficient with her recycling efforts, at home and work. A bit of insight and some practical changes are not always enough though; they can sometimes feel like a drop in the ocean. Monique is suffering from an excruciating sense of guilt about the abdication of responsibility she feels that humanity is culpable of. She knows she is not responsible for all humanity, but she feels it, particularly in relation to those who don't take their stewardship seriously. She talks of her father's use of the environment and its inhabitants to further his own ends; for the West's assumption that it can simply deplete the rich forests of the equatorial belts and replace with palm oil, flowers, coffee and other goods that we might pop into a supermarket trolley without a second thought about how we use it responsibly.

Conversations like this can feel difficult, loaded as they are. They are also overtly political and often related to the 'actuality' of the world. However, when understood in relation to the specific client they can be very personal too. Such discussions are where the personal and the political clearly illuminate a great deal about the client's way of being and the world in which they (and we) exist.

As difficult as guilt can be to work with, Monique's explorations lead us to see that it is just part of a powerful constellation of feelings. For her, it goes something like this: the exploration of guilt is eased by the promise of responsibility; this means that the problem becomes hers and she might be able to do something, she should do something about it. Yet it is becoming clear that responsibility is impossible and this scares her. The fear though is, among other things, a distraction from her powerlessness that she doesn't want to face or admit to because this makes her feel guilty – guilt, responsibility, fear and powerlessness, four difficult states only eased by the process of moving from one to another.

For a while, it seems like all we have done is shift from one irreconcilable dilemma (to be in London or be in the wilderness) to a draining cycle of negative emotions and Monique feels trapped in an impossible spiral. But as autumn turns to winter, her distress becomes less intense; alongside the periods of despair, pleasure is experienced too – in her running or walks in the parks, and in her work and with her friends. This seems to be partly due to the fact that the changes she has made are being maintained and that others, such as Jean, Siobhan and even the Foundation support her changes. In addition to this, her expectations seem to ease and rather than expecting gargantuan, systemic changes to occur before she can feel alright, she has started to understand that even small actions are important and have impact.

As she recognises this I start to see she has pride in her accomplishments. Not an imperious pride, but an experience that leads to smiles, delight and an ability to 'balance the scales' as she put it. She can feel the stress and the pleasure, see how much there is to do and also how much she is doing and has done. She has found ways to keep nature in her heart, whether in the bush or in the boardroom.

V

By the time we finished working together, Monique is feeling more at ease and far less despairing. Despair has not been eradicated, and we think it probably won't be as it is appropriate in some regards. And she is still prone to a demanding set of expectations. But she is now aware of her tendency to expect too much. She is better at recognising these rumblings, at intervening earlier and being more compassionate and realistic towards herself, understanding what she can and cannot do. As importantly, she is able to make space for nature in London; she still runs regularly, but she now also stops to simply spend time there.

While the work of the psychotherapist is very personal and we aim to support or facilitate change in the individual, couple or family we work with, I am also aware that this work has wider repercussions. By understanding the value of the environment as more than just landscape, as a very real relationship, we have validated Monique's experience as well as attending to her dilemma of how to be. The therapy has assisted her in supporting her environmental work, something that is important to Monique and more broadly. In this way, as the personal is political, therapy is environmental.

10

BIG P POLITICS

Andrew Samuels drew the profession's attention to the relationship between 'the political' and the psychological in his seminal text *The Political Psyche* (1993). Of course, this wasn't the first text to take this domain seriously but it placed formal politics – a focus on government and politicians, economic policy, social relations and care of the environment – back in the realm of human psychology, well-being and disturbance and psychotherapy. Previous contributors have included Breggin (1975), Laing (1971) and Pilgrim (1992) to name just a few, and more recent contributions include Proctor (2002), Totton (2000) and Smail (2015). There are, of course, many more in a variety of human science fields.

Every now and again, politics with a big P, enters the public discourse powerfully. As noted in Chapters 1 and 2, recently, it was by way of the impact of austerity, the Syrian crisis, the UK's Brexit referendum and the US election. Such events are clearly linked to increases in rates of depression, anxiety, suicidality and other psychosocial problems in the population over time (see Cooper, 2011; Fountoulakis et al., 2014; Hemingway et al., 2013). Distress is not just a personal, intrapsychic issue.

Large-scale and epidemiological studies are not the only evidence that confirm these impacts. Psychological work with clients also brings this home. Recently, these events and their impacts have been raised in client sessions and supervision groups. Optimistic visions and their more negative alternatives vied for airtime, and the expression of xenophobia, homophobia and misogyny flourished, as did anxiety and fear about such expression. Very few people seem unaffected, individuals are shaken up, families brought into conflict, and communities subject to hostility. As well as the effect on clients, we therapists, those whose work it is to assist with the psychological well-being of our clients, also react to these events; it is impossible not to be affected by politics.

Despite this awareness, therapists and clients too often struggle to see the link between political events and the distress experienced. Maybe it is the urgency of personal despair or perceived hopelessness about being able to impact the political events of the day, but the ability to contribute to the political is often overlooked. Yet psychological contributions to service development and consultations on policy is important, as is reflection on the ways in which we might assist clients in locating their distress in the relationship between themselves and the wider world rather than taking all the responsibility themselves and letting our politicians, (and media and corporations) off the hook. When we do this it means that they are aided in not recognising or ignoring the responsibility leadership holds for the emotional well-being of the population.

The political is personal: Jacinta and Brexit

I

I first meet Jacinta in June 2015 after receiving a rather brief, somewhat terse, email from her requesting an appointment 'at your earliest convenience' and outlining which days and times would be convenient for her. She doesn't explain much about what brings her to seek therapy. I look at my diary and unfortunately the times she suggest don't coincide with my availability so I write back to advise that I either don't run clinics at those times or the appointments are taken with pre-existing client commitments. I do, however, offer her the first appointment I have available. She accepts.

I meet with Jacinta the following week and my overwhelming impression is one of extreme 'professionalism'. This isn't something that often sums up my sense of a client, certainly not on first meeting; I am much more used to being impacted by strong feelings or the absence of these, anxiety and depression for example. However, this is what hit me, a very organised woman, able and efficient and used to making things happen it seems. Jacinta is also dressed professionally, her suit and her entire 'look' are one that fits an elegant setting and she introduces herself in an upbeat manner, with a firm handshake and takes control of the meeting. I almost expect to be invited to sit down in my own consulting room.

'Come in', I say and indicate that she should enter the room.

'You probably want to know why I am here', she says as she checks her nails. Before I have a chance to comment, Jacinta is into her story. She tells me that she is Spanish, twenty-five years old, fluent in three languages and works as a division head for a world-renowned fashion house. I learn that she is very successful, that she has been head-hunted several times, each time securing significantly more status and salary, more than she imagined she would ever earn. 'My parents never had any money you see', she says, suggesting that this was important.

It isn't surprising that clients bring such material, money carries enormous meaning. On one level it is about survival, food on the table, clothes on one's back. Poverty is a root cause of much psychological and social difficulty. But it can have an array of psychological meanings too. When listening to Jacinta, I am aware that her story is an example of the much lauded 'upward social mobility', a frequent notion in our political lives and one which is usually assumed to be a positive and helpful experience. However, these political discourses seldom consider the range of psychological challenges that this may present to individuals, families and communities. While increased resources may well mean access to better diet, enhanced living conditions, health care and the like, psychotherapists also get to hear about anger, disappointment or guilt that what they can now provide was not available to them as children. Sometimes this is understood as inept parenting, at other times as manifestations of 'succeeding' where parents did not, or could not. These emotions are frequently felt as individual and family issues rather than understood in their wider sociological, political or historical terms.

I nod and am just about to ask about her family, but Jacinta is talking again. This time I am told about her wonderful apartment, her 'crazy' schedule, her passion for creative work and her delight that life is going so well. After a while I realise that I have quite enjoyed these first twenty-five minutes with Jacinta: positivity, glamour, pleasure ... all very lovely things.

As is inevitable, there is a lull in the discussion and at that point I realise that I have been sold a vision of a high-flying talented and successful woman, but I am completely clueless as to why she is here, why she seeks help, what isn't right in her world. Well actually, more than that, I am clueless about who Jacinta really is – her history, her likes and dislikes. Is she in a relationship? Does she like animals? Who might she vote for? Is she a person of faith? I have gleaned very little from her initial presentation of herself.

'So ... what is it that brings you here?', I finally ask, 'How can I help?'

And with this Jacinta is transformed. The uber-efficient high-flyer from moments ago has been replaced by a red-faced, teary eyed, tense woman. She drops her head and rubs her eyes before asking, 'Can I trust you?'

Now this is never an easy question, especially on first meeting someone. Trust is at the bedrock of the profession and of good practice. Without at least some degree of trust, any hope of offering a meaningful engagement is significantly limited. Because of this the urge for the therapist is often to say, 'Yes, of course you can'. But you don't actually *know* what the question relates to, what material will follow it, or whether the client is thinking of trust the same way you are. Jacinta spares me from too much worrying though as she starts talking again.

'I mean, you won't tell anyone will you? I mean at work?'

Now *that* I was more confident about, so I reply, 'No, I shouldn't think so ... and if it seems that that would be a necessary thing to do, I would talk to *you* about it and see how best we broach that. But nothing so far seems to be something we should share elsewhere.' It is important to leave some leeway as who knows what she will discuss; for the first time since meeting her I have a thought that maybe she is going to tell me she has plotted the company downfall or is embezzling funds.

Jacinta looks palpably relieved at this point. 'I can't cope', she says before starting to cry. 'I can't sleep ... if I do I wake up terrified, I am worried all the time. I get these palpitations; I thought I was having a heart attack the other day .... It's horrible.'

I push the box of tissues closer to her so that she can use them rather than keep rubbing her snot and tears across her face. 'It sounds horrible', I say. 'Tell me more about it.'

As she wipes her face, Jacinta takes a long deep breath. It seems a lot of effort, especially as she then just whispers, 'No … '

She looks up and asks me, 'Am I going crazy?' Another loaded term in the fact that it can be quite pejorative. But people do use it to capture something about the confusion and distress they feel. It is also far too early for me to know anything much about the distress, let alone whether or not she would find it meaningful.

'Doesn't sound crazy to me, as much as scary and confusing. It sounds like it might be useful to slow down, think about this a bit and see what we can do. How does that sound?' is all I want to say at this point.

And with that Jacinta is in tears again, but somehow these seem different, this is relief as much as fear and the rest of the session has a different feel to it, less pressured, less of a presentation and more of a space for a conversation. I am able to ask about what is behind this sophisticated successful woman and I start to get more of a sense of her.

Jacinta tells me that she was born in suburban Barcelona to parents who didn't have a lot of resources. She can't decide whether they were working class or lower middle class. 'The point being', she says, 'they seemed to work all the hours God sent and yet didn't have any money. I had my one pair of good shoes, which could never get dirty. I had my regular clothes and my Sunday best. I had friends but couldn't play with them on Sundays in case my dress and shoes got messed up.' This is very different to the world she inhabits now.

No matter which therapeutic model psychologists and psychotherapists are aligned to, therapists recognise that early experiences can be very important, allowing us to develop a picture of how the world is likely to be, how safe or at risk we are, what people's expectations of us might be and so forth. This is not the same as saying that we are doomed to live in the past, but simply to note that learning and early expectations are powerful and important, as they are for all social mammals. We also know that factors such as wealth or poverty, sexism, gender and racism are all part of those early experiences. However, whereas we might move away from an abusive parent or a violent bully at school, contemporary capitalist culture with its divisions and hurdles is harder to escape.

Jacinta tells me about her elder sister, Laura, who died very young. Jacinta remembers Laura's death even though she was only three herself. Suddenly everything changed, Mama and Papa were there, 'but not really. Mama couldn't stop being sad and Papa … well he worked a lot. They didn't fight but the house just got very, very quiet.'

She looks at me, hard and says, 'And that's just not ... Spanish! It's like the life had gone out of them. And I had to learn to be quiet too as, well I don't know why, it just seemed that we all froze.'

I listen and am touched by the huge loss – of her sister, her family and their way of being. I am also struck by the powerful and insightful recognition of her, and her family's reaction to the loss, to freeze. To stop being.

I am, however, also aware that our time is coming to an end, and like with so many first meetings we will have to stop before we really understand the problem. So I note: 'We are going to have to stop in a moment, but maybe I can sum up my impression and also see whether there are any questions you might have?'

Jacinta wastes no time and asks, with what feels like an air of desperation – or at least urgency – 'Just one, do you think you can help?'

No pressure then ... but maybe this is an important comment from her, giving me a sense of how desperate she actually is. I reply to her by saying, 'Well ... I am aware that you have only had the chance to tell me some of your experience, and I would like to know more so I suggest that we meet again soon to try.' Jacinta nods as I say this.

'But so far, I have a suspicion that therapy could help. It seems that you have experienced a lot of loss, very painful loss, a sense of it not being attended to, or at least not in the way that would have made sense to you culturally. Instead of talking and being emotional together, it seems you felt that the family had to really hold it in and you, even at the age of three, picked up on this. I need to know more but it sounds like this has become a bit of a habit, almost your way of being, you can perform your role of successful professional, but can't figure out how to share this loss or the other feelings you are experiencing with friends, or with anyone.'

Jacinta is dabbing her eyes and nodding as she listens to this. 'I think you are right', she says as she retrieves her cheque book from her bag. It is clear that she is already transitioning back to her professional persona. By the time we have agreed the next session, she is calm and recovered and looks fine – or at least will do after a quick trip to the bathroom.

II

The following few weeks allow Jacinta and I to unpack her history and her difficulties a little. She is able to tell me more about the death of her sister in a street accident, about her parents' grief and also about their guilt; it transpires that they had been with her when she suddenly darted after a balloon and was struck by a speeding car. I learn that at that moment Jacinta decided to never to be a problem again and never to worry her parents. Mama and Papa seemed to have appreciated her, spent time with her and applauded her success at school, but Jacinta always felt that it was with a sense of half-heartedness. 'I was no compensation', she said sadly one session.

Jacinta tells me that she did well at primary and high school, had a small group of friends, although was never one of the popular girls. She did well academically and also in the creative subjects and as she got older she enjoyed designing and making her own clothes. This turned out to have been a mixed blessing though as while she got kudos from some of her schoolmates for this, there was a negative side to it as well; it meant people could see her 'as the poor kid, the one without money. I didn't have the designer clothes. I was never going to be cool.'

While it may be true that many people are financially better off than in previous generations (see Hamilton, 2004; Wilkinson and Pickett, 2010), the escape from actual poverty is not the only issue at stake in people's psychological and social experience. In recent years we have come to see that 'relative poverty' or the gap between the 'haves' and the 'have-nots' is also an important factor and this gap is growing in many countries (see Shorrocks et al., 2015) with it being reported that 1% of the population own more than the rest of the global population put together. A factor that occurs alongside relative poverty is the conflation of self-worth with material goods. Clearly this plays out more in favour of those with the resources than those without.

As she talks about never being cool, something jars. I am reminded of my experience in our first meeting, when I experienced her as exuding something glamorous and, yes, maybe 'cool'. I made a mental note about the difference between her feeling about herself and the persona she offered me and the wider world. I also found myself thinking about many other clients and pondering whether this is just something about Jacinta or whether this is a modern issue. Capitalism has definitely shaped our lives a great deal – so many advantages, better health care, access to better food and so forth, but equally the difference between the haves and have-nots is so codified now. I have had many clients struggle with this – as do I and my family and friends; I wonder whether this is something Jacinta shares, where clothes, cars, job title (and implied income), where you live, type of mobile phone all signal your status. I wondered whether, in the difficult environment of teenage school years, Jacinta's creativity was overlooked and she was rather seen as the uncool, poor kid. The one people laughed at so as to make themselves feel better.

Jacinta tells me that it was in her last years at school that she started to experience periods of anxiety, usually social anxiety. If a boy asked her out on a date she would freeze and say nothing 'and just be weird'. Having to give class presentations was a nightmare and she would often be physically sick before giving them, despite them usually going down very well. She also started to feel, what she calls, 'paranoid'. She had a summer where she felt she was being followed, but she was never sure who by. The period passed without actual incident but the sense of being vulnerable to some malevolent, dangerous person sometimes feels strong again.

I ask her about who, and how much, she had confided in people about these experiences – about the teasing, about the feelings of threat and paranoia. Jacinta shrugs, 'no one really. If my friends see it I say not to worry, but I never say about the paranoia, what is there to say?'

'Well even if you doubt the presence, it sounds like there were plenty of emotions that are present. So you don't talk about being teased, about feeling vulnerable, about feeling so uncertain?'

'No', she confirms, 'I don't.

At this point I wonder out loud, sharing my updated formulation with her. 'It seems to me that your current worries and anxieties are not that new. Yes, they may have their own shape and form now but they are similar to those you've had for a long time.'

Jacinta looks at me quizzically.

'If we take it that the world is not straightforward, it's uncertain and people can be great support but relationships can also be quite scary; people can be there one minute and can be gone the next.'

She nods at this point.

'So then what we have is you born into this hard-working and loving family, who suffer this awful loss. It's a cruel loss, a hard one to bear for all of you, with each of you, in your own ways, making some sense of it – a dangerous world, we should work harder, we shouldn't bother others with our troubles, not even our family ... Does that make sense?'

Jacinta nods as she wipes her eyes.

'Well, it seems that you decided ... and I don't mean consciously or deliberately, but it made sense that you were secondary, you needed to *not* be the positive centre of attention, your talents and skills might be spotted but you felt that they weren't likely to be celebrated – that would be disrespectful to Laura. So in the family you were good, conscientious and hard-working; at school you kept yourself to your small circle of friends and shied away from competition and being seen too much. You learned that even if being seen was fun, you could be teased, ridiculed and later on you seem to have gotten a sense that it could also be quite dangerous.'

She says nothing but nods quietly.

'And so here is the rub. Maybe you aren't just a quiet person, you are also talented, creative and likeable. You have a job where you are in the public eye, where you are recognised and where you shine. But that's hard. You have learned how to '*do*' that but I don't think you have accepted that you can '*be*'

138

that too. The anxiety is a reminder of the dangers of being all that you can be in case of the judgements and other dangers.'

This seems to make some sense to Jacinta, although over the following months she thinks about aspects of this, what she calls 'tries them on' and sometimes it feels accurate to her and sometimes it doesn't.

The use of formulation is good practice in applied psychology and is a key aspect of technique. It allows psychologists to move away from the problems with diagnosis, including lack of agreement, lack of evidence, the constraints it places on our ability to hear subjective experience, the forcing of identities on people, limiting interventions and so on (see Johnstone, 2000, 2006; Horn et al., 2007). The prioritising of formulation also allows the therapist to construct understandings that can include the personal and the political, the individual and the cultural, strengths and weaknesses too. In this way formulation can be used to challenge superficial binary understandings, be individually tailored and culturally sensitive. In some ways formulation is itself a political act.

Alongside therapy of course, life continues; being asked out gives us plenty of material to consider – the initial delight, then the confusion of how to respond, then the panic as to what a relationship would be like. For a while Jacinta decides she prefers anonymous one-night experiences or Tinder dating; she even has a sexual pseudonym in case she is recognised. This allows her to have temporary connections without any expectations to manage. But she is also curious about a longer-term relationship; is it possible to be herself – vulnerable yet also be able to stand out – with the same person.

Trips back to Barcelona also provide material for her as it is walking back into a highly emotional environment. She wants to visit Laura on her own but she also wants to ask Mama and Papa to visit Laura's grave with her. On her own she wants to get her sister's approval for being successful, to reassure Laura that it isn't a way to out-do her. With her parents she wants to share the deeply felt loss.

Jacinta and I try, and succeed in, holding a relatively secure frame a lot of the time but there are times in the year when it is difficult as Jacinta's role means she is in Milan one week, New York the next and Paris the following. I sometimes see her face in the newspapers or on websites. However, Jacinta's professionalism proves useful here as she suggests that we keep to those times wherever possible by way of telephone or Skype meetings. Contemporary culture brings many new ideas to the practice of psychology and psychotherapy, one of them the possibilities of therapeutic contact via the internet, or what is known as 'digitally mediated therapy'. It, like so many other aspects of therapy, is available for discussion and reflection.

Digitally mediated therapy was a bit of a challenge for me as I am not a great fan of such technology and would never take on a client if that was going to be

THE PERSONAL IS POLITICAL

the main way of meeting a client, but Jacinta is working hard on her therapy and this is a way to limit the disruption of her work, so I agree to give it a try, reassuring myself that we can discuss the experience as we might any other aspect of therapy. Jacinta's commitment is strong as our scheduled sessions in Milan would interfere with her work meetings (which she reschedules ... apparently I was 'an important call from London') and when she is in New York sessions are at 6 am for her. But she is ready and awake and engaged. I suspect that some degree of guardedness is necessary as our session will end and then moments later she is expected to be in the front row of a show.

Jacinta's commitment to therapy and her ability to face up to her fears mean that her explicit episodes of anxiety drop significantly, and quite quickly, and by the Christmas break she is heavily engaged and interested in her wider development and this carries on into 2016 as well.

III

In the introductory chapter, I have written about how the Brexit referendum result affected Jacinta. The strength and nature of her immediate response takes us by surprise. She had of course noticed the newspapers, TV news and social media commentary in the run-up to the referendum and what it might mean, who hadn't? But possibly because it was a little way in the future, maybe because of the liberal Europhile bubble in which she exists or because she, like so many others simply thought this *would not* happen, her reference to Brexit was limited to being confused at some of the absurd claims made and to voice her dislike of some of the key figures. Her response had intensified when one of the campaigns encouraging people to leave the EU utilised an awful poster replicating some of the 1930s racist propaganda suggesting that the UK was facing a never-ending line of migrants. At that point, Jacinta voiced worry about the level of deceit, obfuscation and lies that were made about 'immigrants'.

She also felt it more personally: 'That's me, they are talking about ... me!' This was difficult for Jacinta as the rhetoric tended to paint a singular picture of migrants, claims of threats to space, resources and wider political issues and it failed to accept that migration occurs for a myriad of reasons: people choosing to explore the world, to spend time working abroad and some being displaced due to oppression and war. Very little attention was paid to how that might affect the psychological experience of immigrants to this country, nor the issues that migrants – whether forced or voluntary – might endure, issues such as the loss of home, the feeling different, language issues and the loss of a sense of a belonging.

At the time of the referendum Jacinta's session falls on the Friday, the morning the result is announced, and she is distraught, more than I have ever seen her. More so, even than when considering talking to her sister Laura, at the graveside in Barcelona. People experience an array of feelings in reaction to the vote, some are angry, others are scared and many experience a period of hopelessness. Jacinta's experience is one of huge anxiety, an anxiety that is almost uncontainable with tears, hyperventilation and terror at the face of the enormity of the unknown. She looks me in the eye and asks 'What is going to happen?' An air of desperate expectancy sits between us.

In the face of this question I feel completely helpless, after all what do I know? Not that I tell her but I, too, had hoped that the emotive language and lies of the campaign would have been seen by the electorate and resisted. So I have gotten it as wrong as she did; I have no answers to offer. Very often, when we think of psychotherapy we think of the client – the distress they are experiencing, what it is related to, how we might intervene and so forth. However, it is also important that we understand that therapists are as embedded in the political as anyone else is. Yes, we are trained to listen, while noticing and bracketing aspects of our own experience, but this is never complete – after all, we are not automatons. So there are times when the therapist and client might be similarly affected by the events that unfold. This is true whether we are talking about how the client–therapist relationship embodies difference in gender, sexual identity, faith, level of ability and so forth, or whether the client and therapist are experiencing such impactful political events as the EU referendum.

The questions come and come; it is a tidal wave of anxiety and it illustrates just how destabilised Jacinta feels and how threatening this event actually is. She asks 'How am I going to survive?' imagining as she does that she will have to leave the UK, and painfully she questions 'Why have they done this? What have we, me and people like me, ever done … ?'

The rest of that sentence, 'to people like you', hangs unspoken in the air. And this is what I find so difficult. On this occasion, the option of making the political explicitly personal, to ponder how her reaction may be a coded comment upon me as a specific individual doesn't seem immediately meaningful, it seems too contrived and theoretical at this point; the therapeutic relationship is a strong one, strong enough that she could risk asking this question. But culturally, this is an important question and we embody aspects of this in my quiet south-west London consulting room. I sit there as a white British male with all the privilege that that carries, whereas she is experiencing a huge amount of negativity – not yet face to face, but on posters, social media and news reports. This is more about how we find ourselves in a cultural confusion and shock.

During this session I feel very limited. I listen to the questions and to the underlying themes that Jacinta brings. I try hard to think about what this tells me about her now and also what this adds to what we already know about Jacinta and her distress, how she has long felt an outsider, the one that people made fun of, the one who survived when the other was killed off. But this isn't just personal; it is also important to manage the fact that along with other migrants, Jacinta is subject to negativity and racism in this recent campaign. The London where Jacinta had created her 'wonderful' home no longer feels welcoming or safe.

In the moment I feel slow, stagnant, impotent even. I manage to nod, to agree a few times and take the opportunity to make a couple of comments to try and acknowledge that I am there and I understand the fear and can see the grounds for such fears. 'No, you are not going crazy, but maybe we do have to think about the world and how it is changing.' But that's about all I can manage.

The end of the session comes and the terror has not abated. So much for an immediate sense of relief or respite which even experienced psychotherapists sometimes desire for our clients. I find myself momentarily wanting to reach into some magical bag of psychological tricks and make her feel calm again. I know better, I know so much better, but it is hard to be with someone so distressed and not be able to offer relief. As she leaves we acknowledge how much we do not yet know, that things are changing minute by minute and maybe she can think of how to support herself, to accept that she is scared and that maybe that's OK for now. I also feel unsettled as I know that I will not see Jacinta for a couple of weeks as she is going away on holiday.

IV

In London, the post-referendum period is a whirlwind with all kinds of discussions – there are calls for Article 50 to be triggered immediately – Article 50 being the legal action under the Treaty of European Union whereby a member state can trigger the period of discussion of the terms of their withdrawal from the EU. It is an important step as it sets a two-year countdown to their formal exit. Within that period any laws that the country has set up in relation with the EU have to be reviewed and adjusted in light of the new status. It is therefore an important step and one that has a sword of Damocles feel to it, waiting there just ready to drop.

There are calls reminding us that as a parliamentary democracy the referendum was advisory and so requires discussion and decision by Parliament; there are other speedy calls to reject such points and simply note that 'the people have spoken'. Britain's particular form of democracy comes under scrutiny during this period as issues such as those who were excluded from voting, the problematic first-past-the-post nature of Britain's electoral system and very slim majority were debated. Does the voice of thirty-something per cent of the population actually mean that 'the people have spoken'? Interestingly the government privileges binary perspectives (again), arguing that the vote was clear rather than recognising that it is more complex than this. In speaking, 'the people' have clarified that Britain is actually a very divided country on economic, social and geographical lines. Alongside this, levels of racial insult and violence increase enormously. It is reported that racially motivated hate crime increased after the referendum and the UN Committee on the Elimination of Racial Discrimination says that 'many prominent politicians should share the blame for the outbreak of xenophobia and intimidation against ethnic minorities' (Butler, 2016).

From the outside, I suspect that the three weeks after the result would have been seen as farcical, as leading players come to prominence and then disappear, the Tory Party leadership campaign, brief as it turns out to be, is a nasty and inept affair with those vying for leadership positions stabbing each other in the back and saying one thing and then opportunistically changing their opinion at the drop of a hat. The press picks up on explicit accusations and implied slights.

Sexism comes to the fore in this campaign too. Parenthood and 'kitten heels' are discussed as almost compulsory qualities for the female candidates. Comments are made about having children or being childless (children being constructed as something a prime minister needs, as well as on the female candidates' clothes and the use of different language. As a citizen I am immersed in this but as a psychotherapist I also need to understand what impact this might have on people. Sexism has not been particularly meaningful to Jacinta so far, her attention and distress being focused on her migratory Outsider status.

There were other disturbing interactions, too, and overall they characterise a period where many feel the nation is out of control, maybe even dysfunctional. Psychologically the nation is looking at who would take the parental/leadership role and sadly is offered a cast of characters that appear to have originated in the *Carry On* films.

On 12 July it becomes clear that Theresa May has won the party leadership and will become prime minister. While there are discussions about her policies and whether these will be good for the country or not, at least there is something known, someone to position as leader. Even some of her more confusing political appointees are accepted as the country begins to reorganise its sense of itself.

I feel ambivalent that Jacinta is away straight after the referendum, as I feel bad about not being able to support her through such a chaotic time, the level of her distress staying with me powerfully. On the other hand, I also hope that the trip might be a way of distancing herself from some of the ugliness and nastiness. While I am caught up in the moment-to-moment madness that characterises the post-Brexit discourse, in London at least, Jacinta is holidaying on a Greek island and spending time on a yacht with friends.

V

At our first session after her holiday Jacinta is still anxious. She tells me that the holiday was fabulous. 'I enjoyed the sun, sights, got to spend time with friends, we snorkelled, I saw a turtle, we ate well ... it was paradise.'

I wait to hear more.

'It doesn't feel safe back here though ... I am probably taking it too personally, but the news ... and actually it was on the tube today, too ... I heard some nasty old man tell a young woman in a head scarf to go back to where she came from as we aren't in Europe any more. It's so mean ... and he is stupid, of course we are still in Europe. But do you know what hurts?', she asks. 'No one asks about this ... well OK one person did yesterday as we were leaving work, and she asked in that "apologetic way" in case I hadn't realised it was about me. But I appreciate her asking how I feel, I did and I told her so. She is scared too apparently.'

Jacinta takes a moment and says, 'That's weird, that kinda helps.'

I have heard similar stories from others, from different clients, colleagues and my own family. At our recent conference there was a lot of discussion too. But as well as the general impact such an event has it's the manner in which individual people are treated or experience it that matters so much.

Then Jacinta adds: 'And it's going to be hard getting work – I wasn't looking but on holiday a friend mentioned that they were looking for a new head of division where she works; she got so excited, said I would be perfect for it ... and then she stopped, went quiet and said that they may have frozen that for the moment as they think they probably need to have a British person in post because of all this EU stuff, but they don't know the legality of doing that right now. So I could be screwed ... I could be refused jobs because I am Spanish! What am I going to do?' And with that Jacinta looks scared and starts to tear up again. Up until now Jacinta's 'Spanishness' had been something she enjoys. Yes, it makes her different in many contexts but often in an exotic manner, desirable and it is also linked to home. Comments like this feel more rejecting, more threatening, racist in fact.

While listening to her I realise that we have settled into one singular focus: it is all about the feared unknown; it has become huge and all encompassing and means she is living in this feared future rather than in the present where she might be able to think about the fears, where she might make some sense of what her responses are.

In moments like this therapists have a dilemma. Do we focus on the feared scenario as it is meaningful to the client – they are the ones that bring the issue after all? Or do we also observe what is *not* being spoken about and explore that too, with all the attendant risks of going into domains that are meaningless to the client (and indicative of our own preoccupations)? I am aware of this but remember the level of distress from before. I decide to widen the lens and comment on what seems to be present but unspoken. I also wonder how this fits with our original formulation.

'I know ... I know; it's going to be unclear for a while, isn't it. But maybe that's not the only question right now, maybe right now it's also about what are you going to do right now, to look after yourself? What do you need to do today, this week or this month? I know a lot is up in the air, but aren't we overlooking the fact that a lot also hasn't changed? You still like your job, right?'

'Yes.'

'And that's safe right?'

'Yes, of course.'

'So work-wise there is nothing new, nothing to do now. Your friends seem to be as close as they were? So in some ways it's just the future that's the problem.'

'Just the future?', she asks wide-eyed. 'Well it does seem like a *big* problem.'

'I know, but ... some of this is what you have always struggled with, what will people think. No? That's not surprising because many of us feel scared and hurt when in this situation, and we do ask what will people think of us? Will they like us? Will they accept us? Can we thrive? Can we even keep ourselves safe? There's a question of can you be the person you want to be if others feel different? So, at the moment, part of the problem seems to be what we have spoken about before. You are focusing on the unknowable "what ifs" rather than recognising how creative and resilient you are – or can be. Yes, this may well be a mess but why are you so convinced you *will* crumble? You have overcome so much, why do we imagine this is any different?'

As I speak, I feel torn, with a weird feeling of believing what I am saying but also wondering whether I'm not trying to chivvy her along, cheer her up and rescue her from her despair. But if that is a part of it, it isn't the whole thing; it is more than that. Clarity, a recognition of one's strengths, a sense of hope are all important aspects of psychotherapy and Jacinta has demonstrated that she can think, that she is very resourceful and that while she sometimes loses that capacity, she does have a vision for herself and the future. I need to be careful though so as not to *demand* that of her, but to receive the experience as she has it.

'No, you are right ... it's weird though; it's as if I forget that, maybe not forget it but simply just go to where I normally go. To be honest, who knows how long I will stay in this job even. In two years' time I could be doing something different and could have moved to Paris or New York. Or not, of course.'

The therapy shifts a little after this. While Jacinta still monitors and considers her anxiety and her fear, and spots when she is likely to personalise the dislike or hate-speak that is so prevalent, she seems to engage more with the range of possibilities that exist – yes, there may be challenges ahead, but for her, might there be opportunities too? Yes, she is fearful of the anti-immigrant rhetoric that abounds but she also gets in touch with a sense of anger about it, a feeling that she had always been shy to accept or express. How does one embrace one's anger if you are worried about being teased, bullied or demanding too much attention from people? How does one assert and have confidence in oneself when the papers and social media are full of negativity?

It is early days in relation to anger and disappointment in others, but Jacinta is engaging with these feelings now. Politically she seems to be more confident, having had more passionate conversations with friends, written to the newspapers and even directed an advertising campaign that sheds light on these lines. This growing experimentation and confidence is also there in her personal life and in her therapy, sometimes enjoyable and sometimes a little scary for her. As her therapy continues we work together on the tensions between these big events and the very personal challenges and opportunities it presents.

11

EPILOGUE

It is my hope that as readers met Kenny, Rhonda, Sam and the others, they were offered some insights into ways in which the political dimension and experiences of difference are experienced subjectively, how they inform identity and influence well-being or psychological distress, and that the reliance on binary understandings of the world comes at a price. I also hope that readers will also recognise how psychologists and other therapists have a contribution to make to helping address this – at a variety of different levels.

Perhaps more importantly, I hope that readers have been prompted to reflect on their own practice and have been able to consider the ways in which these issues can be recognised and engaged with, that their interest has been piqued as to how they might come to understand the ways in which difference is at the heart of much subjective experience, both culturally and individually. If so then it may bode well for our ability to utilise the more explicitly social and political information available to us in our professional activity – whether by way of questions being asked in assessment and formulation being enriched by a more deliberate locating of experience in context; or reflections on the ways in which our approaches to service development and theory might be improved when subject to scrutiny through a sociocultural lens (as well as through the psychological and psychotherapeutic lenses we already use). I hope, too, that therapists will be thinking about how we might come together, to cross-fertilise each other's ideas and share theory and practice in wider contexts; how we can challenge tired old visions of the individual being the sole cause of distress. The political domain is an ever-changing dynamic one, as should our theorising and practice be.

Enhancing understandings of psychological health and distress

The stories in this book reflect on the fact that even when working one-on-one in the consulting room, therapists still engage with social and political aspects of existence. As well as bringing our minds and bodies (including the complete physical complement of bones, muscle, blood, gas and hair) into the room, we also bring our sex, gender, race, religious beliefs, affluence or lack of it, levels of ability and so forth – these issues of difference that carry so much meaning. These are not some kind of add-ons that are waiting to be called upon if one of us *thinks* they are relevant. They are there, in the room. The question is when and how do we assess if they are meaningful?

These stories illustrate the fact that our understandings of difference affect the way we perceive and respond to each other. This is the case whether we are considering Sam and Amanda's experiences of gender, Rhonda's of disability or Kenny's of sexual identity, or formal policies such as austerity and the fall-out of Brexit. It is very clear that when hearing about these aspects of a person's experience, we are not facing some kind of value-neutral, random landscape. As Naomi Klein (2015) has so clearly illustrated, differences and political policies are utilised for a purpose, constructed in ways that mean that choices have to be made by individuals, groups, corporations and societies as to how to respond. These choices are often influenced most strongly by those with power and those who have investment in these processes, often those who gain from the status quo. Susie Orbach's work famously identifies the billion-dollar profits that diet companies reap from feeding our bodily insecurities (2009); Clive Hamilton (2004) has shown us the problems of capitalism on psychological well-being across the globe; and Oliver James (2007) offers accessible accounts of the ways in which individuals are hoodwinked for the benefit of corporate profit. The novelist Matt Haig illustrates the link between policy and psychological distress particularly well in his wonderful book *Reasons to Live*:

> The world is increasingly designed to depress us. Happiness isn't very good for the economy. If we were happy with what we had, why would we need more? How do you sell an anti-ageing moisturiser? You make someone worry about ageing. How do you get people to vote for a political party? You make them worry about immigration. How do you get them to buy insurance? By making them worry about everything. How do you get them to have plastic surgery? By highlighting their physical flaws. How do you get them to watch a TV show? By making them worry about missing out. How do you get them to buy a new smartphone? By making them feel they are being left behind.
>
> To be calm is a revolutionary act. To be happy with your own non-upgraded existence. To be comfortable with our messy, human selves, would not be good for business. (Haig, 2015, p. 189).

Of course, we should be wary of emphasising too much the views of individual authors, particularly those who may also have commercial interests in making these points; I recognise that it does no harm to Haig's, Hamilton's, James' and Orbach's sales to be known as critical of these interests. But, as their readers will know, theirs goes beyond mere assertion; they substantiate their arguments exquisitely. These in turn are supported by larger-scale studies that confirm the relationship between individual well-being and social equality/inequality; it is very clear that the greater the level of inequality that exists in a society, the greater the rates of psychological distress, poverty, violence, teenage pregnancy, physical health problems and obesity (Wilkinson and Pickett, 2010). Thus if you are on the wrong end of the experience of difference there is an increased risk of, at best, hurdles to being able to thrive, and at worst, overt damage and distress, oftentimes lasting generations.

So whether thinking about the fictional stories in this collection, the challenges posed by individual authors or the accumulation of studies across disciplines, therapists have to recognise that in order for us to understand psychological distress and interpersonal problems, we have to factor in the socio-political aspects of difference – to do otherwise would be negligent.

Practice as politics

Pearce has recently suggested that 'a political act can be interpreted as any deliberate action that impacts, even in an imperceptible way, on the social context that is itself the sum of human relationships' (2017, p. 30) and this brings politics into the realm of the therapeutic.

Assessment and formulation

Psychologists foreground formulation over diagnosis (Johnstone and Dallos, 2013), and this can be seen as a political statement in itself (Strawbridge, 2010). To eschew diagnosis is to move beyond pre-packaged, reductionistic visions of difficulty and to prioritise more complex and humane accounts of distress, creating understandings rather than labels, stories rather than a status (Corrie and Lane, 2010). This may not be easy though as the political, pharmaceutical and corporate establishments are invested in this view as, alongside the struggles it creates for client and practitioners, it also offers financial windfalls and political control.

Formulation requires us to respond to people's actual experiences, to become more attuned to the person *in* their context. Formulation is a complex and nuanced project, helping us to respond to distress and context in a 'both/and' manner rather than a binary 'either/or' style of thinking. While formulation can appropriately focus on the distress experienced between an individual and their caregivers or in their family or workplace, it is also a process that can incorporate reflection upon a person's position in wider society, so as to understand oppression or opportunity, powerlessness or privilege and the relationships between them.

As well as *thinking* about the person in context, we may also have to *speak* about it. For some clients, a recognition of, and engagement with, socio-political factors will be *crucial* to their ability to reorient and recover. The job of the therapist is to become adept at spotting situational stressors and also to develop sensitive ways to engage with what makes sense to the client. This has been accepted in theory (see Samuels, 1993; Strawbridge, 2006; Szasz, 1960 among others), but many people still wonder 'what does a wider, more contextually attuned formulation mean for intervention, for therapy?' This is, in effect, what was offered in this book, a chance to rethink understandings and explore the ways these insights might be engaged with in therapy, either through reflection, interpretation or even in innovative changes to practice. It might mean advocating for your client as Rhonda needed, or changing the frame and manner of working as was possible with Monique. These all offer a chance to consider the socio-political aspects of difference that can otherwise be so difficult to speak about.

Choosing a focus

While therapists will benefit from considering the wider context, difference and forms of discrimination, that doesn't mean that they will necessarily have to, or be able to, comment on those issues in any particular therapeutic encounter. That decision is a separate one based upon what is going to be of assistance to *this* client at *this* point in time. As the stories of Taye, Amanda and Jacinta (and others) demonstrate, clients often bring too many issues for each one of them to be addressed individually – for example, with Taye, some attention to his lack of financial resources may also have been a useful focus, but this was not as meaningful to him as was an understanding of the racial tensions he was having to navigate. Likewise, with Jacinta, it may have been helpful to reflect on the sexism and misogyny that abounded after the referendum but xenophobia was more pressing. Or I could have noted the ways in which class and its influence on gender were complicit in making it hard for Amanda to think about and speak to her father's abuse and inappropriate behaviour. These may have helped clarify experiences but they were not the *most* pressing contextual factors in those sessions.

It may be that rather than think about single issues, or a number of separate issues, therapists have to, or at least might, think about the fullest understanding of a client's distress, consider *plural* and *intersectional* formulations and then join their clients in choosing where best to focus their considerations. This may mean that, in some instances, aspects of difference are *seldom* discussed. Therapists may find that they *never* comment on the way in which capitalism constructs men and women as oppositional with one client, but they *might* with another; they may *never* comment on how the food corporations benefit from the obesity epidemic and the disordered relationship we have to our bodies, but with some clients it may a *crucial* point to consider. However, we therapists need to be *able* to consistently utilise this lens for it to be available whenever it is needed.

Going beyond the silo: A call to action

The impact of therapeutic work radiates well beyond the therapeutic dyad and the process of therapy itself. Therapists contribute to wider events through personal and professional efforts, so it is important that we periodically remind ourselves that we are not apolitical, we are not without power, nor without influence in the creation and/or challenge of experience. Indeed, Segal noted that:

> psychoanalysts have a specific contribution to make. We are acquainted with the psychic mechanisms of denial, projection, magical thinking. We should be able to contribute something to overcome apathy and self-deception in ourselves and others. When the Nazi phenomenon was staring us in the face, the psychoanalytic community outside Germany was largely silent. This must not be repeated. Mandelstam said, 'Silence is the real crime against humanity'. We psychoanalysts who believe in the power of words and the therapeutic effects of verbalizing truth must not be silent. (Segal, cited in Rust, 2005, p. 3)

This is true for all therapists, wherever located on the therapeutic spectrum. So what contribution can be made outside of the consulting room?

There are a variety of different examples that can be useful, and here are just a few possibilities that include statements by professional bodies, letters to the press and public engagement.

Examples of statements by professional bodies:

The British Psychological Society (BPS), United Kingdom Council for Psychotherapy (UKCP), British Association for Counselling & Psychotherapy (BACP) and other organisations signed a memorandum of understanding confirming that 'conversion therapies' are dangerous and not to be condoned (UKCP et al., 2015). The BPS commitment to this has recently been reiterated (see BPS, 2017a).

The BPS has called for an end-to-end redesign of the Work Capability Assessment (WCA) process – including processes, its outcomes and the periods for reassessment (2016). They have also made a statement about their extreme concern over government plans to stop the transfer of unaccompanied minors to UK (BPS, 2017b).

Psychotherapists and Counsellors for Social Responsibility (PCSR) and the Psychotherapy and Counselling Union (PCU) have recently made a statement about the political situation in the USA (2016).

Examples of letters to the press include:

Four hundred and forty-two therapists and academics signed a letter to *The Guardian* noting the disastrous psychological impact of austerity on mental health that includes increased rates of depression, anxiety and suicidality (House et al., 2015).

Psychologists were included in a letter written to *The Guardian* regarding the damaging impact that political and economic policy is having on the productivity and well-being of those in UK universities (Lesnick-Oberstein et al., 2015).

Examples of public engagement include:

Trainee counselling psychologist's utilising coursework to inform petitioning of the government in respect of weight-based stigma and body image and the offering of public workshops (Ord, 2016, 2017).

Psychologists for Social Change (previously known as Psychologists Against Austerity) have researched and disseminated their findings as to the psychological impact of austerity and other political factors (PAA, undated; PSC, 2017).

Psychologists and psychotherapists have also contributed to public debate by way of newspaper articles on gender and eating problems (Orbach, 2015), Brexit and the referendum (Orbach, 2016; Watts, 2016a), and politics and anxiety (Watts, 2016b).

As a speaker at the 2017 'March for Europe' in London, Emmy van Deurzen has brought a psychological and psychotherapeutic contribution to the political debate about Brexit.

There are, of course, many other examples of psychological and therapeutic contributions being made, and further opportunities available to help tackle harmful and distressing inequality. One of which, and one that I suggest psychologists, psychotherapists and counsellors are eminently qualified to advance on a daily basis, is to challenge the foundational vision of individual psychology being the root cause of most psychological distress. Instead, we need to be vocal with regard to our awareness that society is a key factor in the *creation* of distress, individually and socially. We have the evidence and we are familiar with the results of distressing economic and social policies. We can, for instance, speak to the harmful psychological effects of austerity, effects such as humiliation and shame, fear and mistrust, isolation and loneliness among others (see PAA, undated). We can also offer testimony to the impact of the prevalence and rise of hate-filled narratives; we can vouch for the fact that stigma and oppression, the effects of inequality, conflict and trauma are all factors underpinning anxiety, depression, self-harm, suicide, drug and alcohol use and so much more.

We also need urgently to enrich our understandings and communicate the psychological factors behind wanton environmental plundering that is on the rise, because as well as our physical survival comes the need to tackle social inequality, the uprooting of people and cultures, and war (Klein, 2015). There is work with individuals, communities and at the global scale that confirms social and political factors are central to much distress and inequality.

An associated focus is the hegemony of the medical model of psychological well-being that dominates health and political discourse and this warrants urgent reflection and debate. We see a continued reliance on diagnosis when it is clear that this is not a scientific or evidence-based approach to understanding distress (see Murray, 2016); society overlooks the damage done to many people by having little choice but to accept diagnoses if they want to access professional support; the reliance on powerful chemical treatments locate the problem at the level of the gene rather than recognising the relational and socio-political origins of much psychological distress. It is also a part of the construction of problematic identities and ways of being, as well as having a role in the limiting of practice, reducing it to manualised, impersonal and authoritarian types of intervention. We need also to consider how we show that a different understanding of the causes of mass distress needs urgently to be shared, discussed and acted upon. This biological vision of distress needs continued critique and challenge from psychologists and psychotherapists.

Training issues

Another domain in which therapists can engage with difference and the impact of context is through their professional training programmes. These can help or hinder the development of competences required for working with diversity and influencing services. When we consider this area, there are different foci to consider including *what* should be learnt and *how* trainees and qualified practitioners should approach their learning.

So, first, what should be learnt? As we saw in Chapter 2, it is possible to take an 'additive' approach to the curriculum, and if they do that trainings have to decide how much of course time should be allocated to issues of 'difference' and then which of the 'differences' need to be taught? There is considerable competition for workshops/seminars to kick-start trainees' reflections on working with race, gender, sexuality, disability and other platforms of disadvantage.

Courses have long struggled with the limits of such an approach – the list of worthy 'differences' is long and extends well beyond the time available on most courses. It also leads to explicit and implicit hierarchies of difference (those important enough to teach and those we wish we had time for). The assumption of 'difference' is itself also problematic, maintaining as it does an assumption of 'the norm'. Once this is accepted, we risk overlooking the problems in conceptualising experience and failing to challenge the status quo.

More recently alternative approaches to teaching have been adopted. While it is still common to see sessions on issues related to the psychological and health needs of specific 'minority' groups, we also see reference to diverse experiences being embedded in different types of teaching – research methods courses use examples from diverse populations, theory modules reflect on the speaking positions of different approaches and practice modules reflect on clients from diverse backgrounds. The diversity and interaction of the cohort itself can also be a valuable learning experience to this end.

This brings us to the question of *how* therapists learn? While a traditional 'objective' approach to teaching such as the traditional 'chalk and talk' approach allows trainees to gain intellectual knowledge, learning to work with diverse populations requires therapists to go beyond this; they also need to reflect on their own positioning. So it is helpful when programmes help trainees adopt a reflexive approach to 'being with' clients, fostering curiosity about the myriad ways in which our social positions affect our way of being-in-the-world-with-others.

As well as asking trainees to consider their conscious values and biases, we can also, for example, ask trainees to reflect on how their gender impacts on the demonstration of respect between themselves and their clients? What happens if the therapist only has one language to communicate in and what occurs when this is different to the client's first language? Does race impact on what can truly be understood about the client's experience? How do white therapists grasp the everyday nature of racism? And how do cisgender therapists really grasp the intricacies of constant policing and promoting of binary versions of gender? As Clark and Loewenthal (2015) point out, even the best intentioned among us can still, through ignorance or social positioning, be a vector for Othering.

As well as looking at differences embodied in our clients and ourselves, therapists can help us understand the ways in which privilege and power are embedded in service structure and frames of therapy. It is important to remember, for example, that for a long period of time our models and approaches to practice were heterosexist, making gender and sexually diverse clients rightfully wary of seeking help from services. Why would gender and sexually diverse clients come to a service when it is known that attempts might be made to change orientation rather than offer help in becoming resilient to the tsunami of oppression and discrimination faced?

Alternatively, and more recently, therapists are hearing first-hand accounts of how access to services for migrants is affected when there are discussions of health service personnel vetting a client's right to NHS treatment? The task of engaging psychologically is very different to checking out a person's visa status – such a practice can ruin the possibility of therapeutic efficacy. The political approach to difference has very personal implications and it is important that trainees explore this thoroughly in their training and therapists in their CPD.

The importance of (self) care

While it is clear that there is a call to action, and a *requirement* to challenge inequality and discrimination (see Division of Counselling Psychology, 2008), it is also important to note that a more socio-political approach to the work may, like all other approaches, take effort and extract a toll. This is partly because that's simply what work does; meaningful work usually requires effort (Rafalin, 2010). But equally, it is important to note the specific demands that psychological work places on people because it is personal, it is emotional and it is led by our most cherished of values.

While offering significant advantages and being a powerful way to attune to a wider range of people and contexts, reflecting on our own 'Otherness' can be difficult and can lead to discomfort and distress. Training as, and being, a therapist requires us to *hear* and *see* our own sexism, racism, ableism and other biases; it requires us to *stomach* these biases and to understand our culpability in the traumas we are trying to understand and alleviate. Our society seldom asks the 'majority' to consider their position critically, therefore training might be the first time 'race' or 'sexuality' comes under the spotlight for white or heterosexual trainees; when it does we might feel uncomfortable at how poorly we spot everyday discrimination; we may be appalled about the depth and reach of our privilege. Such awakenings can lead to feelings of shame or the realisation of just how wedded we are to unpleasant biases.

Therapists – both novice and experienced – can recognise both the value and the potential discomfort of such an exploration and need to create opportunities for non-defensive self-care. Trainees benefit when they see that the effort is worthwhile; without such an ethical engagement trainees and qualified therapists alike risk not understanding the issues involved; they risk losing out on their learning and most importantly, of not being able to offer the fullest and most attuned care that all clients need – but especially those who suffer oppression and discrimination.

And finally ...

I hope that readers have found something useful in these tales of difference and that they feel moved, enthused or outraged enough to pick up the challenge that lies before us all. I hope that readers will move forward with their own explorations of the ways in which their practice and our professions can enhance chances for our clients and for our wider communities, whether that be by way of enhanced formulations, more useful practice or ideas about how we might critique, challenge and contribute to an evolution of society in order to break down some of the barbarism experienced and to build bridges rather than walls.

REFERENCES

Adams, M. V. (1997). Jung and racism. *Self and Society, 25*(1), 19–23.

Allport, G. W., & Kramer, B. M. (1946). Some roots of prejudice. *The Journal of Psychology, 22*(1), 9–39.

Antjoule, N. (2016). *The hate crime report 2016: Homophobia, biphobia and transphobia in the UK*. London: Galop.

Antonakakis, N., & Collins, A. (2014). The impact of fiscal austerity on suicide: On the empirics of a modern Greek tragedy. *Social Science and Medicine, 112*, 39–50.

Atnas, C., Milton, M., & Archer, S. (2015). Making the decision to change: Experiences of trans men. *Counselling Psychology Review, 30*(1), 33–42.

Atnas, C., Milton, M., & Archer, S. (2016). The transitioning process: The transitioning experiences of trans men, *Psychology of Sexualities Review, 6*(1), 5–17.

Bagley, C., & Tremblay, P. (2000). Elevated rates of suicidal behaviour in gay, lesbian, and bisexual youth. *Crisis: The Journal of Crisis Intervention and Suicide Prevention, 21*(3), 111.

Barker, M. (2005). This is my partner, and this is my…partner's partner: Constructing a polyamorous identity in a monogamous world. *Journal of Constructivist Psychology, 18*(1), 75–88.

Barker, M. (2014). Open non-monogamies: Drawing on de Beauvoir and Sartre to inform existential work with romantic relationships, in M. Milton (Ed.), *sexuality: Existential perspectives*, Ross-on-Wye: PCCS Books.

Bidell, M. P. (2005). The sexual orientation counselor competency scale: Assessing attitudes, skills, and knowledge of counselors working with lesbian, gay, and bisexual clients. *Counselor Education and Supervision, 44*(4), 267–279.

Blumstein, A. (1982). On the racial disproportionality of United States' prison populations, *The Journal of Criminal Law and Criminology, 73*(3), 1259–1281.

Bor, R., Legg, C., & Scher, I. (1996). The systems paradigm, in R. Woolfe & W. Dryden (Eds.), *Handbook of counselling psychology*, London: Sage.

Borland, S., Spencer, B., & Robinson, M. (2016). NHS fights back against ruling forcing it to hand out 'promiscuity pill' that prevents HIV as the £20m cost will hit its ability to treat cancer and give limbs to amputees, *Mail Online*, 2 August, downloaded from http://www.dailymail.co.uk/news/article-3720706/What-skewed-sense-values-NHS-told-5-000-year-lifestyle-drug-prevent-HIV-vital-cataract-surgery-rationed.html, Downloaded on 6/12/16.

Brantley, T. (1983). Racism and its impact on psychotherapy, *The American Journal of Psychiatry, 140*(12), 1605–1608.

Breggin, P. R. (1975). Psychiatry and psychotherapy as political processes. *American Journal of Psychotherapy, 29*(3), 369–382.

REFERENCES

British Association for Counselling and Psychotherapy (2012). *Ethical framework for good practice in counselling and psychotherapy*, Lutterworth: British Association for Counselling and Psychotherapy.

British Lung Foundation (2017). COPD (Chronic obstructive pulmonary disease), downloaded from https://www.blf.org.uk/support-for-you/copd, Downloaded on 06/01/2017.

British Psychological Society (2008). *Generic professional practice guidelines*, Leicester: British Psychological Society.

British Psychological Society Psychology of Sexualities Section (undated). *History of the psychology of sexualities*, downloaded from http://www.bps.org.uk/networks-and-communities/member-microsite/psychology-sexualities-section/history-psychology-sexualities, Downloaded on 06/12/2016.

British Psychological Society (2009). *Code of ethics and conduct*, Leicester: British Psychological Society.

British Psychological Society (2015). *BPS response to announcement of Government review of sickness benefit system*, downloaded from http://www.bps.org.uk/news/bps-response-announcement-government-review-sickness-benefit-system, Downloaded on 06/08/2015.

British Psychological Society (2016). *British Psychological Society signs statement opposing welfare sanctions*, downloaded from http://beta.bps.org.uk/news-and-policy/british-psychological-society-signs-statement-opposing-welfare-sanctions, Downloaded on 10/02/17.

British Psychological Society (2017a). UK organisations unite against Conversion Therapy, downloaded from http://beta.bps.org.uk/news-and-policy/uk-organisations-unite-against-conversion-therapy, Downloaded on 8/2/17.

British Psychological Society (2017b). BPS extremely concerned over Government plans to stop transfer of unaccompanied minors to UK, downloaded from http://beta.bps.org.uk/news-and-policy/bps-extremely-concerned-over-government-plans-stop-transfer-unaccompanied-minors-uk, Downloaded on 13/02/17.

Butler, P. (2015). Thousands have died after being found fit for work, DWP figures show, *The Guardian*, 27 August, downloaded from https://www.theguardian.com/society/2015/aug/27/thousands-died-after-fit-for-work-assessment-dwp-figures, Downloaded on 13/01/2017.

Butler, P. (2016). Politicians fuelled rise in hate crimes after Brexit vote, says UN Body', *The Guardian*, 26 August, downloaded from http://www.theguardian.com/politics/2016/aug/26/politicians-rise-hate-crimes-brexit-vote-un-committee, Downloaded on 27/09/2016.

Carter, J. (2015). *Why I believe the mistreatment of women is the number one human rights abuse*, TedTalk (Posted June 2015).

Casement, P. (1992). *Learning from the patient*, New York: Guilford Press.

Casement, P. (2002). *Learning from our mistakes: Beyond dogma in psychoanalysis and psychotherapy*, London: Guilford Press.

Cassoni, E. (2007). Parallel process in supervision and therapy: An opportunity for reciprocity. *Transactional Analysis Journal, 37*(2), 130–139.

Cecchin, G., Lane, G., & Ray, W. A. (1992). *Irreverence; A strategy for therapists' survival*, London: Karnac Books.

Clark, D., & Loewenthal, D. (2015). Counselling psychology, in C. Richards & M. J. Barker (Eds.), *The Palgrave handbook of the psychology of sexuality and gender*, Basingstoke: Palgrave Macmillan.

Clarkson, P. (1995). *The therapeutic relationship in psychoanalysis, counselling psychology and psychotherapy*, London: Whurr.

Clarkson, P. (1998). Beyond schoolism. *Changes*, *16*, 1–11.

Clarkson, P. (2013). *Transactional analysis psychotherapy: An integrated approach*, London: Routledge.

Cohn, H. W. (1989). The place of the actual in psychotherapy. *Free Associations*, *1*(18), 49–61.

Cooke, A. (2014). *Understanding psychosis and schizophrenia: Why people sometimes hear voices, believe things that other find strange, or appear out of touch with reality, and what can help*, Leicester: BPS Division of Clinical Psychology.

Cooper, B. (2011). Economic recession and mental health: An overview. *Neuropsychiatr*, *25*(3), 113–117.

Corrie, S., & Lane, D. (Eds.) (2010). *Constructing stories, telling tales: A guide to formulation in applied psychology*, London: Karnac Books.

Coyle, A., & Lochner, J. (2011). Religion, spirituality and therapeutic practice. *The Psychologist*, *24*(4), 264–266.

Dallos, R. & Draper, R. (2015). *An introduction to family therapy: Systemic theory and practice* (4th edn), Maidenhead: Open University Press.

das Nair, R., & Thomas, S. (2012). Race and ethnicity, in R. das Nair & C. Butler (Eds.), *Intersectionality, sexuality and psychological therapies: Working with lesbian, gay and bisexual diversity*, Chichester: BPS Blackwell.

das Nair, R., & Butler, C. (Eds.) (2012). *Intersectionality, sexuality and psychological therapies: Working with lesbian, gay and bisexual diversity*, Basingstoke: John Wiley & Sons.

Davies, D., & Neal, C. (2000). *Therapeutic perspectives on working with lesbian, gay and bisexual clients*, Milton Keynes: Open University Press.

Denman, C., & de Vries, P. (1998). Cognitive analytic therapy and homosexual orientation, in C. Shelley (Ed.), *Contemporary perspectives on psychotherapy and homosexualities*, London: Free Association Books.

Devine-Wright, P. (2009). Rethinking NIMBYism: The role of place attachment and place identity in explaining place-protective action. *Journal of Community & Applied Social Psychology*, *19*(6), 426–441.

Diaz, R. M., Ayala, G., Bein, E., Henne, J., & Marin, B. V. (2001). The impact of homophobia, poverty, and racism on the mental health of gay and bisexual Latino men: Findings from 3 US cities. *American Journal of Public Health*, *91*(6), 927.

Division of Counselling Psychology (2008). *Professional practice guidelines*, Leicester: British Psychological Society.

Douglas, B. (2010). Disorder and its discontents, in R. Woolfe, S. Strawbridge, B. Douglas & W. Dryden (Eds.), *Handbook of counselling psychology* (3rd edn), London: Sage.

Duffell, N. (2000). *The making of them: The British attitude to children and the boarding school system*, London: Lone Arrow Press.

Duffell, N. (2012). Boarding school syndrome. *British Journal of Psychotherapy*, *28*(3), 389–389.

REFERENCES

du Plock, S. (2014). Gay affirmative therapy: A critique and some reflections on the value of an existential-phenomenological theory of sexual identity, in M. Milton (Ed.), *Sexuality: Existential perspectives*, Monmouth: PCCS Books.
Eleftheriadou, Z. (2003). Cross-cultural counselling, in R. Woolfe, W. Dryden & S. Strawbridge (Eds.), *Handbook of counselling psychology* (2nd edn), London: Sage.
Ellis, M. L. (1997). Who speaks? Who listens? Different voices and different sexualities, *British Journal of Psychotherapy, 13*(3), 369–383.
Ellis, S. (2012). Gender, in R. das Nair, & C. Butler (Eds.), *Intersectionality, sexuality and psychological therapies: Working with lesbian, gay and bisexual diversity*, Basingstoke: John Wiley & Sons.
Fanon, F. (1986). *Black skins, white masks* (Trans. C. L. Markmann), London: Pluto Press.
Fletcher, R. (2012). Introduction: Dealing with diagnoses, in M. Milton (Ed.), *Diagnosis and beyond: Counselling psychology contributions to understanding human distress*, Ross-on-Wye: PCCS Books.
Fountoulakis, K. N., Gonda, X., Dome, P., Theodorakis, P. N., & Rihmer, Z. (2014). Possible delayed effect of unemployment on suicidal rates: The case of Hungary. *Annals of General Psychiatry, 13*(1), 12.
Gibson, S., & Hansen, S. (2012). Age and ageing, in R. das Nair & C. Butler (Eds.), *Intersectionality, sexuality and psychological therapies: Working with lesbian, gay and bisexual diversity*, Chichester: BPS Blackwell.
Goodman, L. A., Liang, B., Helms, J. E., Latta, R. E., Sparks, E., & Weintraub, S. R. (2004). Training counseling psychologists as social justice agents feminist and multicultural principles in action. *The Counseling Psychologist, 32*(6), 793–836.
Griffiths, J. (2006). *Wild: An elemental journey*, London: Penguin.
Haig, M. (2015). *Reasons to live*, London: Cannongate.
Hamilton, C. (2004). *Growth fetish*, London: Pluto Press.
Hanisch, C. (1970). The personal is political, in S. Firestone & A. Koedt (Eds.), *Notes from the second year: Women's liberation*, New York: Radical Feminism.
Hannay, D. R. (1980). Religion and health, *Social Science & Medicine. Part A: Medical Psychology & Medical Sociology, 14*(6), 683–685.
Hatzenbuehler, M. L. (2009). How does sexual minority stigma "get under the skin"? A psychological mediation framework. *Psychological Bulletin, 135*(5), 707.
Health and Care Professions Council (2015). *Standards of proficiency: Practitioner psychologists*, London: HCPC.
Heidegger, M. (2014). *Introduction to metaphysics*, New Haven, CT: Yale University Press.
Hemingway, S., Coxon, G., Munday, D., & Ramsay, M. (2013). Austerity is bad for mental health: Implications for mental health nurses. *Mental Health Nursing (Online), 33*(6), 7.
Hepple, B. (2014). *Equality: The legal framework*, Oxford: Bloomsbury Publishing.
Hepple, B., Coussey, M., & Choudhary, T. (2000). *Equality: A new framework*, Oxford: Hart Publishing.
Hodges, N. (2013). Counselling, autism and the problem of empathy, *British Journal of Guidance and Counselling, 41*(2), 105–116. Downloaded from http://dx.doi.org/10.1080/03069885.2012.705817, Downloaded on 28/08/2017.
Høglend, P. (2004). Analysis of transference in psychodynamic psychotherapy: A review of empirical research. *Canadian Journal of Psychoanalysis, 12*(2), 279.

REFERENCES

Hopcke, R. (1989). *Jung, Jungians and homosexuality*, Boston: Shambhala.

Horn, N., Johnstone, L., & Brooke, S. (2007). Some service user perspectives on the diagnosis of borderline personality disorder. *Journal of Mental Health*, 16(2), 255–269.

House et al. (2015). Austerity and a malign benefits regime are profoundly damaging mental health, *The Guardian*, 17 April, downloaded from https://www.theguardian.com/society/2015/apr/17/austerity-and-a-malign-benefits-regime-are-profoundly-damaging-mental-health, Downloaded on 10/02/2017.

Hurrell, K. (2013). *Race disproportionality in Stops and Searches, 2011–12 Equality and Human Rights Commission briefing paper 7*, Equality and Human Rights Commission, Manchester.

Inman, P. (2016). Happiness depends on health and friends, not money, says new study, *The Guardian*, 12 December, downloaded from https://www.theguardian.com/society/2016/dec/12/happiness-depends-on-health-and-friends-not-money-says-new-study, Downloaded on 06/02/2017.

Jackson, J., & Coyle, A. (2009). The ethical challenge of working with spiritual difference: An interpretative phenomenological analysis of practitioners' accounts. *Counselling Psychology Review*, 24(3&4), 86–99.

James, O. (2007). *Affluenza: How to be successful and stay sane*, London: Vermillion.

Jaspers, K. (1963). *General psychopathology*, Chicago: University of Chicago Press.

Johnstone, L. (2000). *Users and abusers of psychiatry: A critical look at psychiatric practice*, Hove: Psychology Press.

Johnstone, L. (2006). Controversies and debates about formulation, in L. Johnstone & R. Dallos (Eds.), *Formulation in psychology and psychotherapy: Making sense of people's problems* (pp. 208–231), London: Taylor & Francis.

Johnstone, L. (2014). *A straight talking introduction to psychiatric diagnosis*, Ross-on-Wye: PCCS Books.

Johnstone, L., & Dallos, R. (2013). *Formulation in psychology and psychotherapy: Making sense of people's problems*, London: Routledge.

Jones, O. (2015). Stonewall is right to bring our trans brothers and sisters in from the cold, *The Guardian*, 18 February, downloaded from http://www.theguardian.com/commentisfree/2015/feb/18/stonewall-trans-issues-neglected-progressives, Downloaded on 09/05/2016.

Jones, R. (2013). Counselling psychology and people with learning disabilities: Some reflections, *Counselling Psychology Review*, 28(1). 47–52.

Jordan, M. (2015). *Nature and therapy*, London: Routledge.

Jordan-Zachery, J. S. (2007). Am I a black woman or a woman who is black? A few thoughts on the meaning of intersectionality, *Politics and Gender*, 3(2), 254- 263, DOI: 10.1017/S1743923X07000074.

Kawachi, I., Daniels, N., & Robinson, D. E. (2005). Health disparities by race and class: Why both matter, *Health Affairs*, downloaded from http://content.healthaffairs.org/content/24/02/343.full, Downloaded on 11/05/2016.

Kinderman, P. (2014). *A prescription for psychiatry: Why we need a whole new approach to mental health and wellbeing*, Basingstoke: Palgrave Macmillan.

King., Semlyen, J., Tai, S. S., Killasoy, H., Osborn, D. Popelyuk, D., & Nazareth, I. (2008). A systematic review of mental disorder, suicide and deliberate self-harm in lesbian, gay and bisexual people. *BMC Psychiatry*. DOI: 10.1186/1471-244X-8-70.

161

Kitzinger, C. (1999). Intersexuality: Deconstructing the sex/gender binary, *Feminism and Psychology, 9*, 493–498. DOI: 10.1177/0959353599009004016.

Kitzinger, C., & Coyle, A. (1995). Lesbian and gay couples: Speaking of difference, *The Psychologist, 8*, 64–69.

Klein, N. (2015). *This changes everything: Capitalism vs. the climate*, New York, Simon and Schuster.

Laing, R. D. (1961). *Self and others*, London: Tavistock Publications.

Laing, R. D. (1971). *The politics of the family, and other essays* (Vol. 5), Hove: Psychology Press.

Laing, R. D. (1990). *The divided self: An existential study in sanity and madness*, London: Penguin.

Langdridge, D. (2014). Gay affirmative psychotherapy: Recognising the power of the social world, in M. Milton (Ed.), *Sexuality: Existential perspectives*, Monmouth: PCCS Books.

Langs, R. J. (1989). *The technique of psychoanalytic psychotherapy: Theoretical framework: Understanding the patients communications* (Vol. 1), Lanham, MD: Jason Aronson.

Langs, R. (2004). Death anxiety and the emotion-processing mind. *Psychoanalytic Psychology, 21*(1), 31.

LaVeist, T. A. (2005). Disentangling race and socioeconomic status: A key to understanding health inequalities. *Journal of Urban Health, 82*(3), iii26–iii34.

Lesnick-Oberstein, K. et al. (2015). Let universities do what they do best: Teaching and research, *The Guardian*, 6 July, downloaded from http://www.theguardian.com/education/2015/jul/06/let-uk-universities-do-what-they-do-best-teaching-and-research, Downloaded on 08/05/2017.

Lockwood, G., Henderson, C., & Thornicroft, G. (2012). The Equality Act 2010 and mental health. *The British Journal of Psychiatry, 200*(3), 182–183.

Lofthouse, J. (2010). The 'R' word, in M. Milton (Ed.), *Therapy and beyond: Counselling psychology contributions to therapeutic and social issues,* Chichester: Wiley-Blackwell.

Louv, R. (2006). *Last child in the woods: Saving our children from nature-deficit disorder*, Chapel Hill, NC: Algonquin Books.

Ludwig, J., Ladd, H. F., Duncan, G. J., Kling, J., & O'Regan, K. M. (2001). Urban poverty and educational outcomes [with comments]. *Brookings-Wharton papers on urban affairs*, pp. 147–201.

Macfarlane, R. (2007). *The wild places*, London: Penguin.

Malley, M., & Tasker, F. (1999). Lesbians, gay men and family therapy: A contradiction in terms? *Journal of Family Therapy, 21*, 3–29.

McClelland, A. (2000). Effects of Unemployment on the Family, *The Economic and Labour Relations Review, 11*(2), 198–212.

McGeorge, C., & Stone Carlson, T. (2011). Deconstructing heterosexism: Becoming an LGB affirmative heterosexual couple and family therapist. *Journal of Marital and Family Therapy, 37*(1), 14–26.

McLeod, J. (2003). The humanistic paradigm, in R. Woolfe, W. Dryden & S. Strawbridge (Eds.), *Handbook of counselling psychology* (2nd edn, pp. 140–160), London: Sage.

McNamee, S., & Gergen, K. (Eds.) (2006). *Therapy as social construction*, London: Sage.

Merleau-Ponty, M. (1996). *The phenomenology of perception* (Trans. by C. Smith), London: Routledge and Kegan Paul.

Milton, M. (2005). Political and ideological issues, in E. van Deurzen & C. Arnold-Baker (Eds.), *Existential perspectives on human issues: A handbook for therapeutic practice*, Basingstoke: Palgrave Macmillan.

Milton, M. (Ed.) (2014). *Sexuality: Existential perspectives*, Monmouth: PCCS Books.

Milton, M. (2016). Forming a relationship: A phenomenological encounter, in B. Douglas, V. Galbraith, E. Kasket, B. Douglas & R. Woolfe (Eds.), *Handbook of counselling psychology* (4th edn), London: Sage.

Milton, M., Craven, M., & Coyle, A. (2010). Understanding human distress: Moving beyond the concept of psychopathology, in M. Milton. (Ed.), *Therapy and beyond: Counselling psychology contributions to therapeutic and social issues*, Chichester: Wiley-Blackwell.

Moon, L. (2011). The gentle violence of therapists: Misrecognition and dislocation of the other. *Psychotherapy and Politics International, 9*(3), 194–205.

Moore, D., & McAweeney, M. (2006). Demographic characteristics and rates of progress of deaf and hard of hearing persons receiving substance abuse treatment. *American Annals of the Deaf, 151*(5), 508–512.

Morgan, P. (2010). Towards a developmental theory of place attachment. *Journal of Environmental Psychology, 30*(1), 11–22.

Murray, R. M. (2016). Mistakes I have made in my research career. *Schizophr Bull* (2016 sbw165). DOI: 10.1093/schbul/sbw165.

NHS England, et al. (2015). *Memo of understanding on conversion therapy in the UK*, London: NHS England.

NICE (2010). *Update: Guidance on the use of electroconvulsive therapy*, London: National Institute of Clinical Excellence.

Norcross, J. C. (Ed.) (2011). *Psychotherapy relationships that work: Evidence-based responsiveness*, Oxford: Oxford University Press.

Norcross, J. C., & Wampold, B. E. (2011). Evidence-based therapy relationships: Research conclusions and clinical practices. *Psychotherapy, 48*(1), 98.

O'Connor, N., & Ryan, J. (1993). *Wild desires and mistaken identities: Lesbianism and psychoanalysis*, London: Virago Press.

Office of National Statistics (2011). *2011 Census: KS201 UK Ethnic group, local authorities in the United Kingdom*, ONS.

Office for National Statistics and Ministry of Justice (2013). *An overview of hate crime in England and Wales*, London: The Home Office.

Orbach, S. (2009). *Bodies*, London: Profile Books.

Orbach, S. (2015). Obesity isn't the half of it: Fat or thin, our eating is disordered, *The Guardian*, 14 December, downloaded from https://www.theguardian.com/commentisfree/2015/dec/14/obesity-chief-medical-officer-war-on-fat-troubled-eating, Downloaded on 15/03/17.

Orbach, S. (2016). In therapy, everyone wants to talk about Brexit, *The Guardian*, 1 July, downloaded from https://www.theguardian.com/global/2016/jul/01/susie-orbach-in-therapy-everyone-wants-to-talk-about-brexit, Downloaded on 15/03/17.

REFERENCES

Ord, C. (2016). *Put an end to discrimination, bias and stigma based on a person's bodyweight and size*, Online petition downloaded from https://www.change.org/p/the-equality-and-human-rights-commission-include-weight-as-a-protected-characteristic-under-the-uk-equality-act-2010?source_location=minibar, Downloaded on 15/02/17.

Ord, C. (2017). *Live more, diet less*, downloaded from https://www.eventbrite.co.uk/e/live-more-diet-less-how-to-reshape-your-body-and-your-life-using-acceptance-and-commitment-therapy-tickets-30457292582, Downloaded on 17/02/2017.

PAA (Psychologists Against Austerity). (undated). *The psychological impact of austerity: A briefing paper*, downloaded from https://psychagainstausterity.files.wordpress.com/2015/03/paa-briefing-paper.pdf, Downloaded on 15/03/17.

Pearce, R. (2017). Towards a radical psychotherapy, *Existential Analysis, 28*(1), 20–33.

Petersen, A. (2006). An African-American woman with disabilities: The intersection of gender, race and disability. *Disability & Society, 21*(7), 721–734.

Phoenix, A. (1987). Theories of gender and black families, G. Weiner & M. Arnot (Eds.), *Gender under scrutiny*, London: Hutchinson.

Pickett, K. E., & Pearl, M. (2001). Multilevel analyses of neighbourhood socioeconomic context and health outcomes: A critical review, *Journal of Epidemiology Community Health, 55*, 111–122.

Pilgrim, D. (1992). Psychotherapy and political evasions, in W. Dryden & C. Feltham (Eds.), *Psychotherapy and its discontents* (pp. 225–242), Buckingham: Open University Press.

Proctor, G. (2002). *The dynamics of power in counselling and psychotherapy: Ethics, politics and practice*, Ross-on-Wye: PCCS Books.

PSC (Psychologists for Social Change). (2017). *The psychological impact of austerity: A briefing paper* Downloaded from http://www.psychchange.org/uploads/9/7/9/7/97971280/paa-briefing-paper.pdf, Downloaded on 30/08/2017.

Psychotherapists and Counsellors for Social Responsibility (2016). *The political situation in the United States: Statement from the psychotherapy and counselling union (PCU, UK) and psychotherapists and counsellors for social responsibility (PCSR, UK)*, downloaded from http://pcsr-uk.ning.com, Downloaded on 08/05/2017.

Radlett, M. (2017). Therapy beyond its remit, *Existential Analysis, 28*(1), 34–47.

Rafalin, D. (2010). Counselling psychology and research: Revisiting the relationship in the light of our 'mission', in M. Milton (Ed.), *Therapy and beyond: Counselling psychology contributions to therapeutic and social issues*, Chichester: Wiley-Blackwell.

Reeve, D. (2000). Oppression within the counselling room, *Disability and Society, 15*(4), 669–682.

Richards, C. (2010). Trans and non-monogamies, in D. Langdridge & M. Barker (Eds.), *Understanding non-monogamies* (pp. 121–33), London: Routledge.

Richards, C., & Barker, M. (2013). *Sexuality and gender for mental health professionals*, London: Sage.

Richards, C., & Barker, M. J. (Eds.) (2015). *The Palgrave handbook of psychology of sexuality and gender,* Basingstoke: Palgrave Macmillan.

REFERENCES

Riggle, E. D., Whitman, J. S., Olson, A., Rostosky, S. S., & Strong, S. (2008). The positive aspects of being a lesbian or gay man. *Professional Psychology: Research and Practice*, *39*(2), 210.

Rivers, I. (2004). Recollections of bullying at school and their long-term implications for lesbians, gay men, and bisexuals, *Crisis*, *25*(4), DOI: 10.1027/0227-5910.25.4.xxx

Rizq, R. (2011). IAPT, anxiety and envy: A psychoanalytic view of NHS primary care mental health services today. *British Journal of Psychotherapy*, *27*(1), 37–55.

Rogers, C. R. (1966). *Client-centred therapy*, Washington: American Psychological Association.

Rudmin, F. W. (2003). Critical history of the acculturation psychology of assimilation, separation, integration, and marginalisation. *Review of General Psychology*, *7*(1), 3.

Rust, M. (2005). Making the Sea Change: From Chaos and Inertia to Creativity, Keynote speech for the PCSR Conference, 2005, downloaded from http://www.mjrust.net/downloads/Making%20the%20Sea%20Change%20.pdf, Downloaded on 02/02/2009.

Rust, M. J. (2008a). Climate on the couch: Unconscious processes in relation to our environmental crisis. *Psychotherapy and Politics International*, *6*(3), 157–170.

Rust, M. J. (2008b). Nature hunger: Eating problems and consuming the Earth. *Counselling Psychology Review*, *23*(2), 70–78.

Rust, M. J., & Totton, N. (2012). *Vital signs: Psychological responses to ecological crisis*, London: Karnac Books.

Ryan, C., & Rivers, I. (2003). Lesbian, gay, bisexual and transgender youth: Victimisation and its correlates in the USA and UK. *Culture, Health & Sexuality*, *5*(2), 103–119.

Samuels, A. (1993). *The political psyche*, London: Routledge.

Samuels, A. (2006). Working directly with political, cultural and social material in the therapy session, in L. Layton, N. C. Hollander, & S. Gutwill. (Eds.) , *Psychoanalysis, class and politics: Encounters in the clinical setting*, London: Routledge.

Schavarien, J. (2015). *Boarding school syndrome: The psychological trauma of the 'privileged' child*, London: Routledge.

Searles, H. (1960). *The non-human environment in normal development and in schizophrenia*, New York: St Martin's Press.

Shorrocks, A., Davies, J. B., & Lluberas, R. (2015). *Global Wealth Databook 2015*, Credit Suisse

Smail, D. (2015). *Taking care: An alternative to therapy*, London: Karnac Books.

Smith, D. L. (1991). *Hidden conversations: An introduction to communicative psychoanalysis*, London: Karnac Books.

Smith, D. L. (1999). *Approaching psychoanalysis: An introductory course*, London: Karnac Books.

Smith, D. L. (2003). *Psychoanalysis in focus*, London: Sage.

Spinelli, E (2001). *The mirror and the hammer: Challenges to therapeutic orthodoxy*, London: Continuum.

Spinelli, E. (2005). *The interpreted world: An introduction to phenomenological psychology* (2nd edn), London: Sage.

Spinelli, E. (2014). *Practising existential therapy: The relational world* (2nd edn), London: Sage.

Spivak, M. (1990). *The joy of TEX: A gourmet guide to typesetting with the AMS-TEX macro package,* Providence: American Mathematical Society.

Stone, J. (2016). Brexit: Surge in anti-immigrant hate crime in areas that voted to leave EU, *Independent,* 31 June, downloaded from http://www.independent.co.uk/news/uk/crime/brexit-hate-crime-racism-immigration-eu-referendum-result-what-it-means-eurospectic-areas-a7165056.html, Downloaded on 02/09/2016.

Strawbridge, S. (1994). Towards anti-oppressive practice in counselling psychology. *Counselling Psychology Review, 9*(1), 5–12.

Strawbridge, S. (1996). *Myth of the self-contained individual in counselling psychology.* A paper presented at the Third Annual Conference of the British Psychological Society's Division of Counselling Psychology, York.

Strawbridge, S. (2006). Thoughts on becoming, being and developing as a counselling psychologist. *Counselling Psychology Review, 21*(1), 27.

Strawbridge, S. (2010). Telling stories, in S. Corrie & D. Lane (Eds.), *Constructing stories, telling tales: A guide to formulation in applied psychology,* London: Karnac Books.

Stolorow, R. D., Brandchaft, B., & Atwood, G. E. (2014). *Psychoanalytic treatment: An intersubjective approach,* London: Routledge.

Strasser, F., & Strasser, A. (1997). *Existential time limited therapy,* Chichester: John Wiley & Sons.

Szasz, T. S. (1960). The myth of mental illness, *American Psychologist, 15*(2), 113–118. http://dx.doi.org/10.1037/h0046535

Totton, N. (2000). *Psychotherapy and politics,* London: Sage.

Totton, N. (2011). *Wild therapy: Undomesticating inner and outer worlds,* Ross-on-Wye: PCCS Books.

Townsend, M. (2012). Stop and search 'racial profiling' by police on the increase, claims study, *The Guardian,* 14 January, downloaded from http://www.theguardian.com/law/2012/jan/14/stop-search-racial-profiling-police, Downloaded on 13/01/17.

UKCP (United Kingdom Council for Psychotherapy) et al. (2015). *Memorandum of understanding on conversion therapy in the UK,* downloaded from https://www.psycho-therapy.org.uk/wp-content/uploads/2016/09/Memorandum-of-understanding-on-conversion-therapy.pdf, Downloaded on 10/02/2017.

UKCP (United Kingdom Council for Psychotherapy) (2009). *Ethical principles and codes of professional conduct,* London: UKCP.

United Nation (1948). *Universal declaration of human rights.* United Nations General Assembly.

Valdes, F. (1996). Unpacking hetero-patriarchy: Tracing the conflation of sex, gender & (and) sexual orientation to its origins. *Yale JL & Human, 8,* 161.

van der Merwe, A. C. (2006). *Moffie,* New York: Europa Editions.

van Deurzen, E. (1998). *Paradox and passion in psychotherapy: An existential approach to therapy and counselling,* Chichester: Wiley.

van Deurzen, E. (2015). *Paradox and passion in psychotherapy: An existential approach,* Chichester: Wiley.

Ward, C., Bochner, S., & Furnham, A. (2005). *The psychology of culture shock,* London: Routledge.

Watts, J. (2016a). The EU referendum has caused a mental health crisis, *The Guardian*, 29 June, downloaded from https://www.theguardian.com/commentisfree/2016/jun/29/eu-referendum-mental-health-vote, Downloaded on 15/03/17.

Watts, J. (2016b). This has been a year of high political anxiety. Here's how to survive it, *The Guardian*, 8 November, downloaded from https://www.theguardian.com/commentisfree/2016/nov/08/keep-calm-and-carry-on-brexit-donald-trump, Downloaded on 15/03/17.

Whatascript (2016). Dustin Lance Black: A passionate story-teller, downloaded from http://www.whatascript.com/dustin-lance-black.html, Downloaded on 27/03/2017.

Whitman, J. (2015). Mental health disparities and minority stress, a paper given in the symposium entitled. *An international declaration for global LGBT psychology and psychotherapy standards.* British Psychological Society Annual Conference, Liverpool: May 2015.

Wilkinson, R., & Pickett, K. (2010). *The spirit level. Why equality is better for everyone,* London: Penguin.

Wink, P., Dillon, M., & Larsen, B. (2005). Religion as moderator of the depression-health connection: Findings from a longitudinal study. *Research on Ageing, 27*(2), 197–220.

INDEX

simplistic   23, 76
split   18
terms   15
understandings   139, 147
visions   16–17, 115
Biology   15, 51
Biopsychosocial   27
Birth certificates   51, 93
Bisexual   66, 72
Black, Dustin Lance   xii
Blame   8, 14, 85, 86, 98, 110, 143
Blank Screen   67
Blindness   103
Body   30, 93, 111
  image   152
Boredom   33, 48, 120
Boxing   68, 73, 75
BPS   15, 66, 151, 152
  Lesbian and gay psychology
    section   16
  Psychology of sexualities
    section   16
Brexit   1–4, 6, 12, 132, 133–146, 148,
  152
British Psychological Society
  (see BPS)
Buddhism   83, 84, 86
Buddhist   83
Bullying   26, 31, 38, 83, 107
Bush, George   80

Cameron, David   87
Camp   71
Capital
  -ism   7, 9, 14, 137, 148, 151
  -ist   20, 119, 120, 135
  social   25
Carbon
  footprint   124
Carter, President Jimmy   18
CBT   8, 9, 19
Cheetah   116
Chromosomal pairing   51

XY   51
XX   51
Cisgender   18, 20, 83, 98, 154
Civil partnership   17
Class   10, 28, 54, 135, 150
Climate change   125
Closet   100, 102
CMHT   83
Cognitive behavioural therapy
  (see CBT)
Colonialism   31
'Colour blind'   19, 20, 28
Community Mental Health Team
  (see CMHT)
Conservationists   115, 124, 125
Contact hypothesis   90
Continuing professional development
  (see CPD)
Control   18, 31, 71, 99, 129, 133, 149
  lack of   35, 64, 82, 89, 109, 143
COPD (Chronic Obstructive Pulmonary
  Disease)   105, 108, 113
Counselling   27, 31, 51, 86, 102, 103
Counselling Psychology   10, 115
Cox, Jo   12
CPD   103, 155
Creativity   137
Criticism   71
Crusades   80
Curiosity   xii, 46, 48, 53, 56, 72, 99, 100,
  101, 118
Cutting   34

Deaf
  community   13
Death 74, 76, 86, 87, 112, 135, 136
  threats   12
Democratic   30, 127
Denial   151
Dependence   6
Department of Health   15
Department of Social Security
  (see DSS)

INDEX

170

INDEX

NHS 15, 109, 155
Non-binary
  gender 93–103
Non-human world 115
Normal 18, 104, 120
  are you normal? 17
  -isation 2
  -ised absence, pathologised
    presence 19
  -ity 122
  gender development 93
'Normalised absence/ pathologised
    presence' 19
Normate 104
Northern Ireland troubles 80

Obesity 149, 151
Oestrogen 51
Ontic 40, 64
Ontological 40
Oppression xii, 7, 8, 14, 140, 150, 153
  and discrimination 13, 16, 18, 21, 80,
    155, 156
  and gender 52–65
  and trauma 21, 80
  self 61
  social 13, 66
  targeted 17
Orbach, Susie 148
'Other' 9, 16, 20, 22, 25, 41, 66, 80, 88, 90
  Dangerous 86
  -ed 24
  environment as 115
  hate of the 89
  -ing 25, 43, 80, 86, 90, 101, 115–131,
    154
  judging 33
  -ness 87, 155
  therapist as 23, 41
Outdoor working 126, 127, 128
Outsider 37, 39, 50, 107, 142, 142

PAA (Psychologists Against
  Austerity) 152

Pathologis
  ation 20, 25
  ing terminology 23
Parallel process 36, 57
Parliament 14, 142
PCSR (Psychotherapists and Counsellors
    for Social Responsibility) 152
Penis 51
Persecution 80
Pharma 7, 14
  -ceutical company 15
Phenomenological
  method 76
Phenomenologically
  oriented 62, 99
Phenomenology 56
Planet 115, 124, 126, 129
Plural 150
  interpretation 29, 30, 87
  istic 27
Poker face 68
Policing 5, 27, 57, 71, 98, 154
Politicians 14, 86, 132, 143
Political xi, xii, 2, 10, 65, 71, 87, 99,
    103, 115, 132, 134, 140, 141, 148,
    150, 152, 153, 155
  acts 27, 139, 149
  allegiances 16
  and personal 4, 8, 93, 131, 133–146
  appointees 143
  aspects of life 4
  change 12
  codes 51
  contributions 8
  control 149
  dimension/ domain 6, 11, 13–14, 22,
    27, 30, 97, 147
  discourse 89, 133, 153
  engagement 6
  experiences 16
  informed therapy 7
  leaders 7
  mindsets 26
  overtones of language 23

Druck:
Canon Deutschland Business Services GmbH
im Auftrag der KNV-Gruppe
Ferdinand-Jühlke-Str. 7
99095 Erfurt